# E.P. Thompson

## Objections and Oppositions

*SOCIAL & BEHAVIORAL SCIENCES*    History, Geography & Area Studies    *Europe*

**32-5820**        HX244        94-21908 CIP
Palmer, Bryan D. **E.P. Thompson: objections and oppositions.** Verso, 1994. 201p
index ISBN 1-85984-975-X, $59.95; ISBN 1-85984-070-1 pbk, $18.95
    Palmer wrote *The Making of E.P. Thompson: Marxism, Humanism, and History* (Toronto, 1981)
and was Thompson's friend and close follower. Thompson, who died in 1993, was a Marxist historian
most renowned for his *The Making of the English Working Class* (CH, Jul'64) and was a leader of various antiestablishment causes. Along with Eric Hobsbawn, he was one of the most important leftist historians in postwar Britain. He influenced and befriended a great many historians, as well as students,
some of whom have now become extremely prominent in their own right. Palmer states at the outset
that this is not a biography, and indeed it is not. Instead, it is a work written lovingly by one of
Thompson's loyal friends and followers, and contains anecdotal discussion of Thompson's childhood
and adult life, and the influences on him, including that of his father, from whom he inherited anti-
imperialist and antiestablishment attitudes. This short work is not only valuable for a flavor of a
remarkable life, but is also indispensable for an understanding of Thompson's ideas and scholarship.
All levels.—*R. D. Long, Eastern Michigan University*

# E.P. Thompson
## Objections and Oppositions

BRYAN D. PALMER

VERSO

London · New York

First published by Verso 1994
© Bryan D. Palmer 1994
All rights reserved

**Verso**
UK: 6 Meard Street, London W1V 3HR
USA: 29 West 35th Street, New York, NY 10001–2291

Verso is the imprint of New Left Books

ISBN 1–85984–975–X
ISBN 1–85984–070–1 (pbk)

**British Library Cataloguing in Publication Data**
A catalogue record for this book is available from the British Library

**Library of Congress Cataloging-in-Publication Data**
Palmer, Bryan D.
E.P. Thompson: objections and oppositions
Thompson / Bryan Palmer.
p.    cm.
Includes bibliographical references and index.
ISBN 1–85984–975–X. – ISBN 1–85984–070–1 (pbk)
1. Thompson, E.P. (Edward Palmer), 1924–93. 2. Communism.
3. Socialism.  4. Dialectical materialism.  I. Title.
HX244.7.T45P35  1994       94-21908
335.43'092–dc20       CIP


Typeset by Solidus (Bristol) Limited
Printed and bound in Great Britain by
Biddles Ltd, Guildford and King's Lynn

# Contents

*In an age of nationalist tragedies and the politics of difference/identity, this book is dedicated to all internationalists who continue to hold high the banner of humanity. For my friend Greg, and his many indulgences over the years, I offer my thanks. Mike Sprinker delivered this book, holding my hand and urging me on like an unselfish midwife. I won't forget his support, especially as so much of it was given freely on the very ground of intellectual 'difference'.*

# Preface

Readers are entitled to know what they are *not* getting. What they do get is often not what they imagine they should receive or what they want. Authors are not responsible for this, but there is no reason to complicate matters further by overt acts of deception. So I will state clearly at the outset that this is not a biography of Edward Palmer (E.P.) Thompson. Such a book will no doubt be written some day, but it will of necessity entail deep researches into archival sources, family papers, far-flung correspondences, personal relationships, and the political and intellectual history of the mid-to-late twentieth century. It will require resources of expertise and sensitivity rarely found in any individual student of history; knowledges and appreciations that reach across the chronologies and academic boundaries, politics and poetics, that Thompson traversed in his life as a chronic objector. This will be a long and important treatment of a life of significance and complexity. What follows will prove a mere footnote to this study, a memoir and a homage that skirt as much as they probe, introducing sets of reflections that are meant to illuminate suggestively more than they aim to provide definitive detail.

For twenty years I had known Thompson. My first contact was

with the public E.P. Thompson, author of *The Making of the English Working Class*, a text which I read, like so many others, on my journey to becoming a working-class historian. I was captivated by this large book, exhilarated by its way of seeing class anew, energized by its tone, so resolutely defiant of the ideological posturing of supposedly detached scholarship, unashamedly engaged with the struggles of labour, past *and* present. That contact deepened as I began to write social histories of class experience, offering along the way a small statement on the relationship between Thompson's historical writing and his political activism.[1] Our relationship was not, however, overly close in these beginnings, nor was it without its rocky moments. But gradually, through the peace movements of the 1980s and through letters and visits almost always associated with the twinned projects of historical writing and left politics, my contact evolved into one with the more private Edward, where our exchanges were marked with the jesting, sparring and mutual concern of an odd friendship, separated by great distances of geography and culture, age and upbringing – even, at certain points, politics and personalities.[2] Yet there was an awkward mutuality there, and certainly a tone of reciprocal humours and self-deprecations, as there was between Edward and so many others. Internationalism, he knew, was 'a concourse, an exchange. Argument is its true sign.'[3] As an objector himself, he felt strong loyalties to those who lived their objections as he did, openly.

Edward's death literally stopped me in my tracks. His health had been in a pronounced state of deterioration for at least six or seven years. Letters were punctuated with acknowledgements of recurrent and diverse disabilities; visits required getting over the initial shock of actually seeing Edward debilitated, a troubling experience made all the more difficult because of the vigorous, intensely physical way he carried himself into the late 1970s and his early campaigning for peace. I knew, as did others, that Edward was dying, even remarking sadly to people who had recently seen him and were upset by the state of his health that he could not keep battling back for ever. But this abstract knowledge was somehow countered by Edward's resistance, his persistent objection to his end, registered in his relentless engagement with his own writings and the political causes that had dominated his life for fifty years. When I learned of Edward's death, then, it was as though I were unprepared for what I should have known was going to happen.

For days afterwards the phone rang. Callers from afar who had been close to Edward wanted to talk; there were requests from various quarters to write short obituaries and memorial statements, or appear on panels paying tribute to him. There was a Sunday gathering in mid-September at Wick Episcopi (Thompson's Warwickshire home), where his wife, Dorothy, hosted some two hundred people who came to celebrate Edward's life. It was not a solemn event: food, wine, conversation and memories flowed around the rooms, spilling out into the garden where Edward had died, adults and children mingling. The talk of disarmament activism, 1956, the historiography of nineteenth-century England, plebeian resistance in the eighteenth century, Warwick University, the Romantic critique of capitalism in the 1790s, C.L.R. James, St Paul's Church and Edward's anti-Althusserian finale, and Eastern European dissidence – to name but a few of the topics alluded to – cut across the causes and analytic points of departure long associated with E.P. Thompson.

I returned from England to Canada and sat down to write an obituary for a journal of Canadian labour studies, *Labour/Le Travail*, with which I had been associated for much of the period I had known Edward. (It later appeared in two parts in 1993 and 1994, and this text is an extension of that original lengthy essay.) There were trips to the library to acquire published writings; my files started to spill out on to the floor of the study – yellowed newspaper clippings, Xeroxed articles, fading notecards from the past, piling up and out in a chaotic disregard for order;

letters shoved into shelved books were unfolded, read, and rethought; pictures came out of albums and off the wall. I would find myself, at 2.30 a.m., staring into the word-processor screen with tears in my eyes. After about a month of this – no more than five weeks – I stood tearing the computer paper perforations of approximately 180 pages. I don't know how this happened.

What follows was thus written quickly and too closely on Edward's death to provide the kind of distanced reading and assessment of Thompson that is necessary, and requires so much research and careful interrogations of varied subjects and experiences. It is too personal in its origins to claim to be much more than a memoir and a homage, of the sort that Thompson himself often wrote in appreciation of figures both dead and alive.[4] I felt strongly that there was a need to locate Thompson historically, and in so doing I attempted to touch down on the formative influences and historical contexts out of and within which he wrote, thought and acted. Much will have been missed, but enough, perhaps, is there in these pages to introduce E.P. Thompson to an audience that will continue to grow. And if there are times when counter-readings and alternative interpretations are not only possible, but probable and necessary, something of the importance of Thompson's themes and the tone in which they came to be articulated should be apparent from this account.

There is no simplistic summing up of these themes, and no formulaic structuralist ordering of Thompson's tone is possible. It is not so much that he created a systematic elevation of human agency, a rational theoretical edifice that repositioned the subjective in relation to the collective, situating desire and need in their complex historical accounting with determination. Thompson did this, I think, and he did it in ways that enriched and energized the materialist tradition. But more important was the way he accomplished it. If we look to Thompson for a programmatic statement, a command of theory, we will not find what will pass muster as either 'moral law' or methodological imperative, largely because he intuitively rejected any such act of intellectual and political closure. Such statements can be read out of his writing; this is especially the case in the famous 'Preface' to *The Making of the English Working Class*. But behind each statement lies the more fundamental creativity of Thompson's unwavering commitment to *refuse* the analytic boxes within which much of historical writing and political practice incarcerates humanity. This *was* his theory, and more: it was the politics *and* the poetics of his life.

Theoretically, this turned on Thompson's understated insistence on seeing past, present and future with the vision of dialectics. 'Oh, but one must be a dialectician to understand how this world goes!' he exclaimed, tongue only somewhat in cheek, in his letter to Kolakowski.[5] The lessons of 1956 – political and analytic – stayed with him for the remainder of his life, and they turned on the need to understand 'the way in which the most contradictory elements can co-exist in the same historical event, and opposing tendencies and potentialities can interpenetrate within the same tradition'.[6] Three decades later he was insisting on the importance of seeing cultural mutations as arising from 'the contradiction within the contradiction',[7] an interpretative injunction he offered by way of comment on his friend, the communist poet Tom McGrath, but one that could just as easily apply to his study of the plebeian ritualistic sale of wives, or his futuristic Swiftian satire *The Sykaos Papers*.[8] 'History knows no regular verbs,' Thompson once concluded, with a typical metaphorical flourish. (Politics, he might have added, has few truly simple nouns.)[9]

Practically, this conceptual premiss translated into Thompson's penchant for objection. Behind every statement of 'Thompsonian' intent – rescuing the poor from the 'condescension of posterity' or the experiential validity of aspiration – lies a fundamental politics of rubbing against the grain of conventional wisdoms: of left, right and centre. 'I have been conscious, at times,' he wrote in *The Making of the English Working Class*, 'of writing against the weight of prevailing orthodoxies.'[10] Thompson constantly clarified his positions – not with propositions, but with counters and challenges. Self-deprecatingly referring to himself as an extinct mythological species, a great bustard, he claimed that he could never be gagged by opposition alone. 'For the great bustard, by a law well-known to aeronautics, can only rise into the air against a strong headwind. It is only by facing into opposition that I am able to define my thought at all.'[11] Polemics and rejoinders commenced with 'certain refusals', and even at the point of his most academic comment, as in a *London Review of Books* discussion of an account of Wordsworth and Coleridge, Thompson seemed proudly defiant in his announcement that in some small matters of interpretation he stood the ground of privilege in relation to most literary scholars. 'I have myself been involved in editing oppositional publications,' he explained in support of his dissent concerning a critic's assessment of Wordsworth's relation to a journal of opposition, adding that parts of his life had been spent 'immersed among beautiful and ineffectual utopians and hissing factionalists'.[12] Of a friend Thompson wrote:

> McGrath's is an implacable alienation from all that has anything fashionable going for it in the past four decades of American culture – and from a good deal of what has been offered as counterculture as well. There need be no suspicion that this alienation is worn as a pose, as the distinguished sorrow of a lonely soul; it is *suffered* with bitterness and with anger; it is *opposed*; and the official culture is seen as (without any qualification) menacing and life-destroying, not only in the most direct political meanings but also to historical and literary values[.][13]

The words are respectful. They apply as much to Thompson as they do to McGrath.

In his last, posthumously published work, *Witness Against the Beast: William Blake and the Moral Law*, Thompson staked a historical claim for his own allegiance to an antinomian tradition that reached through the ranting impulse of sixteenth-century dissent into sects such as the Muggletonians – a continuity which, he argues, touched Blake in an oppositional dualism that marked an established culture and political economy of Works, Morality, Legality and Bondage as challenged by Faith, Forgiveness and Freedom. 'Never, on any page of Blake,' writes Thompson in the concluding sentence of his study, 'is there the least complicity with the kingdom of the Beast.'[14] And in a final comment on the European Nuclear Disarmament movement (END), which he helped to found and lead, Thompson took his objections to nuclear annihilation and placed them alongside his objections to the contemporary ideological construction of the end of the Cold War as merely yet another victory for capitalism. He drew out of these objections yet further commitment to widening the constituencies of minority oppositions, East and West. 'Today there is nothing to prevent these minorities, East and West, from growing in strength and discovering common strategies,' he claimed, arguing that 'The citizens' search for a common project . . . in a direct discourse unmediated by Cold War agencies or media, is the urgent task of our time.'[15] From Blake to the Bomb and beyond, Edward Thompson objected to the end.

# Introduction

Edward Palmer (E.P.) Thompson, described in 1980 as 'our finest socialist writer today – certainly in England, possibly in Europe', died at his home, Wick Episcopi, Worcester, approximately one year ago, on 28 August 1993. Born on 3 February 1924, he is survived by his wife of forty-five years, fellow historian and political comrade Dorothy, their daughter Kate, sons Mark and Ben, and numerous grandchildren. He left us – whom I define as those interested in and committed to the integrity of the past and the humane possibilities of a socialist future – a most enduring legacy, his *example*. In the words of a former student, Anna Davin, Thompson's greatness did not lie only in his published writings: 'It was also the example he set. . . . He was a man of feeling, reason, and commitment, and he set for us the standard of what an intellectual should be.'[1]

There are those who would disagree. For as long as I have been a historian there has been an uncomfortable respect for Thompson's histories, a recognition that they occupy a special and influential place. But there has also been a nagging denigration of his accomplishments that runs through an honest and understandable articulation of critique and intellectual difference into less benign realms of malice. Much of this

*1*

is developed as caricature, but its distortions and disfigurements are fundamentally political, even as they are, at times, trite. From some quarters this is so much to be expected that it can almost be regarded as a phenomenon of political nature; from others it is more disturbingly noteworthy. Seemingly 'naturalistic', the antagonism to Thompson within elite circles of complacent scholasticism has been longstanding, whatever its softening in recent years. In England it often reached heights difficult to comprehend in North America.[2]

It must not be forgotten that the first academic response to Thompson's *William Morris: Romantic to Revolutionary* (1955) was a stifling silence, punctuated by a *Times Literary Supplement* review – a mere 600 words in length – titled 'Morris and Marxism' that bemoaned the book's 'splenetic' tone, castigated its ideological 'bias', and identified the author's 'remarkable feat' of sustaining a 'mood of ill-temper through a volume of 900 pages'. While *The Making of the English Working Class* (1963) played to a more appreciative audience, the reviews were not without the shadows of this Cold War posture, which Gertrude Himmelfarb, for one, cast promiscuously across the pages of *The New Republic*. It is perhaps too easy to declare, in hindsight, that the book 'was instantly recognized as a classic', as does E.J. Hobsbawm in an appreciative passage in his recent Thompson obituary; this is a voice that speaks through the obviousness of the book's importance over three decades. But in the early-to-mid 1960s, other voices spoke, shrill and often faltering with fear. In 'A Tract of Secret History', Himmelfarb declared: 'Thompson is not merely *engagé* ... [he] is positively *enragé.*' This, apparently, was not good; nor did it produce history of value. Thompson's *Making* was 'large deduction from very little evidence ... stance rather than substance'. Many reviews carried their sneer in titles of condescension: 'Hard Times', 'Enter the Cloth Cap', and 'The Common Man as Hero'. There was obviously worry that Thompson's prose, unique in its almost sexual seductiveness, carried with it a libidinal charge capable of corrupting impressionable youth. J.D. Chambers, writing in *History*, thought it imperative that the 'residue of ideological importation be laid bare', lest it lure the unsuspecting innocents of scholarship into its nefarious lair of 'sheer fantasy'.

Dazzled by 'the apocalyptic vision of a minority of desperate men', obsessed by 'the colour of a bloody revolution', Thompson was an author who, in certain quarters, conjured up the symbolism of the black-coated, anarcho-communist writer-as-bomb-thrower. Worse, there was an audience for this curdling stuff. Students were not only 'reading his book – they [were] sometimes buying it'. Maybe they were 'punch-drunk', like the miserable hand-loom weavers and others who formed the insurrectionary core of Thompson's imagined revolutionary underground. Clearly, the dangers were great. To use words such as 'psychic masturbation', applying them to a reading of aspects of Methodism's history, or to allude metaphorically (and perhaps problematically) to Francis Place's cautious constitutionalism and ultra-respectability as posing for the portrait of 'the White Man's Trusty Nigger', disturbed academic proprieties, freezing the professional disciplinary countenance in a look of shocked disbelief.

Decades later, as Thompson's historical researches took him back into the eighteenth century, on to ground less immediately politically threatening and less littered with the anti-communism of the 1950s academy, the reaction to his *Whigs and Hunters* (1975) and the edited volume *Albion's Fatal Tree* (1975) appeared slightly more generous. The crude ideological dismissals of Cambridge's J.C.D. Clark were offset by the more knockabout casuistries of the *New York Review of Books'* Lawrence Stone, the latter taking great pleasure in pointing out: 'And so the old Marxist turns out to be a new Whig after all.' Revolutionaries of the *NYRB*, unite! But the mainstream, by and large, gave little to Thompson, and that begrudgingly. By the early-to-mid-1980s, the reinvigorated New Right refocused generalized conservative sights on Thompson. His peace journalism prompted one Conservative member of the

House of Lords to pontificate: 'I think this passes the bounds of decency in journalism (Cheers). It was not a thing which anyone, not even Mr. E.P. Thompson, should have written, and having written it, it is not a thing which a great newspaper, read throughout the world, should have been willing to print (Cheers).' Roger Scruton opened his 'philosophical' case against the sentimentality of Marxism with a treatment of Thompson, including him in his diatribe against 'thinkers of the New Left'.[3]

As the obituaries rolled off the press in late August and September 1993, and as a series of large public memorials celebrated Thompson's life in the months following his death, proclaiming him 'the foremost historian in the English-speaking world', 'the most eloquent historian of his English generation', 'the most widely-cited 20th-century historian in the world', it was necessary to stop and recall that within established historical and academic circles Thompson was an opposing force, and the counter-strikes against him were persistent and often petulant. As Christopher Hill rightly reminds us: 'He was not universally appreciated by lesser minds in the English historical establishment: to its shame and disgrace the British academy delayed electing him to a fellowship until 1992.' Hobsbawm, writing with less of a political edge and slightly less sympathy, comments that while Thompson 'derived some comfort from not wearing the badges of the Establishment', it was nevertheless true that these were 'unjustly withheld from him'.[4]

When I suggest that Thompson's legacy is his example, then, I do not imply a uniform embrace. Clearly he will be rejected by many, among them that species of *Academicus superciliosus*, consumed by the enormous pomp and self-important propriety of *the* University, whose preening and mating habits Thompson satirized so tellingly in *Warwick University Ltd.*[5] From the 'philistines' of both the capitalist right and the Stalinist left, whose understanding of human need was and is ordered by 'things' to the point where the creative, intellectual and moral foundations of life are exiled,[6] Thompson would expect no warm reception. As a figure who knew that he had jeopardized friendships and exaggerated differences so that he could face into an opposition the better to define his own thought, Thompson himself would not have been likely to hold his own *example* up to anyone as a statement of anything, let alone a legacy to future generations.[7]

Yet his example is there to think through. He took from Marx and Morris and Blake the absolute *necessity* of countering 'intellectual error', of refusing to abstain from battle: 'Where is the battlefield', asked a *New Reasoner* editorial, 'if it is not within the human reason and conscience?' Blake's dictum 'He who desires but acts not, breeds pestilence' was a powerful injunction, which Thompson was early to quote against those who let the revolutionary impulse of Romanticism rot in the sentiment of solitude. Ironically, given his historical reading of Methodism's place in English class formation, his father's missionary Methodist past reinforced his commitment to commitment. 'He groaned sometimes under [this] sense of duty,' recalled his friend Sheila Rowbotham.[8]

It weighed on him heavily, especially when the often-painful choices that he knew he had to make ran up against the usually fickle face of historical process:

> Crime and compassion, then, statistics, ecstasy,
> Struck like a match from chaos. It's all an accident:
> This town beneath me meaning no more than a stonecrop,
> Lichen of banks and offices: fungus on a stone wall,
> Spawning into the night a pretty stitchwork of lights
> Like swarming midge spiders, bringing someone money.
> Widows and acrobats, clowns, suicides:
> It's all in the luck of the draw. Man makes what he can get.
> The kids play at bandits. Blood issues on the speedway.
> The gunmen point from the hoardings, indicating manhood:
> Virility slouching in a soft hat and an oil-stained raincoat,
> Getting girls at a bargain, going loaded to the cash-tills,

Educating the young in the ethics of business.
The weak get cracked like grapeseed, chewed into digits.
On the corner by the Palace
Without malice or logic
Death waits in a slumped indifferent posture,
Sticking his knuckles in the eyes of all comers.

I once took Edward and Dorothy to see a Kingston showing of Rick Salutin's *The Farmer's Revolt*, a dramatization of the Upper Canadian rebellion of 1837. Edward's favoured line from that evening's theatre came towards the end of the play, as the blacksmith, Samuel Lount, was asked, on the gallows, what had brought him to this sad end. 'I do not know exactly how we came to this,' he replied, 'except by a series of steps, each of which seemed to require the next.' This was not all that far removed from what Thompson had long ago identified as 'the central theme' of Morris's *A Dream of John Ball*: 'I ... pondered how men fight and lose the battle, and the thing they fought for comes about in spite of their defeat, and when it comes turns out not to be what they meant, and other men have to fight for what they meant under another name.' For Thompson, this echoed passages in Engels's *Ludwig Feuerbach and the End of Classical German Philosophy*, and it would ring loudly in his own declarative statements on socialist humanism and agency and choice in the *New Reasoner*. Choice itself was struggle, uncertain in its outcomes, related to past choices and campaigns, but in ways that were not always simply a matter of logical progression. It was driven by the possibility of possibility, not by any promises or assurances of success or laws of historical motion:

It's time to speak one's mind.
I'm sick of an 'anxious age'.
I am fed to the teeth with the cant
Of 'guilt' and original sin.
From all the fires that raged
In England's youth I find
A grocer's timid candle
Is all that is left behind:

And life being unassuaged
By the fuel of cant and cash
Consumes us in the flames
Of unfulfilled desire
Down to sarcastic ash
And threatens to disown
Fire with terrible fire,
Air, water, and stone
Resume what was their own.

Whatever evil there is
I declare was first let in
By timid men with candles
And abstract talk of sin.
Man is what he has made,
Chipping bone with bone,
Shaping the teaching spade:
Urged by his human needs
Changes the world, and then
Transfigured by his deeds,
Changes necessity,
Becoming whole and free.

I stand upon the earth
And watch the hursts of space,
And at last I raise my voice
In the teeth of the swarming wind:
I declare that man has choice
Discovered in that place
Of human action where
Necessity meets desire,
And moors and questioning wind,
Water, stone, and air,
Transfigured in the soul,
Can be changed to human fire
Which man, becoming whole,
Will order and control.

These lines of verse, penned in 1950 under the title 'The Place Called Choice', summarize much of what Thompson's *example* is about.[9]

It was an example that never wavered in its insistence that choice had to be made, and that such choice entailed action. It was an example that never lived to become 'whole and free', but it was, equally, an example that was never timid. Edward Thompson carried no candles for the causes of humankind; his sense of human need and commitment was too great. He shouldered more than mere light; his blasts of intervention were powered by rage as well as by love. Even when he was whispering for effect his voice was loud, his presentation dramatic, his every word and gesture theatrically explosive. When Thompson set his sights on an evil, it was with a cannon, and he would never let it slip by: wrongs and dangers that pressed moral commitments and the unrealized potential of humanity into misshapen containments or worse he could never let stare him in the face and drift freely away in a breeze of abstraction. His place of choice, like that of Lount, was one of opposition, a tone of unfulfilled political engagement registered in refusals that were as consistently powerful as they were unfailingly impolite. As Perry Anderson acknowledged more than a decade ago, 'his has been the most declared political history of any of his generation. Every major, and nearly every minor, work he has written concludes with an avowed and direct reflection on its lessons for socialists of his own time.'[10]

Even in times of seeming desperation – 1973 appears to have been one such period – he never turned the cheek of apostasy to accept willingly the slaps of accommodation and acquiescence to capitalism and its doctrine of government by market values.[11] To Kolakowski he acknowledged prematurely that 'The voice of the bore is doomed in the end to tail off into silence. And that, in a nutshell, is my own history as any kind of political voice.' In 'My Study' he expressed a sense of futility:

> The mills that grind my own necessity.
> Oh, royal me! Unpoliced imperial man
> And monarch of my incapacity
>
> [. . .]
>
> I rush out in this rattling harvester

And thrash you into type. But what I write
Brings down no armoured bans, no Ministers

Of the Interior interrogate.
No one bothers to break in and seize
My verses for subversion of the state:

Even the little dogmas do not bark.
I leave my desk and peer into the world.
Outside the owls are hunting. Dark

Yet 'no matter how hideous the alternative may seem,' he continued to Kolakowski, 'no word of mine will wittingly be added to the comforts of that old bitch gone in the teeth, consumer capitalism. I know that bitch well in her very original nature; she has engendered world-wide wars, aggressive and racial imperialisms, and she is co-partner in the unhappy history of socialist degeneration.' This first and fundamental step in Thompson's choice ensured that he would again walk in oppositional politics, striding out of silence and into major theoretical and historiographic debates, and on to the stage of international public mobilizations:

Standing above the lamplit town I watch this crime,
Cruel and beaked, crushing all comprehension,
Killing whole streets of men, sticking his horny knuckles
In the eyes of whoever comes. Man, who is changed by his hands,
Evolved the man of business, within whose mind
The clawed beast of possession gnawed all bonds until
Man fell apart, and split from self to self,
The acquisitive brain cutting off the creative hands.

Now crime, compassion, have reached the place called choice.
I hear at last the voice of resolution, loud
From the flagstones and setts, the commons engrossed for sheep,
From the mullioned windows, the lighted bulk of the mills,
And the living killed in their streets. In the frost-blue flames
Of the handloom weaver's rushlight the heroic shadows leap:
Mellor at Cartwright's mill: Jones on the hustings: names
That merge with anonymous shadows, shaping that man who crowds

Every room of the human house, opens the windows, stands

Warming the winds of space at his compassionate hands.[12]

Within the moving relationships of opposition and choice, Thompson looked to the past to renew the present, the better to recover possibility in the future.

Thompson's example, then, is one of consistent refusals. It is a legacy worth nurturing and passing on, yet again. But there are signs that understanding of this will be lost in the very political spaces where it is needed most. Among a fragmented and fragmenting left, the voices one hears, speaking *at* the legacy of Thompson, are, however subdued, often voices of quiet reproach: his 'trope' was not 'ours'; his tone was not congenial; his prose, whatever its power, lacked discipline; his understanding did not extend to 'us'; his idiom was parochial; his method lacked theoretical moorings. . . .[13] This, too, can be refused, with *reasons*. Those reasons take us into a history that encompasses internationalism and insight, forcing appreciation of a body of historical writing guided by a politics of socialist humanism and embattled engagement, insistent integrity and the imagination of the poet. They are reasons which changed the way many of us approached the very project of seeing a past layered in depths of obscurity; reasons which, at certain points, made history when it seemed that its future was at risk. Understanding Thompson's own history is pivotal in understanding ourselves.

# 1

# Family Tree as 'Liberty Tree'?

There has long lingered on the left a conception of Thompson as a parochial populist, narrowly nationalistic in his understandings and style. To be sure, this owes much to the sharp polemics of the mid-1960s, in which Thompson and Perry Anderson and Tom Nairn squared off in acidic and personalistic debate over the question of Englishness, its 'peculiarities' or 'mythologies'. Anderson took decided aim at 'the astonishing contrast in Thompson as a socialist intellectual, between the brilliance and richness of his imagination as a historian, and the poverty and abstraction of his intelligence as a political analyst'. This gulf was attributed to Thompson's populist idiom and its corollary, '*messianic nationalism*'. Whatever the olive branches extended by the opposing camps of the 1960s, the charge of 'cultural nationalism' continued to stick as an assessment of Thompson's political character, and even sympathetic comment at the time of his death tended to collapse his essence into a 'thoroughly English' container: 'he wrote about history or anything else', noted Eric Hobsbawm, 'in the persona of a traditional English (not British) country gentleman of the Radical Left.'

For his part, Thompson refused such readings, claiming an

unambiguous allegiance to socialist internationalism, confessing that his own awkwardness marked him as always 'alien', however much his idiom was, understandably, 'English'. Survival as a socialist, he once wrote, was a constant struggle in 'this infinitely assimilative culture'. It necessitated putting 'oneself into a school of awkwardness', making 'sensibility all knobbly – all knees and elbows of susceptibility and refusal'. That alien awkwardness was forged within the friction occasioned as English experience and traditions of radical dissent collided with the oppressions, record of exploitation, and challenges of international developments, both theoretical *and* practical. Thompson never denied that he had learned much from an increasingly sophisticated international theoretical discourse; on the contrary, this dialogue he embraced. But he was adamant that it was as an exchange that theory would prove productive – an exchange between concept and evidence, among divergent analytic trajectories. Nothing was to be gained by mere imitation, by lying prostrate before the theorist of the month; this was to evacuate 'the real places of conflict within our own intellectual culture'. Just as the main enemy was at home, so too were possibilities of socialist renewal:

> Talk of free-will and determinism, and I think first of Milton. Talk of man's inhumanity, I think of Swift. Talk of morality and revolution, and my mind is off with Wordsworth's Solitary. Talk of the problems of self-activity and creative labour in socialist society, and I am in an instant back with William Morris – a great bustard like myself, who has never been allowed into the company of such antiquated (but 'reputable') eagles as Kautsky or Plekhanov, Bernstein or Labriola – although he could, if given the chance, have given them a peck or two about the gizzards.

Such a passage can be construed as nationalistic only if other passages of Thompson's are in fact ignored:

> we are not at the end of social evolution ourselves. In some of the lost causes of the people of the Industrial Revolution we may discover

*12*

insights into social evils which we have yet to cure. Moreover, the greater part of the world today is still undergoing problems of industrialization, and of the formation of democratic institutions, analogous in many ways to our experience during the Industrial Revolution. Causes which were lost in England might, in Asia or Africa, yet be won.

It was on Spain and Indian independence, after all, that Thompson cut his teeth of political consciousness, as he noted in a 'Foreword' to *The Poverty of Theory*. His internationalist arguments were never distanced from moments of engagement and mobilization: World War II, Yugoslavia and Bulgaria, the Korean War and the campaigns for peace and disarmament that developed out of and beyond this initial hot flash in the Cold War, 1956, Suez, Cyprus, Algeria, Cuba, Vietnam, Chile, the implosions of 'actually existing socialism'. . . .[1]

Thompson was in fact born at the fault line of this England/ not England divide; his internationalism and his imaginative capacities were products, in part, of his own negotiations with his family tree. One branch – ironically enough, given an entrenched view of Thompson's anti-Americanism[2] – had deep roots in the United States. His mother, Theodosia Jessup Thompson, could trace her lineage back to seventeenth-century New England. Judge William Jessup, Thompson's great-great-grandfather, was prominent in the early Republican Party, chairing the platform committee of the Chicago Convention that nominated Abraham Lincoln, and the family was favoured with offerings of diplomatic posts.[3] His son Henry founded the American Mission in Lebanon. A writer himself, he penned a rambling paternalist tract, *Fifty-Three Years in Syria*, confident in its proselytizing zeal. Quoting Matthew 10:34 – 'Think not that I am come to send peace on earth: I came not to send peace but a sword' – Jessup was a man of uncomplicated religious certainty: 'Light dissipates darkness. Truth antagonizes error.' Islam he was capable of seeing as a 'gangrene'. 'Oh, the depths of corruption in Islam!' he wailed. Thankful that two-thirds of the world's Muslims were under Christian imperialist rule, Jessup could acknowledge some positive traits of the peoples of the Middle East, but many, such as the Bedouin, were little more than 'robbers and murderers'. Their salvation lay in compelling them 'to abandon their nomad life and internecine wars, settle down, and cultivate the soil and live in peace. This will come when there is a strong and honest government in Syria, Palestine, and Mesopotamia.' Without Christ and Empire, Muslims, it seemed, were destined to be 'lost'.[4] Theodosia, who would become a Methodist missionary in India,[5] spent her childhood in the Middle East, undoubtedly moving off the nineteenth-century ground of evangelical colonialism of her predecessor, Henry Jessup, and into a tough-minded liberal critique of imperialism. She was not likely to have been one of those itinerant Christians bent on a simple-minded Westernizing of 'the natives'.[6]

First introduced to the United States at the age of five in 1929, Thompson regarded the faces and gestures of the American people as 'reassuring and familiar'. (More than once I noticed Edward's penchant for observing the 'collective countenance' of a geographical region or socioeconomic locale.) Seventeen years later, fresh from his war service, having secured an introduction to the American communist poet Tom McGrath, a young Edward Thompson visited Manhattan. It seemed 'electric with life'. He attended one of the Madison Square Garden rallies, and heard Robeson, Marcantonio, and Harlem's communist councilman, Ben Davis; International Ladies Garment Workers' Union banners flew in defiance of the congealing climate of the Cold War. New York he remembered as 'a great city with an internationalist consciousness; a great anti-Fascist city, its diversity churning into a common torrent of solidarities'. It was a time when 'the causes and arguments of New York' mattered in an internationalist world.[7]

So too did those of India. Thompson's father, Edward John, was born in 1886, the son of Methodist missionaries who had worked in southern India. His father, the Reverend John Moses Thompson, eldest son of a small English farmer, died before Edward John reached the age of ten, and his mother was left with six young children and little means to support them. She charted much of the early course of her first-born son, sending him from his studies at the Methodist Kingswood School, Bath, to work in a bank in Bethnal Green, where Thompson sacrificed a university scholarship to provide for his mother and siblings. Writing to a friend in the 1920s, he would later claim that he had 'always been one of the depressed classes'. Along with his later war service in Mesopotamia and Palestine, and aspirations in the literary area (nine volumes of poetry were published between 1907 and 1922, the first seven at Thompson's own expense), this added to his life dimensions that were quite extraordinary in missionary circles. Graduating from the University of London with a BA in 1909, Edward John was quickly ordained and, under pressure from his influential mother, entered into Methodist 'service'. For the remainder of his life Thompson was engaged in a creative dialogue with his parents' past, his present, and the future of the land where so much of this came together – India. The result, E.P. Thompson would later insist, was a unique interface of English and Bengali cultures, profoundly unequal but none the less not reducible to a merely exploitative footnote in the history of British imperialism and Western Orientalism. The elder Thompson 'was a marginal man, a courier between cultures who wore the authorized livery of neither', a complex individual caught in the predicament of an 'alien homage'. One aspect of his dilemma was his resistance to the 'gulf so often alleged to exist between the East and West':

> Look in my eyes, and see what memories rouse
> At glimpse of your soft leaves and silken sheen.
> No alien this – whose spirit understands
> Each scent and sound of these beloved lands.

In the certainties of Edward John Thompson's judgements and passionately held liberal beliefs lay an awkwardness of principled effort that would result in a series of difficult oscillations and encounters over the years 1910 to 1946. Culture and politics, independence and Empire, poetry and personalities were but some of the discursive locales within which the elder Thompson shifted ground in tension-ridden engagements with Indians and others, balancing an ostensibly uncomplicated view of 'truth' against an always precarious appreciation of power.[8]

Edward John Thompson spent thirteen formative years (1910–22) in the Far East, travelling educationally in the footsteps of his parents. His 'mission' had surprisingly little to do with Christian proselytizing. Ending up in one of the more impoverished districts of West Bengal, he joined an expanding Bankura College. By 1920 the school had grown to 800 students and encompassed a College and a High School. The former became an affiliate institution of Calcutta University, which recognized some of its offerings, but for most students in both the upper and lower schools, rote-learning and a highly ritualized theatre of 'education' by expedient exam-taking and deferential discipline were the norm. Thompson freewheeled it, making his friends mostly among the educated Indian literary elite, ignoring the syllabus, and learning Bengali. He jostled gaily with the local culture, spent time on cricket and soccer, prepared anthologies and handbooks on poetry, and managed to manufacture precious few Christians, although as a gifted teacher working within a system he deplored, he was capable of stimulating his best students, one of whom graduated to the heights of international scholarship. But Thompson was also constrained by administrative responsibilities, among them those of Vice-Principal of the College and Principal of the High School. After meeting Rabindranath Tagore at the very time when news of the Indian poet's Nobel Prize reached him at his Santiniketan colony, Thompson told another Englishman of his mystic aspirations. '*You're* not a mystic, Thompson,' was the response, 'though I dare say you'd like to be one. No man in charge of a high school can possibly be a mystic.' Thompson offered a defensive rejoinder: 'I'm by way of being a mystic in my spare moments.' The reply was terse: 'From all I hear, those are precious few.'[9]

In these years of Wesleyan teaching, Edward John Thompson was renegotiating his relationship with religion. 'The missionary was beginning to undergo a conversion of some sort by heathen legend, folklore, and poetry,' commented his son in 1993, while his wife saw his fictionalized autobiographical statements in *Introducing the Arnisons* (1935) and *John Arnison* (1939) as inventing socialistic, irreligious characters 'to provide an escape from the Ministry'. He took his leave more directly into the Indian landscape, where he learned to love the rivers and jungles, the flora and fauna, that marked the Far East as much as its spirituality:

> Earth! I have loved thee so,
> That, going hence, I swear I do not know
> On what celestial lawn
> Hereafter I shall find
> A garden to my mind!

A few years later, while serving in another 'eastern' region during World War I, Thompson mourned the disappearing forests, cherishing what man could not kill:

> But there are things no axe can destroy, no builder blot out. . . . There is the view over leagues of sea to Cyprus. There are the dripping glens, and the ancient brooks making their way, the red sand stretches by Beirut, the multitude of olives far below. For posterity this generation might have left how much more! But at least we cannot help but leave all this.[10]

War further separated Thompson from any traditional sense of Methodist mission, his chaplain service from 1916 to 1919 taking him first to the hospitals of Bombay and then to the

Mesopotamian front. *Crusader's Coast,* his writing on this period of anguish and exhilaration, conveys a deep love of the physical beauty of the areas of the Middle East as well as poignant hurt at the carnage of battle. Increasingly, Thompson's gaze seemed fixated on the cruelties of power, the inequalities that scratched sorrow into the human condition. He saw dearth in what should have been a land of plenty. Famine he had known in India in 1916, and it moved him closer to a concern with the agricultural poor of the colonies. But it ill prepared him for what he would face in Lebanon:

> It is hard to think that such a land can suffer famine. From the earliest times it has sent out food to other lands. But during the War Turkish rule to its other infamies added yet this, the use of famine as a weapon of political massacre. When we entered Beirut the streets were full of people dying with a docility and despairing acceptance of misery which are impossible of belief, unless you saw. Gaunt crowds dragged themselves past well-stocked food shops, so drilled into submission that they never thought of looting. They eagerly gathered the bacon-salt we flung away; they picked the undigested grain out of the dung on the streets; there were queues outside our men's billets. A woman could be bought for a tin of bully beef. Even in the Hauran the wash of the famine was sufficient for men to be seen walking beside our troop trains, collecting the orange peel and melon rinds our feasting Indians threw down. In the Lebanon villages were blotted out, even to the dogs. American ladies visited a large village to give the people employment, and found themselves in a solitude of empty huts. The people had not emigrated; they had died.

Years later, in Syria, Thompson was guided to a hill that had once sustained a king and queen and their summer palace, a place where subjects were routinely hanged. 'Man's agony was stamped deep' into the rock, he wrote: 'man's imagination had filled this valley with passion; the record had been kept by a handful of folk, whose own sorrows had faded out with each generation, while they handed on these symbols mightier than their own realities'. War was clearly a disquieting experience. In verse Thompson offered his protests against the 'so-called *right* of making war'. The horrors of 'Death, in the blinding sands;/ Death, in the desert's stench', appeared in a poem, 'Spring, 1916'. This left Thompson adrift in an intense interrogation of the established colonial culture and its assumptions. He remembered one wounded 'coloured' hero, who bore the loss of an arm with pride: 'We boys stood the test *well*.' 'Many an Englishman must have wondered how his race could prove worthy of such loyalty,' mused Thompson. Yet war also consolidated a comradeship of the front which, in its sacrifices and solidarities, impressed him far more than his educational missionary experience: 'When I remember all the ways I went,/ Companioned as was never man before/Companioned, even so the heart grows sore/With too much pain of musing, memories bent.'[11]

As he moved beyond and outside stereotypical missionary concerns, Edward John Thompson may well have rethought many relationships, among them race and class. There are indications that in his early days at Bankura he could lapse into the role of patronizing paternalist, a managerial element in the educational factory of 'babuism', whose product was the ill-paid, servile, aspirant Indian middle class desirous of ensconcing their sons in the petty administrative posts of colonialism. He found amusement in the 'howlers' of his Bengali pupils, and could be moved to irritation at the stoic worshipful incapacities exhibited by peasants confronting 'sahib' Englishmen. 'I was very ignorant, ill-informed, & John Bullish,' Thompson would later remark concerning his Indian days. This was an overly severe self-judgement. He was never easily accommodated to this role of simple acquiescence in the stations of Empire, but there were limitations within which he lived. Even the most sensitive of Thompson commentators, Sumit Sarkar, acknowledges that while the educational missionary could communicate with Indian intellectuals – Tagore, Nehru, and others – he was ill at ease with the 'rank-and-file cadres of middle-class nationalism' who came out of colleges such as Bankura. More distance still stood between Thompson and the common folk of the Indian countryside. Other writers – predominantly E.P. Thompson and Amit Chaudhuri – suggest a more subtle, if awkward, relationship in which Thompson was somewhat uniquely attempting a negotiation of the strains of difference that structured English–Indian contact. In this there was no doubt an abstract attraction to overcoming the barriers separating patrician and plebeian. Certainly one of the central attractions of Tagore for Thompson was the Indian poet's 'intimacy of knowledge of the common people'. Whatever the actualities of this personal encounter between Thompson and ordinary Indians, there is no question that he grappled with the oppression he saw clearly all around him:

> Beneath this pipal, on a verminous mat,
> With skin-clad ribs and withered shank she lies,
> Dying by inches, after her fierce day
> Of labor – carrying water, bearing babes,
> And nameless menial tasks – the anguished toil
> For the scant meal which came with so much fear.

In 'Lepers' Thompson perhaps presented a metaphor that reached into the centres of power associated with race, class and imperial authority, personalizing the social relations of 'superiority' and subordination in ways that were all too familiar to the high school administrator:

> Sullenly friendly, watching me they sit,
> Their battered hands drawn close across their knees,
> What should he say, this saheb who means them well,
> Yet in whose veins the blood runs clean, whose limbs
> No furies of anguish eat?
>
> [...]
>
> A woman thrusts out knuckled palms – to these
> Will fingers come back again? I talk of cures,
> Of life given slowly back, of the fell plague
> Quenched in the crumbling limbs, that break no more.

> But, as I go, about my head there scatters
> A rain of bitter, unbelieving mirth.

Such verse calls into question who is diseased, how, and why? It perhaps also reconfirmed in Edward Thompson's thought something of an ambivalent Christian commitment, sustained increasingly by the apparent need not to let go of faith in human betterment:

> I have sought a city that I shall not win,
> Until my broken body they bear in;
> I serve a King whose courts I shall not find,
> Till I can never see his face, since blind.
> Vain service! Effort vain! yet I but know
> One fear, that I should cease to wish it so;
> And out of failure make no other prayer
> But this – when that last dimness holds the air,
> When crushed I reel, with dying eyes that glaze –
> Let not Faith fail, at crowning of her days.

On Christ, Edward John Thompson was now adamant: 'His life was with the common people.'[12]

Such convictions, solidified at the war's end, unsettled Thompson. He wrote to his mother:

> If I live thro this War, I stand, finally & without question, with the Rebels. What we need is entire *Reconstruction* of Society. The old order is gone, & it was inestimably damnable when here. The east does things better, in a thousand things, than we do, with our hideous industrialism ... our cowardice of thought in politics & the Churches ... I am a nonconformist on principle, because this War has shown with sheets of flame that the whole system of things is wrong, built on blood & injustice & issuing in blood & tears, & unChristian as any Rome or Babylon.

Bankura took on new meanings, and tensions once bypassed assumed more centrality. Quarrels with colleagues were frequent. There were additional pressures. When Thompson returned to Bengal from the war early in 1920 he was no longer able to consider only his own modest material needs and those of his mother, whom he had long supported. During his war chaplaincy in the Lebanon, he met and courted Theodosia Jessup, writer and daughter of American missionaries. They married in 1919, and by 1920 Theo was expecting a baby. Conditions were not favourable. The pregnancy was difficult, both parents were not in the best of health, their son (named William Frank after Edward's beloved youngest brother, Frank, killed on the Western front in 1917) was born a month premature, and Theo and Edward were separated – she living in a Darjeeling boarding house, he at Bankura. It was also a period of intense political turmoil associated with the massacre at Amritsar, or Jallianwala Bagh, in which hundreds of Indians attending a prohibited meeting in April 1919 were gunned down by a British officer. This unleashed a torrent of repression, racist public humiliations, floggings, and ceremonial endorsements of loyalist British terror. Thompson embraced the unpopular cause of indignation, signed a letter of protest authored by twenty-five missionaries, and drew the fury of the Empire's extremists down upon his head. Theo cautioned him against such seemingly rash acts of provocation, and – perhaps ambitious for her new husband – urged him on with his scholarly work. At any rate, Edward's involvement in the politics of protest was short-lived. Having made the appropriately liberal gesture of differentiating himself from the ugly reaction of imperial terror, he withdrew into his work on Tagore, which involved some translation but, more importantly, a futile attempt to bring the Indian poet to the West.

In the aftermath of Amritsar, Thompson cultivated Tagore and sidestepped the rising nationalist tide of Gandhi and the early 'non-co-operation' movement. War and nationalist rebellion, from 1916 to 1922, threw him into politics, only to result in a postponement of his reckoning with the unequal exchange of India and the British Empire. Critical of brutal repression, he could lapse into a defensive posture concerning the benevolence of British rule and the care that some Englishmen, such as himself, had for Indian culture; drawn to the literary accomplishment of Eastern writers, Thompson extended them in his commentary the critical compliment of being 'truthful'. Such a stand – for *and* against what was at stake in an India fractured along lines of obvious oppositions – won Edward Thompson few allies. By the early 1920s talk of being with 'the Rebels' gave way to a stubborn resignation to finish his work on Tagore and take his leave. Few Bengali friends seemed to remain. Early in 1923 Edward John Thompson left India, 'bruised but impenitent'.[13]

The Thompsons settled into their Boar's Hill Oxford home, and one year later, on 3 February 1924, a second son, Edward Palmer Thompson, arrived. The neighbourhood was one of distinguished literary accomplishment, and the Thompson home life was apparently lively, a cultivated culture of conversation and cricket that drew regular visitors. Resigning from the ministry, Edward John Thompson, who apparently contemplated becoming a Buddhist, took up the seemingly prestigious post of Lecturer in Bengali at Oxford University. The title meant little: he was not on the regular Oxford faculty until much later; he was employed part-time at £160 per annum, his income to be supplemented by a piece rate of £5 a term per student. His job was mainly to teach candidates for the Indian Civil Service the Bengali vernacular. But there were few takers for such an offering; only one student awaited the professor's arrival from India. When he presented his first public university lecture on Tagore, Edward Thompson found his colleagues even less receptive. He talked to an empty hall, his wife Theo, two disgruntled Indians, and the Chair of the meeting being the sum total of his audience. No doubt things improved, but for a decade Thompson had the time to write. Eventually he was appointed Oxford Leverhulme Research Fellow (1934–6), and then Research Fellow of Indian History, Oriel College (1936–46). Thompson was also an occasional Professor of

Greek and Latin at Vassar College for Women at Poughkeepsie, New York, where he would write *The Reconstruction of India* (1930), declaring: 'I am in America and have been drawn into defence of the Indian government and my own people.'

During this Oxford period Thompson published dozens of volumes that ranged broadly and eclectically across the disciplinary boundaries of fiction, poetry, literary criticism, biography, history, political commentary, polemic, and even social anthropology. A staunch and outspoken liberal critic of British imperialism, eloquent and volatile, he offered qualified (followed, later in life, by more categorical endorsement) support to the cause of Indian independence, and maintained personal relations and critical dialogue with leaders such as Mahatma Gandhi. Nehru and other Indian scholars, poets and activists were favoured visitors to the Thompson home, where they contributed to a young Edward's stamp collection and schooled him in his batting technique. (Decades later, Thompson would impishly close a brief appreciative note on C.L.R. James's eightieth birthday with the words 'I'm afraid that American theorists will not understand this, but the clue to everything lies in his proper appreciation of the game of cricket.')

His love of India expressed best in his poetry, novels and translation, as well as in his admiration for Tagore, Thompson deplored the crimes of British imperialism at the same time as he refused to pander to what he considered the backwardness of communalism, caste inequality, bigotry and violence. He would come to be revered among a segment of Indian literary society, acknowledged to be 'the human bridge of understanding between India and England'. But his 'sharp criticisms' of close friends within the nationalist movement 'pained' some, such as Tagore. Quoting Thomas Hardy – 'Nought remains/But vindictiveness here amid the strong,/And there amid the weak an impotent rage' – Thompson often seemed to cast a plague on the leadership houses of both Empire and Independence: 'The angry ghosts of nationalism and imperialism must be exorcized from a region where they have stalked so long.' The British he saw for many years as 'the only guarantee of … ordered progress. … If India would kill communal hatred, would overhaul her systems of thought and social practice, and would bring into the full stream of national effort her despised minorities and her women, she would be rid of nine-tenths of her miseries.' But he could not close his eyes to the dishonour of British shame, especially the racially edged brutality with which his country – 'the last in which free and unregimented thinking is still possible' – had historically suppressed uprisings such as the 1857 Sepoy Mutiny. When Tagore, knighted in 1915, relinquished this British honour in protest against the terror with which the Punjab disorders associated with the Jallianwala Bagh massacre of 1919 were put down, Thompson commented: 'Knighthoods are not for poets.' From all of this an impressionable Edward Thompson remembered: 'I grew up expecting governments to be mendacious and imperialist and expecting that one's stance ought to be hostile to government.' This was no doubt part of what he inherited from his father.[14]

But the subtle ways in which the legacy of a father such as Edward John Thompson, a man of cosmopolitan reach, cultured intellect, passionate 'Englishness', Methodist mission (however lapsed), attracted to the spiritualism and civilization of Indian accomplishment but repelled by the seeming gulf separating East and West in matters of liberal humanitarianism, was assimilated by a 'non-believer' son who would join the Communist Party at the age of eighteen are by no means straightforward. The Thompson household was obviously one in which the power of rhetorical persuasion and poetic imagination was not so much extolled as lived. Poetry was no mere amusement, but humanity's 'best effort down the ages to distill some wisdom from the inarticulate depths of [its] soul'. Belief in human potential and the transformative possibilities of genuine respect for difference, which alone could bring down the walls of racial separation in recognition of common needs

and origins, clearly drove the elder Thompson's pen. It structured his faith in the deity of possibility, the weapon of verse:

> This sword of verse I bear within my hand
> The years have fashioned; thus, and thus, I bade;
> But they, for higher mandate that they had,
> With patient eyes elsewhere to my command
> Not hearkened, neither wrought it as I planned
> But damascened with shining joys and clad
> The hilt with gems that make the gazer glad,
> And plunged in hissing griefs the bitter brand.
>
> Yet men, that dream not of the heats which made,
> Chide the sure poise and beauty of the blade,
> Till cold its master seems and wrapt apart.
> The brightness blinds. – To you this truth appears:
> No warrior wields it, but a child, whose heart
> Is weak and troubled oft with causeless tears.

Important as remaking the present was to Edward John Thompson, it was the dream of a new future, liberated from the
entanglements of messy, disputatious change, that was ultimately paramount. That future could be built out of generosity
and a renewed appreciation of history rooted in 'free grace and
love of truth'. This drew the elder Thompson rather more to the
poet (and the poetic side of) Tagore than to those, like Gandhi,
for whom the immediate end was of ultimate importance. And
as Benita Parry has commented, this 'conquest of estrangement
by goodwill' figures forcefully, if increasingly ambivalently, in
Thompson's fictional trilogy, a search for meaning in the
British–Indian encounter: *An Indian Day* (1927); *A Farewell to
India* (1931); and *An End of the Hours* (1938). That same
exploration was central to Thompson's most notable excursion
into social anthropology, a hostile discussion of *suttee*, the Hindu
ritual of widow-burning. In other writings, which included
criticism and biography, he stepped outside his concern with
India, but sustained a democratic temperament through peri-
odic outbursts of blunt denunciation. Of the years of Jacobite

repression to which his son would later be drawn, Thompson snorted: 'The reader cannot remind himself too often that this half-century was the most contemptible and venal in English parliamentary history.'

While he was a man of letters and apparent gentle grace, Thompson's father never believed in keeping his convictions to himself, or quieting his principled voice. Poetry was clearly the love of his life, but it never quite stilled his political discomforts. As he wrote to Nehru in 1936, once his 'brain [was] convinced', he could be 'relied on to stand firm'. 'I cannot do this when I disagree and will not pretend to do it,' he stated with finality. To grow into one's teenage years in this kind of milieu – which regularly welcomed Poet Laureates such as Robert Bridges, and breathed a 'tolerant, international sympathy' that encouraged a 'steady flow of Indian visitors' alongside a principled refusal to compromise when integrity, truth and justice were at stake – must have been, at times, a daunting experience. Edward was undoubtedly in awe of much that went on and passed through this remarkable house. But it could not have left those living within it untouched. The Thompsons' Boar's Hill home culti-vated poetic aspiration and commitment to the principles and causes of freedom, as well as gruff denials of the importance of individual indulgences. As his father lay dying of cancer in 1946, Edward asked him if Jawaharlal Nehru should be told of the state of his health. 'He told me to mind my own business,' Thompson recalled in 1978; that 'Nehru had far more import-ant matters to attend to'. Thompson sent the letter anyway; Nehru replied immediately.[15]

It is not hard to see the sensitivities and style of his father, their grounding in internationalism and the imagination, in Thompson's later politics, polemics, and historical prose. Thompson acknowledged, late in his life, that – at least unconsciously – he had 'modelled' himself partly on his father. Indeed, Amit Chaudhuri's assessment of the elder Thompson as a personality always 'awkward but receptive ... with a caricaturist's gift for exaggeration and a realist's eye and ear for the true and human', fits the Edward I have known and read with uncanny accuracy.[16] But it is possible that Thompson, in his remembrance of his father, opted for an appreciation of Edward John Thompson's general commitment to India and independence which, over the course of the 1920s and 1930s, placed the lapsed missionary and Oxford Fellow firmly to the left of British intellectual and political thought on colonialism and 'the question of India'. This was a longstanding entrenched 'anti-imperialism', to be sure, but it was more complicated than that, and the matter was made more complex by historical context and chronology, and the elder Thompson's shifting locales and concerns. When he was actually resident in India, his strength was his capacity to learn from what the culture had to offer; his weakness was a tendency to filter his vision of India through a sieve which, for all its capacity to bleach the 'races' clean of animosity and misrepresentation in the reciprocal solution of universal humanity's commonalities, was not fine enough to accommodate the profound and overriding author-ity (both as practice and as perception) of imperialism's exploitative essence. This failure blinded him to the impossi-bility of his liberal programme of 'atonement', in which the sheer goodwill of Britain, combined with the advantageous efficiency of administration it could, for a time, offer an India in need of preparation for home rule, might reverse gener-ations of misunderstanding and mistrust.

To read Edward Thompson's relationship with his father in this overtly political way, whatever the complexities involved, is appropriate, for it is how Thompson himself came to grips with his family legacy at the end of his life. But it is difficult not to make a speculative, Freudian detour. Thompson's youth, regardless of his father's movement away from Methodism, could not have helped being stamped with the mark of Wesleyanism. This experience obviously left its scars. Some of the most vividly hostile pages of *The Making of the English Working*

*Class* turn on a merciless spit of condemnation, a relentless polemic against Methodism's 'essential disorganization of human life, a pollution of the sources of spontaneity bound to reflect itself in every aspect of personality'. Pillorying Methodism as a 'moral machinery', E.P. Thompson as a young adult interpreted Wesleyanism as falling 'ambiguously between Dissent and the Establishment', doing its apologetic utmost 'to make the worst of both worlds'. Quick to defend Lecky's late-nineteenth-century characterization of Methodism as an 'appalling system of religious terrorism', Thompson's argument in *The Making* exposed how Wesleyanism's 'pitiless ideology of work' could be circumvented by those at whom its rituals of 'psychic masturbation' were directed. But it could not forgive 'the psychological atrocities committed upon children', the purposeful assault on sensuality that attempted to submerge anything approximating a humane sexuality in a deluge of 'useful labour'.

At Wesley's Kingswood School (where Thompson's father and Thompson himself had sat in attendance), students of the first Industrial Revolution learned 'workful "recreations"', since 'games and play were "unworthy of a Christian child"'. Wesley promised these youngsters that he would 'kill or cure', and Thompson added that 'he rarely said things he did not mean'. Toddlers were taught to sing that they were, 'By nature and by practice too,/ A wretched slave to sin'; the Methodist young lived in a state of intimidation and fearful terror, their nights a restless negotiation with images of death and everlasting punishments. At the onset of puberty children were expected to come to a sense of religious wrong, their baptism taking the form of immersion in the obsessional Wesleyan teachings on the sinfulness of the sexual organs. Later in life, Methodists were expected to displace life's passions in Sabbath orgasms of Wesleyan emotionalism, causing Hazlitt to describe them as 'a collection of religious invalids'. In Thompson's words: 'The obsessional Methodist concern with sexuality reveals itself in the perverted eroticism of Methodist imagery . . . by turns maternal, Oedipal, sexual, and sado-masochistic.' The symbolism of Wesleyanism opened out into a perverse assimilation and eroticization of Christ's wounds, blood, sacrificial love, pain, guilt, sex and sin: humanity, as a sinful 'worm', found 'lodging, bed and board in the lamb's wounds'.

This was nothing less than 'the psychic process of counter-revolution'. How could E.P. Thompson's obviously antagonistic *understanding* of a Wesleyanism he had literally been schooled in – a Methodism that was, in his own family, deeply historical and embedded in *generations* of his forebears – not be rooted in a highly ambivalent relationship with his father? Over time, perhaps, that ambivalence may have softened, and the politics of Edward John Thompson's advocacy of India no doubt became elevated in E.P. Thompson's appreciation of his once-Methodist father. But for a part of his life, at least, the Methodist meaning of his father and his family might well have been a matter of inner conflict for Edward Thompson.

E.P. Thompson himself left little indication of how he may have wrestled with his father's Methodism. His concerns with his father's legacy had little to do with a Wesleyanism that figured less and less forcefully in his family's history, and more to do with rehabilitating the possibilities inherent in the political and cultural meeting of East and West that Edward John Thompson embodied. Along with Sumit Sarkar, E.P. Thompson has forced reconsideration of the bluntly leftist reduction of Edward John Thompson to a 'vestigial imperial-ism', a reading associated with Benita Parry. Sarkar, in partic-ular, suggests that in Parry's depiction of Thompson as embodying a paradox of moral conscience and paternalist supposition, the urge to atone for British oppression coupled with an acute desire to have the world – and India – recognize the accomplishments of 'the' British, much is missed of his shifting 'structure of feelings'. Thompson's gestural reach for 'atonement', for instance, as expressed in his 1924 play of the same name, and in some of his historical writing, especially *The Other Side of the Medal* (1925), could have had a more far-reaching cathartic effect than Parry appreciates, moving the uncomfortable otherworldly paternalist towards concrete political endorsement of the need for Indian self-government. In his puritanical (*and* humanist) disdain for the brutalization of women, evident in his substantial statement on *suttee*, Thompson confronted 'the dangers of falling into the western ethnocentric trap of complete condemnation' at the same time as he faced the recognition that '"orientalist" patronage could hide behind a romantic glorification of the exotic'.

In the process he explored tentatively, but insightfully, the relationship between gender and imperialism that historians and theorists of seventy years later are only beginning to address. In *Atonement*, an Indian character proclaims:

> 'We are fools, and we have fallen long ago in love with the English spirit, which is so hard and masculine and – so contemptuous of us. . . . I begin to see that there is more justice in the world than I thought. We have always refused freedom to our women for the very reasons for which it is now being refused to us – because they are emotional, swayed by their passions and loyalties, and cannot be calm and collected.'

Thompson, in Sarkar's words, was repeatedly reaching 'the outer limits of liberal discourse and his ambiguities are interesting and moving precisely because of the honesty with which he exposes the crisis of his liberal concern in the colonial situation'. This was an extremely complex and irregular reckoning, involving overlapping and conflictual chronologies, as well as discrete but connected realms; encompassing religious and spiritual matters, politics, literature, and personal friendships. Yet even Sarkar concludes that the extension of Thompson's discourse did have its limits. In his 'search for human understanding across political, racial, and cultural divides,' the lapsed Wesleyan 'could at most admit British failure to tackle poverty, not colonial responsibility'.

*31*

The interface of British and Indian culture was, in Thompson, a conjuncture of cultures, deeply personal, in which economies tended to be understated. Oppression moved him; to reach beneath its surface to appreciate exploitation was not something he usually attempted. When Reginald Reynolds wrote *The White Sahibs in India: British Imperialism from the Days of the John Company to Date* (1937), he relied on much of Thompson's historical writing. But a footnote to Thompson's *A History of India* (1927) commented that while the unofficial corruption of the early history of the British in India was acknowledged, 'the *official* activities' of the East India Company in draining the wealth and production of the populace went largely unrecorded. One Indian reviewer responded to Thompson's *The Other Side of the Medal* – an anguished account of British brutality in the suppression of the Sepoy Mutiny of 1857, where captured Hindu and Muslim rebels were branded, impaled on stakes, bayoneted in the face, smeared with pork fat before public executions and hangings, burned, and shot from cannons – with the statement that such atrocities were 'as nothing to the long-drawn-out agonies of a whole nation of 247 million people, exposed daily to starvation, disease, ignorance, and life-long misery'.

An honest, impassioned idealist who could have one of his fictional characters proclaim 'Idealists do a lot of mischief', Edward John Thompson demanded, for much of his life, British repentance and Indian patience, insisting that ruler and ruled alike open up in sensitive embrace of the civilizing tendencies of the culture of 'the other'. It was a dream which, given the hard realities of power, was doomed to drift in the direction of nightmare for the culture of those subjected to domination. Displaced from India, settled in Oxford, Thompson engaged throughout the 1920s and early 1930s with the politics of Indian independence, but he was – as Parry indicates, and his letters to Nehru show – temperamentally radical but moderate in his programmatic attachments: he was actually estranged from

Gandhi and distanced from Nehru politically for much of the later 1930s, friendships and respect aside, and he was no advocate of the Indian National Congress until very late in life.

By 1936 Thompson's dream of an Indian independence fuelled by liberal humanitarian modernization among Indians and an invigorated commitment to respect and atonement on the part of the British – which he himself proclaimed 'pure "Liberal"' – was fading. A character in one of his novels states: 'We neither govern nor misgovern. We're just hanging on, hoping that the Last Trump will sound "Time!" and save us from the bother of making a decision.' He was losing faith in both sides of the independence equation, troubled not only by Indian tactics and the tendency to impose silence on those like himself, but also by a British state that was sacrificing any sense of 'fair play' at home, intensifying its intolerance into 'sedition' by monitoring and opening his own correspondence. Towards the end of the year he wrote two letters to Nehru:

> Being now old and profoundly disillusioned and depressed by every-thing, in India as well as the West, I am going to concentrate, for the little time left to me, on my own country's affairs. I now know, after 26 wasted years in trying to help forward what seemed to me truth and decency, that any Englishman who troubles himself about India is a fool. . . . I take away no anti-Indian feeling whatever. But I know we are a poor kind of animals, in India or England; and I feel profoundly pessimistic. I think at the back of your mind, as of other Nationalists' minds, is the demand that no Englishman, if he wishes to be considered a friend, should ever criticize. Our own Labour Party (which has behind it such a deplorable record of betrayals, desertions, and anti-democratic stiffness) makes the same demand. I cannot meet it. You must consider me an enemy, if you feel I must never say I think any action mistaken. . . . As to your own socialism, I have no doubt that superficially viewed, it is bad tactics. But here I believe your instinct will be proved right in the long run. The whole economic and social (and, especially in India, religious) structure is monstrous.

Letters were now signed E.F.I., Emeritus from India. While some have interpreted Thompson's *You Have Lived Through It*

*All* (1939) as a totalizing interrogation and rejection 'of the fact and concept of Empire', in 1943 he was able to begin a book with unqualified acceptance of independence, and close it with praise for the early-nineteenth-century colonizers: 'The work they achieved was to stand the test of over a century, and when all empire and dominion at last are finished their work will still win toleration and sympathy, and not in their land only.' As Sarkar emphasizes: 'Rethinking about received "John Bull" attitudes, as always, [was] accompanied in Thompson by rethinking about aspects of received Christianity.' In *The Youngest Disciple* (1938) Thompson offered an unorthodox reconciliation of Buddhism and Christianity, while a year later he would write to Nehru: 'I think religion is the greatest pest in the world.'[17]

As Edward W. Said has recognized, Thompson's liberal anti-imperialism was an idealism that did, historically, cloud understanding of the British–Indian relationship. For all the admirable artistry of his exploration of imperialism as a 'cultural affliction for colonizer as well as colonized', it could ultimately only reproduce the very representational dichotomies it was struggling to overcome. In *The Other Side of the Medal* (1925) Thompson's genuine humane revulsion at the historical act of brutal repression of the Sepoy Mutiny (1857) extends usefully beyond a mere recovery of the savagery of the event itself (no inconsiderable accomplishment) to address the *meaning* of history's presentation as suppression. Writing to a missionary friend, Thompson identified the impulse behind his book:

> I cannot bring myself to believe that hanging of – say ten thousand, I believe it was nearer to twenty thousand – blowing to pieces of hundreds, burning of hundreds of villages, and a war without quarter, has passed unremembered and unresolved. The Indian government has suppressed all the evidence of resentment. I'm afraid I feel too bitterly about it. I'd like as an individual Englishman, to do my bit of prayaschitta [ed.: a Sanskrit term for gesture]. ... It's obsessed me of

recent months. I've thought of little else. ... You and I hitherto have both been very distinct moderates. ... But now I'm becoming a left-winger very fast, and I feel how patronising nearly all propaganda, political *and* religous, and education must seem to an Indian. I can hardly imagine an Indian accepting Christianity – an educated and thinking Indian that is – as it comes to him to-day, from missionaries who've got *all* their knowledge of India from books written by British. ... I marvel that they bore with me in my India days. We *are* a gauche, crass lot.

But in his battle to transcend misrepresentation, in which the unfeeling superiority of the English and the seeming squalor of uncivilized India are pitted relentlessly against one another, Thompson could fight on a consistent independence plane only for so long. As a moderate mediating between the inflammatory misrepresentations of both sides, he aspired to 'help root out of the Indian mind some of its "inferiority complex"'. This, he knew, was regarded by the pro-colonial forces surrounding him at Oxford as highly subversive, to such a point that it could threaten his university post. 'They think I have done a very shocking thing,' he wrote to a friend just after the publication of his account of the Mutiny. Eventually, however, this narrative of outrage collapsed inward in 'atonement', returning to a relationship of inequality. *The Other Side of the Medal* makes the case for colonized want and paternalist gift: Indian men and women 'want their self-respect given back to them. Make them free again, and enable them to look us and everyone in the eyes, and they will behave like free people and cease to lie.' As Said notes, Thompson's limitation was that he was 'bound to the notion that there [was] "a truth" to events involving both sides that transcends them. Indians "lie" because they are not free, whereas he (and other oppositional figures like him) can see the truth because they *are* free and because they are English.' But, Said concludes, the Empire 'cannot *give* Indians their freedom', which must be extracted from it by protracted struggle. Moreover, British attitudes, whatever their merits, can, in such circumstances, be defended, and proposed as possible values, only at the point where their imperialist supports are dashed in defeat.

*The Other Side of the Medal* is thus a profoundly two-sided text, encompassing core chapters on the brutal, racist terror unleashed on Indians in the Mutiny and its aftermath (where Thompson explores the shadows of this episodic repression in similar events in 1872, 1879 and 1919), introduced by a defensive account of British contributions and Indian weaknesses, closing with a plea for an egalitarian passing over the cruelties of history by *both* sides. To read Thompson's 1925 text is to hear the troubled thoughts of a loyalist who loved India, a country where 'savage hatred' permeated a 'seditious and envious and unthankful' culture. For the nationalist 'extremist' press Edward John Thompson had little patience, and it is of considerable significance that he used the opening pages of a text of 'atonement' to launch what he recognized in his 1924 play as the colonizer's penchant for talking 'to Indians as if they were a class ... instruct[ed] for confirmation'. One part of the problem, surely, was Thompson's inability to discriminate in terms of his audience: refusing the separations of East and West, *The Other Side of the Medal* was addressed to English *and* Indian, a seemingly even-handed repudiation of Empire's vicious excesses and Indian 'foolishness'. Alongside the sensitive repudiation of a self-serving colonial historiography, and prefacing a detailed accounting of his countrymen's history of atrocity, were passages such as this:

> Every Englishman who has been in any position of responsibility in India knows how often he has had to interfere to save Indians from their own kin. The measures of self-government granted from time to time, municipal and parliamentary, have frequently been worked listlessly or – I am afraid it is impossible to avoid repetition of the word – dishonestly. The world's literature of abuse might be ransacked, and still the crown for utter irrelevance and reckless unfairness allowed to rest with the Indian extremist press. Nor is it (in my judgement) possible to exaggerate the services which Britain has rendered to India or the greatness of the individual contribution of many of her sons and

daughters. I know that the heroisms of this Empire are innumerable, and that they throw about its daily traffic a splendour brighter by far than any which imagination flings about the thought of Caesar's outposts on the Rhine or in Libya. These things will be seen and acknowledged one day, and no honest and competent mind will judge our rule hardly when its day has passed. It is no use looking for gratitude; the whole world is raw and bleeding, and we have all got memories that we had better forget.

Thompson looked forward to the day when the British would not always be assailed as 'hypocrites or fiends', when the altruism of the outposts of Empire would be appreciated for the quiet dignity and righteousness that often lay at the core of their human endeavours. For this to happen, the 'unavenged and unappeased ghost' of the Mutiny's horrific suppression needed to be broached by an honest British accounting. Thompson thus sent Tagore an inscribed copy of his book, 'R.T. An individual Englishman's act of atonement', and ended his statement on the Sepoy Revolt:

> But the last word seems to me this. Seventy years ago our two races were mad, with an awful homicidal insanity. We cannot afford to perpetuate their feud nor to carry their deeds, which were not ours. That we should probably have shared in them, had we lived when their madness could have drawn us in also, is nothing to the point; it is true of ourselves and of every evil action ever done, the crucifixion of Jesus or the burning of Joan. We can at least refuse to ratify those deeds, or to misrepresent them to flatter our own national esteem. This is a world of fallible men and women, who had no power of choosing their race or land of birth; all we can choose is whether our attitude shall be generous and courageous, or ignoble and cowardly. We who are British can sweep our minds clear of all the poison and untruth that our books have placed there, and we can create an atmosphere in which a new beginning of thought is possible. To many who have read my pages, after the first shock of horror and shame must have come relief, that a monster had been shown to be unreal. Our own madness we can understand, and it is a matter for humiliation but not for perplexity; and there is seen to have been no inexplicable Indian madness, but only the passions of suffering men like ourselves. With such men an understanding is possible, and friendship and forgiveness. And this new attitude, I believe, is the *atonement* that Indians are seeking.

This was, of course, greatly to simplify the resolution of the tensions and inequalities at the core of the Britain–India relation. Sarkar characterizes *The Other Side of the Medal* perceptively: a text rich in 'tensions, ambiguities, and silences which underlie its surface smoothness of polemic. For what emerges is a contradictory, indeed tortured, sensibility.' Thompson's 'atonement' was, in the face of a century and more of imperialist distortions, the last gasp of liberalism's dream of Empire's redemption. By the 1930s and 1940s, other dreams, in the growing nationalist, socialist and communist movements, were being voiced, and in the process Edward John Thompson was too often vulgarly dismissed as little more than an 'apologist of imperialism'.[18]

This was ironic, for Thompson apparently moved more decisively to the side of categorical support for Indian independence as Britain declared the country 'a belligerent' in 1939. There was the expectation of nationalist acts of civil disobedience, and fear of the subsequent imperialist repression. Thompson travelled to India on a kind of unofficial mission of mediation: he hoped that if protest could be called off by Indian leaders, the British would commit themselves to independence after the war. Bound to Nehru by friendship and the politics of opposition to appeasement and anti-fascism, Thompson also gravitated more warmly towards Gandhi. He was treated with great respect by the nationalist leadership and gentle cordiality by ordinary Indians. Two decades of thought were opening out into reconsideration. But the war proceeded; it elevated ugliness everywhere. Thompson returned to England. And India came apart: the declaration of civil disobedience; the British reaction of repression. Nehru, of course, was jailed. There were protest meetings in Oxford: young Edward went; his father was thrown into the cause in a more public and prominent way, especially with the publication of *Enlist India for Freedom!* (1942). Eventually Thompson was banned from visiting India until the war's end, and his letters to the subcontinent were intercepted.

The English voices raised against this repression spoke as liberals, socialists and communists. Among the Indian voices, the message was firm. No paternalist gift was wanted; what was demanded was liberty itself. 'We are not asking you to "give us freedom". We will take it when we want to. I am not here to ask you for your help but to remind you of your duty.' For the first time in his life, Edward John Thompson embraced an unequivocal pro-independence stance, putting forth a 'staunchly pro-Congress' position, rubbing political shoulders with H.N. Brailsford, Kingsley Martin, Fenner Brockway, Harry Pollitt and the India League of Krishna Menon. A final letter from Nehru allowed a dying Edward John Thompson to pass ironic judgement on his own movement from religion to politics. 'Now Lord, let thy servant depart in peace,' he said with a smile as his last days were 'blessed' by the Indian nationalist's communication of gratitude and affection.[19]

Just how this was digested by an Edward Thompson barely out of adolescence will never, I suspect, be adequately known. But young people grew up quickly in those days, when a trip to Europe was anything but a holiday for nineteen-year-olds. There can be no mistaking that his family nurtured a particular kind of appreciation of 'the liberty tree'. Planted in this soil of internationalism, imagination and insight, its branches would grow in different directions, but they would remain rooted in a common base. India, after all, figured centrally in the Marxist reading on imperialism that young Edward Thompson must have done to be in a position to quote Marx on the destructive progressivism of British colonialism on the subcontinent, where human advance often seemed fated 'to resemble that hideous pagan idol, who would not drink the nectar but from the skulls of the slain'.[20] One of E.P. Thompson's last projects was an attempt to try to come to grips with his father's tempestuous relationship with Tagore, which one reviewer considers to be a window looking out over the intimate relations of 'humane' colonialism and ordinary Indians.[21] Towards the end of Edward

John Thompson's life Edward worked with his mother to offer criticism and advice on the selection for publication of a hundred poems written by the aging Oxford Fellow over the course of forty years. A year before, Edward John Thompson's last substantive historical writing had gone to press. In it he remained true to humanist principles even as they were seemingly swamped by 'realist' politics and philosophies, popularly discredited as a weakness of will or a failure of energy. If his subject continued to be the reciprocities and dualities of Britain/India, Thompson also chose to allude to the internal class frictions of English society. 'The discrepancy in England, between the highest and the ordinary levels of our civilization, has always been immense,' he wrote, 'I doubt if there is anything like it in any country with which we should wish to be compared, and it is a discrepancy that lessens so slowly that it often seems hardly to lessen at all.' These words appeared in 1943, in a book entitled *The Making of the Indian Princes.*[22]

For E.P. Thompson, then, breaking from the limitations of his father's liberalism was by no means a process of totalizing repudiation; as he moved in more radical directions in the late 1930s and 1940s, Edward's branches of the family tree remained connected to a particular intellectual genealogy. Both he and his older brother, William Frank, as well as Oxford friends and neighbours, were sent as children to the Dragon, one of the most esteemed preparatory schools in England. Later Frank would attend Winchester and go on to Oxford, while Edward went to his father's school, Methodist Kingswood, in Bath, and then found his way to Corpus Christi, Cambridge. There he was elected President of the University Socialist Club, and read Christopher Hill and Christopher Caudwell with interest. If his attraction to these authors reproduced his father's aesthetic, in which history, verse, and engagement overlapped, it did so on decidedly Marxist ground and, in the case of Caudwell, also addressed frontally the theoretical dimension of language, with which his Classicist brother Frank, drawn to linguistics,

Romance and Eastern European tongues, and poetry, was much concerned.[23]

Frank, three-and-a-half years older than Edward, was the bridge from their father's liberal limitations to the potentials of communism. Remembered by a former Winchester dormitory mate as 'the largest, the loudest, the most uninhibited, and the most brilliant' of his group, Frank was dubbed 'College Poet'. Hobsbawm claims that he 'was supposedly more brilliant and certainly more favoured' than his younger sibling, a view also suggested in a 1980 *Times Higher Education Supplement* 'Profile' of Edward; but if this was true, little has survived to indicate anything resembling a rivalrous resentment. Thompson may, of course, have been overshadowed by his brother: 'I grew up firmly convinced I was stupid,' he once confessed. Out of a good-humoured mischievousness and romantic attachment to the mythical T.E. Lawrence (long a subject of conversation at Boar's Hill), drawing on his father's willingness to face into the wind of orthodoxy and convention, and attracted to the necessity of acting to better the world, Frank began to be governed by the Communist Party. By 1936 he was reading the CP poet, Cecil Day Lewis, and the *Daily Worker*, but it was Spanish atrocities and Hitler's persecutions that pushed him hardest to the left. A friend and neighbour, one of the three Carritt brothers, lost his life in the Spanish Civil War, and when his younger sibling Brian joined the Young Communist League at Eton, Frank, too, began to adopt a more open political stance:

> I see a man
> Last heard of alive on a hill-crest
> In Spain, expecting to die at his gun,
> Alone, his youth and work over,
> His stars and planets
> Reduced to yards of ground,
> Hoping others will harvest his crop.

In Frank's case the harvest began with symbolic, personal and

*41*

poetic acts. He wore red ties, jersies or shirts, drawing the ire of Establishment boys. When Chamberlain bowed in appeasement to Hitler late in 1938, Frank donned a black tie and mourned the disgrace:

> Our last chance and that vanished. In the night
> A rumour like an east wind chilled the land,
> Of cowardly betrayal calmly planned.
> The pass was sold. It was no use to fight.

But he remained, into his first year at Oxford in 1938, in the Officers' Training Corps, joining not the Communist Party but the Oxford Labour Club, which he would later find 'needlessly bohemian'. By May Day 1939 he was a Communist, marching in what he must have felt was a new and disciplined procession. A schoolmaster commented that he had come to this political decision out of 'intellectual conviction and frustration at what to him seemed the helplessness of other political parties to deal effectively with the problems of the time'. Fascism, Frank obviously thought, would triumph unless it was stopped.[24]

Edward was probably thinking similar thoughts, living through the same times, looking up to his elder brother as much as – perhaps more than – his father. This was a moment of political maturation that obviously divided father and sons. 'To join the Communist Party was, for my older brother, a cause of conflict in the family,' Thompson noted. 'He broke open the way,' he remembered in gratitude, 'and when I did the same there was less conflict.' Indeed, Thompson's father was himself looking to Russia with some openness. Like Tagore, by the 1940s Edward John Thompson saw hope for a regenerated Indian peasantry in the example of the transformed Russian countryside, insisting, however, that 'no alien administration has the authority to remove them'.[25]

Frank, like many young communists, 'staggered' under the news of the Hitler–Stalin non-aggression pact, but he was an implacable anti-fascist and he volunteered for military service when war was declared a month later, in September 1939. His early service was spent in England, in an officers' training unit. Commissioned in March 1940, he was beset with ambivalence about his class place as a commissioned officer and the possibility of fighting fascism as a communist when the Soviet Union had already signed off into abstentionism. He volunteered for service in Greece, ended up in North Africa on an intelligence assignment, and eventually found his way to Persia – crossing, no doubt, many ancestral paths, including those of his father, who had been stationed in the region throughout World War I. He chafed under the inaction of a desert campaign, but the implosion of the Nazi–Soviet pact in 1941 reinvigorated him, and he soon connected with James Klugmann in Cairo. An intelligence officer who headed the Yugoslav Section responsible for liaisons with Tito's Partisans, Klugmann was a former secretary of the Communist Students' League at Cambridge, and he would later be prominent in the British Communist Party. Late in 1943 Frank was accepted for training in the Balkan section responsible for reconnaissance activity behind enemy lines. His language skills, as well as Klugmann's assessment that he was an ideal officer who could work sympathetically and productively with anti-fascist Partisans, secured him the opportunity to be air-dropped into war-torn Bulgaria. In January 1944 Captain Frank Thompson parachuted into the Mission of 'Mulligatawny'. He was to contact the underground Resistance movement in Bulgaria, serve as British liaison officer, suggest possible supply options, and establish radio communications with the Allied Command in Cairo.[26]

As he left Cairo, however, Thompson became an 'official secret'. His Mission, like many others, has never been acknowledged by the British state. Secrecy covered many things: uncertainties; chaos; incompetence; the cross-purposes of politically oppositional operations (there was even reported to be a fascist contingent, with its own Mission); betrayal. It gave those committed to maintain capitalism in Europe and Britain's slice of the imperialist pie, especially those who worked hard at this project through the intrigues of Whitehall or the posh Shepheard's Hotel in Cairo, all the cover they needed. These were the people who abandoned those they had sent into exposed positions or, worse, double-crossed them when they were there, under fire. They used their own cloistered inner circle to shield their superiors from the knowledge they needed about the state of popular resistance to fascism. Such resistance carried with it the odour of unthinkable outcomes, not at all pleasant in the already foetid atmosphere of 'the secret state within the state'. Churchill's own representative to Tito, Sir Fitzroy Maclean, for instance, was thwarted by these moles of monopoly capitalism. There was a planned and deliberate effort in Cairo to refuse him transport and slander him in the officers' messes as 'consistently cowardly and unreliable'. The 'dirty trick' campaign's ace-in-the-hole was to be the final allegation that Maclean was a 'hopeless drunk, an active homosexual'. This was, too often, the stuff of secrecy.[27]

At least Maclean was not a communist; Thompson was, and his beliefs were by no means hidden. Ultimately, secrecy denied an official accounting of 'Mulligatawny', which faltered in tragedy and courageous loss: Thompson's superior officer was killed and he assumed command, temporarily promoted to the rank of Major. He witnessed brutal butcheries of village populations and the heroism of his Partisan comrades; to survive, he led his own 'long march'. In the end Thompson and others were captured by the Bulgarian state forces: brutally interrogated, beaten and subjected to public humiliation, Thompson responded with declarations of his communist commitments and insistence that he and others be treated as prisoners of war. After ten days of captivity, weakened by malnutrition and a festering wound, Frank Thompson was subjected to a mock trial. He stood firm, speaking in Bulgarian: 'The most vital thing in the world today is the struggle of anti-Fascism against

Fascism. . . . I am proud that I die together with my comrades, partisans of Bulgaria.' His clenched-fist salute in the name of the Partisan Fatherland Front was struck down by a gendarme. As he led the condemned men to the firing squad, all raised their fists in defiance. 'I give you the salute of freedom,' said Thompson, before he and twelve others were executed:

> Write on the stone no word of sadness,
> Only the gladness due
> That we, who asked the most of living
> Knew how to give it too.

'When a democrat dies – that is, a man who has shown, as they [the Partisans of Yugoslavia] have, by word and action that he cares more than anything for democratic freedom – then one, or ten, or a hundred new ones are created by his example,' wrote Frank Thompson in the very year of his death, concluding: 'one or ten or a hundred existing ones are strengthened in their resolve. But when a fascist dies the effect on his confederates is the reverse. Only in the most confused and darkest periods of history does this not appear to be the case.'[28]

As these words were being written, Frank's younger brother was a tank troop commander in Italy, part of the Allies' slow march up 'the Italian boot'. It was an 'advance' that pressured the beleaguered German rearguard, to be sure, and in the process, like Major Thompson's Bulgarian Mission, it bought time and resources needed elsewhere. But the cost was great: weekly, if not daily, the leading tank, infantrymen and engineers were sacrificed, not to mention any and all who happened to find themselves in the midst of the incessant shelling. Thompson chose to make as little as possible of this experience of war service, his sensibilities offended by the crass self-promotion of those who have made a business of equating loyalty, patriotism and war service with the cause of lawless repression of the left. But like any veteran, he bore the scars of war. Many were in his mind. First, he remembered, above all else, *the death*: the never-ending battle to cheat it; its constant presence; the ways in which it could come, without logic or warning; the dozy unreality of it all, which lulled many into a kind of personal acceptance that it would get you next, no matter what you did; even the smell of it. 'Save some in England all of Europe knows/ So I'll not tell you how a dead man smells/Nor what five days of sun can do to flesh.' It was a theme his father had also addressed in the previous war. Second, in the minute-by-minute unfolding of war's actual war, Thompson recalled the living failure – not of courage, conviction and comradeship, but of *reason*. In his overture to the Battle of Cassino, which he lived through, written in 1947 or 1948 – the first instalment of a 'war novel' destined never to be written – Thompson acknowledged that amidst all the death and destruction, war's foot soldiers were occupied with the struggle to live through the intensified minutes that made up, day after day, the moment of survival's sudden possibility:

> Few of them remember what is their objective. They give no thought to history and they have lost count of time. These twelve minutes have severed them from the past, and this new pattern seems to stretch out in all dimensions and to encompass them forever. Time-future and time-past have been exchanged into an everlasting now in which the anguished consciousness throbs until time-never falls.

Third, however, Thompson placed these scarred memories in the space between necessity and desire, where human agency found a resting place of honour, however despoiled by later events and machinations. 'We were disgusted by war but we assented to its political necessity, a necessity which might – although we hoped most ardently that it would not – entail our own deaths,' he wrote, adding, like his brother:

> Then as now there was an active democratic temper throughout Europe. There was a submission of self to a collective good. Then as

now there was a purposive alliance of resistance to power, a 'popular front' which had not yet been disfigured by bad faith. And there was also an authentic mood of internationalism which touched the peasants in the Umbrian villages and the troopers in our own tanks.

1944 was this, and more. It was the tide, already ebbing by 1945, that brought Labour to power in Britain, an electoral victory that was often a cautious parliamentary reflection of a more 'leftish volatility'. The future head of the Foreign Office saw this as presaging 'a Communist avalanche over Europe, a weak foreign policy, a private revolution at home and the reduction of England to a 2nd class power'. There was a new theatre of democratic, socialist and internationalist symbolism: it made the powerful defensive; political manners were mindful of class inequalities and the need for welfare provisioning. And then, in the partition of Europe and the sclerotic Cold War hardening of the arteries of democracy, internationalism, heroism and sacrifice, these human achievements that had been fought for against the press of war were turned into 'a pile of shit'. But that did not erase them from the past. Many who fought in World War II, Thompson was convinced all his life, were conscious anti-fascists and anti-imperialists, infused with socialist ideas and purpose. 'Our expectations may have been shallow,' he noted in 1978, 'but this was because we were overly utopian, and ill-prepared for the betrayals at our backs.' His own brother, he thought, could have been 'bargained ... out of captivity if only the first frosts of the cold war had not begun to glint in Sofia'. 'I was too bloody innocent by half,' he would later remark. But innocence was and is not a hanging offence, and it can be learned from in ways that duplicitous treachery and disregard for human life cannot. What Thompson took from his own war service was a fierce commitment to those who fell in battle for freedom and the defeat of fascism. A part of his life's work would be to liberate 'the intentions of the[se] dead', one of whom, of course, was his own brother.[29]

In September 1944, mere months after Major Thompson's

death and Edward's tank troop's participation in the misconceived Italian campaign, the Red Army liberated Bulgaria, the Fatherland Front took over the government, and Frank was proclaimed a national hero. Prokopnik, a railway stop where the Partisans had fought a particularly fierce battle, was renamed Major Thompson Station. But the darkness came quickly. Five years later, Stalinism's regime having sunk the hopes and heroism of the Resistance fighters in show trials, repression and hypocrisy, Thompson was for a time unceremoniously removed from the edifice of National Heroes, there being room within the new cult of personality-building for only so many politically expedient rivals to the Great Leader. He became, instead, an 'agent of Anglo-American imperialism', not unlike his recently deceased father.[30]

But before this shameful reversal, two related 'agents' travelled to Bulgaria in 1947 at the invitation of Georgi Dimitrov and the government. After re-enrolling at Cambridge at the close of the war, Edward and his mother paid homage to Frank, Edward retracing his brother's war march and visiting the villages where Partisans remembered the Major with affectionate comradeship. Later in the summer he served as commandant of the British Youth Brigade on the Yugoslav Youth Railway construction project, in which socialist peasants, workers, soldiers and students built a 150-mile railway from Samac to Sarajevo. Finished ahead of schedule, the railway was constructed without supervision and with only the most primitive tools. 'It was not built by underpaid Irish navvies or by unemployed drawn from a pool of "labour reserves",' noted the British–Yugoslav Association pamphlet account. 'It was not built slowly, shoddily, and at great expense, by a foreign company, remaining as a tentacle to suck more wealth out of the impoverished peasantry.' Edward's companion and future wife, Dorothy, recalls the work routine and the socialist meaning that lay behind it:

There were Fabians, there were Communists. We saw people as good workers or bad workers. ... We didn't really look at people's politics very much if they were good workers. ... Mostly the youth workers were from different parts of Europe [ed.: Soviets excepted] and they all worked together, they had camp fires together, they sang songs, shouted, went to meetings, or slept through meetings, together ... there was a great sense of international cooperation and of course an enormous sense of hope. We got up at half past five, washed in cold water, then went off to work at the rock face at six o'clock. We had a break at half past eight, then we had a sandwich of black bread and that apple jam stuff and some acorn coffee, and then we worked on till about midday. At midday we went back and had the main meal of the day which was eaten on the campsite, you know big dishes of tea and vegetables and things. In the afternoon everyone could do what they liked. ... In the evenings we had camp fires and political speeches and singing and dancing.

Thompson could be quick, in later years, to deflect gruffly what he took to be a scholastic – as opposed to a socialist – interest in the Yugoslav project. 'The Railway will not interest the great transatlantic academia,' he wrote to me early in our relationship, his words carrying a particular sting: 'it is about building a railway, with wooden wheelbarrows, which is not a proper academic subject.' Yet for Thompson this was an experience of immense importance, pointing directly to the alternative values of a co-operative and collective social order, a socialism bound up in 'a new emphasis on man's obligations to his neighbours and society'. In a Bosnian valley, E.P. Thompson saw hard labour and democratic leadership coexist co-operatively; it was an 'excellent school' in which 'imagination and decision, resourcefulness and patience, were demanded at every level'. He would carry the experience of this transformative revolutionary possibility with him for the rest of his life, citing it against the cynicism of Kolakowski, drawing on it in the 1980s in a call for a new 'vocabulary of mutual aid and of plain duty to each other in the face of power'. This, one senses, was what Frank had come to mean to Edward, who would, as W.L. Webb has noted in a moving obituary, revere his 'admired and beloved elder brother' as 'a touchstone . . . an emotional and moral reference point in all his writing and political thinking'.[31]

As World War II came to a close, then, Thompson's own family tree had been ruthlessly assailed by death, but its consciousness and conscience, as liberty tree, was deeply rooted. Thompson translated his father's and mother's experience into a personal narrative of uncompromising anti-imperialism, his brother's martyrdom into a resolute anti-fascist stance. Thirty years later he would refuse to paper over the failures of the labour movement in these areas, challenging Tony Benn's unduly complacent presentation of the virtues of British trade unionism. Thompson never stopped thinking, as he did in 1947, that 'We must place our bodies between fascism and our freedom.' These were the politics of the past, present and future, the refusals that were ordered, again, by a family aesthetics of internationalism, poetic imagination and historical insight. Barely into his twenties, Edward Thompson knew that his place was the choice of resistance, refusal – even, at this juncture, revolution. His die was cast as a heretic who could never forget the centrality of imperialism, the need for internationalism. Inspired by the insurgent popular anti-fascist mobilizations of 1943–7, Thompson was guided by the unfolding human possibilities of struggle, by the ways in which resistance could become *the* Resistance. His 'popular front' had little to do with the programme and practice of Stalinism, although he was at this time a loyal member of the Communist Party of Great Britain:

> In liberated Italy I would mooch around the town, find the blacksmith's shop – the oxen lifted on a hoist to be shoed – notice the PCI posters, introduce myself as a comrade, and in a trice I would be seated on a bench, incongruous in my British officer's uniform, sampling the blacksmith's wine. It was the same with my comrades in India, Iraq, Egypt. (One good friend of mine, masquerading as a sergeant-major, was able to second himself to work for some weeks with the Communist Party in Calcutta – against British rule!) It was the same also with many of our American comrades, who were moved by the same internation-

alism and optimism. A million informal transactions and discourses were going on in those years, which historians will never recover and which the hard-nosed party organizers knew nothing about.

Thompson would never renounce this historical act of creation, however much he was repelled by the parallel – and ultimately triumphant – history of betrayal and traitorous complicity, a history that buried not only his brother but also the ideals and sacrifices of a significant sector of an entire generation. History – as lived through power's dictates and written by that authority's handmaidens – might well have boiled all this down to a 'lost episode', perpetuating a 'foul historical con', but Edward Thompson would keep the watch of loyalty to this moment of human possibility for the rest of his life. Not to be forgotten was the role of the Labour government:

> Labour's leading Ministers were active – and, in the case of Ernest Bevin, eager – accomplices in these developments. ... A zealous ideologically-motivated anti-communist already, this able, forceful, and philistine bully [Ernest Bevin] ... was perhaps the leading actor on the Western side in that foul interactive process which led to the Cold War. ... Bevin had archaic imperialist impulses which out-Churchilled Churchill [,] ... an architect of NATO, and also ... a member of the secret Cabinet committee (GEN 163) which (unknown to the rest of the Cabinet) took the fateful decision to manufacture British nuclear weapons.

That Thompson kept this vigil the way he did – through metaphor and memory, as well as the poetics of historical imagination – owes much to the liberty tree that was his family.[32]

# 2

# Romanticism and Marxism

## I Cold War Containment, 1945–55

Thompson joined the Communist Party in 1942, while he was studying history at Cambridge. During his war service years his Party membership apparently officially lapsed, but he rejoined upon leaving the army. There was no doubt of his political commitment: everything suggests a young Communist proud of the heroism and accomplishment of the anti-fascist war, cognizant of the immense importance of the Red Army and Soviet sacrifice in the victory over Hitler, secure in his allegiance to the Party leadership. There were reasons why civilization was not destroyed, learning and art were not throttled, and history was not 'scrubbed out':

> We know that we have ourselves to thank that this did not happen – ourselves, and the Red Army and the resistance movements. What happened instead was glorious and inspiring. Deserted often by their leaders, with traitors in their midst, the common people of the world took up the challenge. In the great expanse of China and the dry sierras of Spain men and women took up arms. The slogan 'They Shall not Pass' greeted the fascists on the walls of Madrid and in the streets of Bermondsey where the Blackshirts tried to march. The fascist tide reached out as far as Stalingrad, Indonesia, El Alamein – and then the

people hurled it back. Surely we have not forgotten already the days of the great Red Army offensives, when we clustered round the wireless to hear Marshal Stalin's Orders of the Day, and the people of Moscow celebrated with salutes from a hundred guns? Or the final assault on the fascist blockhouses of Cassino, the bloody wrestling for Caen, and the great leap over the Rhine? Or yet the first news which came through to us from Yugoslavia, of how the peasants had taken to their wooded mountains, fighting without boots or equipment, and with only the arms which they tore from the enemy's hands?

Edward Thompson travelled in a milieu where such allegiances were deep and unmistakable. There was a 'ready-made network of contacts and friends . . . a circle of comrades'.[1]

His lifelong partner would be one such figure. Finishing his degree at Cambridge, reading mainly in literature and history, Edward met Dorothy Towers. A third-generation Londoner, displaced to a village in Kent, Dorothy was the only daughter of shopkeeper/teacher parents schooled in the arts, especially music. Adept at modern languages, immersed in the mythologies and oral traditions of an artisanal family that encompassed Huguenot East End London silkweavers and seafaring patrons of the theatre and the music hall, Dorothy was drawn to history as 'being at the interface' of 'literature, politics, and family traditions'. Educated by strong-willed women who never married, brought up in a household where women's talents were recognized and encouraged, she faced few gender barriers blocking her aspirations and intellectual/political development. The family leaned noticeably to the left, reading progressive journals and newspapers, backing the Labour Party, but was not composed of joiners or fervent advocates of radical causes. By the age of fourteen, Dorothy changed all that. Quick to join the Young Communist League in 1939 she was, like Edward and Frank Thompson, part of a generation that saw no options in the stale politics of traditional electoralism and appeasement. She remembers the mammoth demonstrations in Trafalgar Square, and the intense atmosphere of politicization which sustained huge socialist clubs and large communist groups. And for her, as for Edward, this commitment would be sealed in a sense of loss: Dorothy appreciated the great sacrifice of the anti-fascist war effort.

After two years at Cambridge she was conscripted for the war effort herself, opting to train as a mechanical draughtswoman – the first such woman to work at the firm she ended up with – in order to get industrial employment. Since she had long been involved in socialist and communist seminars on working-class history, shared political and academic interests brought her and Edward together; their circles crossed in the post-war politics of the University, and by the end of 1945 they had set up home together, delaying a marriage ceremony for a few years. Because Dorothy had been married during the war, and could not remarry for three years, she and Edward had to wait until 1948, one week before the birth of their first son, Ben. For almost fifty years they were partners in an amazing array of movements and political causes, their personalities, temperaments and styles complementing one another, writing their histories of eighteenth- and nineteenth-century Britain separately but relying on one another's support, encouragement, ideas, criticism and shared research, sustaining a relationship that Richard Hoggart considered 'a model'. No political couple on the English-speaking left since the Webbs had registered more of a *combined* influence; no academic historical couple since the Hammonds had dominated the field of social history so decisively.[2]

Edward and Dorothy worked together on the Yugoslav Youth Railway, seeing and living a rare equality of the sexes. When they returned to England they had no intentions of working within the academic establishment, which in any case was rigidly excluding communists by 1948. Neither took advanced degrees. Edward was as much interested in literature as he was in history, and was adamant that he 'never "took a decision" to be a historian' (he would, rather, adopt Lount's appreciation of the series of steps, one leading from the other, which moved him in specific ways). He and Dorothy did decide that they wanted to live in the North and raise a family. Settling in Halifax, they saw working in adult education as an 'obvious choice', and Edward secured a full-time tutorship in English at the Department of Extra-Mural Studies, University of Leeds, where he would teach for seventeen years; Dorothy took part-time employment in the same area and also did research, often of a sociological sort, for various university departments. In and around the University, they were just not of it. With much of their work concentrated in the evenings, there was time for shared childcare and domestic responsibilities during the days, although Dorothy no doubt shouldered the greater burden of such labours. Money was tight – Edward's annual salary was £425 – but they managed, in part because there was a familial 'safety net'; relatives helped out with toys and children's clothes for Christmas, and the household was something of a democratic centre of political socializing. Integrated into the West Riding community, the Thompsons lived in a whirlwind of activism and generosity. Visitors remembered 'huge cakes ... after pay-day while cats scampered about and slid through a hole cut in the solid front door; sometimes an attempt would be made to press a kitten into a ... pocket as a parting gift'. Dorothy recalls that they lived 'in a shambles, house and garden were rarely far away from complete chaos, one project only ever got completed by putting off something equally important and what money we had tended to get absorbed into political activities instead of into clothes, furniture, or redecoration of the house'.[3]

The political activities were communist activities. Both Edward and Dorothy were involved in the Communist Party Historians' Group, Dorothy more so than Edward, who was the single member of the group influential enough to get himself elected to his District Party Committee. They were equally inspired by Dona Torr, a lifelong communist with academic training in history, literature and music, a woman who, more than anyone else, provided an example and a push for Edward and Dorothy to move increasingly in the direction of historical research. Yet at this time Edward also remained the communist activist, spending half of his busy days and nights in Party work. He was chair of the Halifax Peace Committee, secretary of the broader Yorkshire Federation of Peace Organizations, editor of a regional peace journal, and a member of the Yorkshire District Committee of the Communist Party. He is still remembered, 'all elbows and knees', as the 'tall rangy sort of fellow' heading up the peace marches of Leeds and elsewhere, his speeches 'devoid of dogma'. (His writing, however, was gaining note for its 'polemical and even abrasive style'.)

With hindsight Thompson has suggested the ambivalent current within which he found himself: participating in an affirmative, grass-roots movement of protest and opposition, he was also growing wary of the manipulative practices of London's King Street CPGB officials, who seemed to want to squeeze the broad peace movement within their own controlling grip. Intellectually he has noted, in passing: 'There were a good many frustrated proto-revisionists in the Communist Party in those days; in my own circle we designated the enemy as "King Street" and as "Jungle Marxism", of which we increasingly came to see *The Modern Quarterly* as the leading ... organ.' But in the intense anti-communist climate of the early 1950s, politics seemed to be frozen in the polarities of the Cold War. 'So far from dismaying one,' Thompson has commented apropos of another context, 'it was a tonic to one's fighting-blood: ... self-righteous sectarian errors were confirmed within the circular field of antagonism':

> And Order sent its orderlies about
> Lest any disaffected innocents might still be hid –
> Not the Old Testament said so much grace
> Before and after meat as those guns did.
>
> So many souls were liberated on that day
> Out of their cage of skin and freed into the airs
> It is curious that a buzzard ate the speeches
> And odd that flies should have blown on the prayers.

It was remarked upon. But the turnout was splendid.
'Quite like old times,' the vizor and goggles said.
Now, children, hallowed be this memorable service,
Which you may meditate upon until you are dead.

When Morality, that immaculate lady, came in season,
And Nobadaddy mounted her in rut,
And she was conceived by him of a white millennium
When all are cleansed of sin, their throats being cut.

What mattered to Edward Thompson was the desperate need to avoid a repetition of the fascist carnage of the 1940s, to protest, to survive: 'Never has there been a time in the history of the world when the real moral issues before man have been clearer. Perhaps the issues are so clear and so big that we sometimes fail to grasp them. We are offered Life or Death.' If he remained incarcerated, in part, in an overly reverent notion of Marxism as a particular received orthodoxy linked, in part, to the Communist Party of Stalin, it was because the pressuring congealments of the Cold War and loyalties to the memory and meaning of 1944 kept him there. William Morris would begin the process of his liberation.[4]

Thompson was never the 'pure-and-simple' communist. Listen to the language of urgency in his 1947 exhortation to fight fascism:

If the jackboots are not to march again; if the tormented weight of human flesh is not to hang from the trees of our parks; if the voices of those who love freedom are not to be heard through prison walls; if we are not to meet in secret, distrusting our families, our children, our friends; if we are not to listen for the footsteps at night; if we are to save civilisation.

This is a communism driven less by economic necessity and the logic of determinative forces than by moral passion and desire, as Thompson's attraction to Morris's May Day 1896 article for *Justice* indicates: 'Now at last we will it; we will produce no more for profit but for *use*, for *happiness*, for LIFE.' To divorce these seeming oppositions of 'hard' economics and 'soft' aspiration, of course, is a fatal error, for they were always twinned in Thompson's own political and intellectual understanding of the impulses behind socialist transformation. But Thompson's tone was *always* drawn most substantially from the side of the moralities of opposition: by 1950 he had read Marx and experienced 1944; teaching as much literature as history, and obviously drawn to culture and its analysis rather than to economics (where he saw his comrades Hobsbawm and Saville as 'very sound' and more able to write effectively on the topic than he was), he knew capitalist immiseration and ideology through *Hard Times* and Mr Gradgrind, which he *did* teach, as much as through Engels's *The Housing Question* and Adam Smith, which he probably alluded to only in passing in his extra-mural work. Against 'official' Communist Party Marxism's tendency to shy away from 'sentimentalism' and rhetorical flourish, Thompson reached neatly into the very body of an impoverished tradition to extract support for a new aesthetics of communist presentation. The pioneers of British communism, he stressed, always carried 'strong moral conviction'. Quoting Harry Pollitt's *Serving My Time*, Thompson made the point that 'We have all become so hard and practical that we are ashamed of painting the vision splendid – of showing glimpses of the promised land. It is missing from our speeches, our Press and our pamphlets . . . [yet] it was this kind of verbal inspiration that gave birth to the indestructible urge . . . to keep . . . fighting for freedom.'[5]

It is now commonplace to argue the influence of Morris on Thompson: the relationship figures centrally in a virtual industry of Thompson commentary, which draws, of course, on Thompson's own statements in various interviews and publications. Morris, in Thompson's words, 'claimed me'. Thompson was 'seized' by Morris, driven deeper and deeper into the source materials. In what would prove a recurring pattern, what started out as an article on Morris, aiming polemically to settle scores with two books '*so* dreadful and so ideological . . . that I thought I *must* answer these', ended up as an 800-page book. In the process Thompson became both a historian and a dissident communist, developing a 'fascination in getting to the bottom of everything', a compulsion that would lead to the archives and away from King Street. This is now conventional wisdom.[6]

But to be claimed and seized in this way requires a certain receptiveness, temperamentally, politically and intellectually. In Thompson's case this came, no doubt, from his own inter-rogation of Romanticism and its moral critique of capitalism. Yet he was prepared to receive the moral message of aesthetic rejection of capitalism associated with the 1790s by his partic-ular embeddedness in the 'liberty tree' that was his own family and history. Morris's passionate *refusal* of the hideousness of 'progress', his insistence that a past of poetic imaginative possibility could be liberated from the limitations of history to inform consciousness and conflict in the present so as to create a future of socialist beauty, was in form – if not necessarily in political content – congruent with the otherworldliness of Thompson's father as well as his own experience of the transformative potential of the resistance of the 1940s. K. Mukherjee's memoriam to Edward J. Thompson noted that he 'had the spiritual loveliness of a poet in his heart, the loveliness of a far other world from ours'. And E.J. Thompson ended his 1921 treatment of Tagore with allusions to the forerunners 'of such types of *beauty* and of *goodness* as Athens never knew', seeing in the Bengali poet a reconciliation of East and West: 'Neither he nor we have entered into the greatness of our heritage.' Thus Morris's youthful Romantic rebellion 'of value, of aspiration, against actuality', parted paths with Thompson's father only at the point of struggle and revolt. Even after he joined the CPGB, Frank Thompson, in training as a potential gunnery officer in 1939–40, spent much of his evening leisure time reading classical verse.

As Morris moved from the Romanticism of *The Defence of Guenevere* (1858) – 'The knights come foil'd from the great quest, in vain,/In vain they struggle for the vision fair' – through the despair of mid-century, into his age of socialist commitment, he crossed the class politics of a river of fire that alone could build Blake's Jerusalem. It was the failure to make this political leap into the possibilities of working-class revolution that had soured the Romantic critique of capitalism of Wordsworth and Coleridge, Ruskin and Carlyle, returning them to the 'forms of paternalist sensibility'. Morris made no such return, but revolutionized Romanticism. 'I can't help it,' he told his friend Georgie Burne-Jones. 'The ideas which have taken hold of me will not let me rest. ... One must turn to hope, and only in one direction do I see it – on the road to Revolution.'

Morris's transformation of Romanticism worked within Thompson's communism because 'the moral critique of capitalist process was pressing forward to conclusions consonant with Marx's critique, and it was Morris's particular genius to think through this transformation, effect this juncture, and seal it with action'. In the words of Morris himself, 'what romance means is the capacity for a true conception of history, a power of making the past part of the present'. Like the artisanal Romantic Blake, who distinguished himself among the Jacobin radicals of the 1790s by his avoidance of disenchantment, Morris's *refusals* were unmistakably anti-capitalist: 'Shoddy is King,' he roared, 'From the statesman to the shoemaker all is shoddy!' John Bull he saw as 'a *stupid, unpractical* oaf'. 'That's an impossible dream of yours, Mr Morris,' a religious figurehead once said to the old socialist, 'such a society would need God Almighty Himself to manage it.' Morris offered the complacent clergyman his fist: 'Well, damn it, man, you catch your God Almighty – we'll have Him.' Morris's revolutionary Romanticism was driven by *anger*, but it was an anger – again like Blake's – which was cut with satire, polemic, mockery, hyperbole, abuse, provocation, framing a personality that was 'humorous, brusque, shy, meditative, vehement by turns'. This did not just *claim* Edward Thompson; it *was* Edward.[7]

Morris seized Thompson, then, because he filled the silences in Marx to which Edward had listened in his father's and mother's homes – silences that he had heard, loudly, echoing from Cassino to the Po Valley, silences that were sung as the railway snaked its way slowly to Sarajevo, silences that he would recognize in Althusserian theory:

> The injury that advanced industrial capitalism did, and that the market society did, was to define human relations as being primarily economic. Marx engaged in orthodox political economy and proposed revolutionary-economic man as the answer to exploited economic-man. But it is also implicit, particularly in the early Marx, that the injury is in defining man as 'economic' at all. This kind of critique of industrial capitalism is found in Blake and Wordsworth very explicitly and is still present in Morris.

Thompson drew on Morris to argue, in 1951:

> If we wish to save people from the spreading taint of death, then we must win them for life. We do not wait for a new kind of person to appear until after Socialism has been won, any more than we wait for Marxism to arise within a Communist society. We must change people *now*, for that is the essence of our cultural work. And in this work, all the forces of health within society are on our side: all those who, in whatever way, desire a richer life, all those who have warmer ambitions for Britain than those of tedious insolvency and rearmament, all those, indeed, who desire any life at all, can be won to our side if we take to them the message of life against that of the slaughter-house culture.

In a distinctly non-revolutionary age, Morris, similarly, reminded the young Marxist tradition that 'a Communist community would require a moral revolution as profound as the revolution in economic and social power':

> Though every battle, every augury,
> Argue defeat, and if defeat itself
> Bring all the darkness level with our eyes –
> It is the poem provides the proper charm
> Spelling resistance and the living will,
> To bring to dance a stony field of fact

And set against terror exile or despair
The rituals of our humanity.

To this end the Victorian socialist stood before audiences of working people and, defiant in the face of the political climate, struggled to instil in them a sense of discontent: 'It is to stir you up *not* to be content with a little that I am here tonight,' he once proclaimed. He needed labour to know, collectively, with all its potential power, that 'these uglinesses are but the outward expression of the innate moral baseness into which we are forced by our present form of society'. That Morrisian insight, when conjoined with intelligence, courage and power – the coming together of consciousness and labour-power – would ensure that 'the thing will be done', and revolution accomplished. Increasingly, Thompson himself came to see this as a comment not only on the bounded consciousness of the insurrectionary working class but on his own Communist Party orthodoxy as well. Stalinism was too little morality, too much inhumanity.[8]

But in the climate of the mid-1950s the 'muffled revisionism' of Thompson's Morris text could not break out of the Stalinist straitjacket. To do so, at the height of the Cold War, seemed an act of apostatical default too disturbing to contemplate. The lessons of Morris, then, were often drawn in stark political strokes whitewashing the failures and crimes of a degenerating socialist state. It would take two decades for Thompson to negotiate his way through the searing rapids of his own particular river of fire, breaking finally and decisively from the CPGB. According to Thompson, Morris was his guide: 'When, in 1956, my disagreement with orthodox Marxism became fully articulate, I fell back on modes of perception which I'd learned in those years of close company with Morris, and I found, perhaps, the will to go on arguing from the pressure of Morris behind me.'[9]

No doubt this is true, as far as it goes. But I would like to suggest that Thompson's particular Stalinist political stasis at the zenith of the Cold War is explainable at the conjuncture of structure and agency. On the one side, the boundaries of his experience were the imposed constraints of rabid anti-communism, capitalism's ascendant ideological confidence, and the aggressive acquisitive individualism that was reflected in philistine consumerism and a possible nuclear holocaust waged in the name of global conquest. These imposing barriers made repudiation of actually existing communism seem a dirty stain on the memory of 1944 – or, worse, a material contribution to human destruction: 'Beneath all the nice quibbles about means and ends, all the clever things which Orwell or Koestler or Eliot or their American counterparts have to say, will be found the same facts: napalm, the Hell Bomb, and the butchers of Syngman Rhee.' Yet on the other side, as Morris increasingly told Thompson, the means did matter: in an age of shoddy, they were often all that socialists could actually touch, a revolutionary end being beyond reach. And those means included commitment to an end that was more than simple quantitative economic change. 'I hold that we need not be afraid of scaring our audiences with too brilliant pictures of the future of Society,' Morris thundered, 'nor think ourselves unpractical and utopian for telling them the bare truth, that in destroying monopoly we shall destroy our present civilization.' Against those 'one-sided Socialists' who were always 'preaching to people that Socialism is an economic change pure and simple', Morris placed himself and the cause of larger possibilities.[10] As Thompson grappled with the Morris example in the early-to-mid-1950s, then, he was tugged in one direction by structure, in another by his invigorated Morrisian appreciation of agency, which began the process of severing the heroic accomplishments of popular front resistance from the programmatic squeeze of Stalinism. Thompson, I suggest, negotiated this balancing act between structure and agency, containment and cultural renewal, largely through his own experience of the 'education of desire'. It allowed him to refuse Cold War accommodations at the same time as it presented a more free and open space where King Street Marxism could be side-stepped with some subtlety.

### Education and Experience: Mediating the Marx/Morris Encounter

For the better part of two decades, Edward Thompson was employed in adult education. His students were workers, housewives, and a broad mix of the 'middling' sort: teachers, commercial travellers, social workers, clerks, even the odd bank official. The Leeds Extra-Mural Department emerged in the post-war period of welfare and educational extension, a bridge between the University and the old commitments of the Workers' Educational Association (WEA), dedicated since 1903 to practical training for workers, 'healing the divorce between the institutions of higher education and the centres of social experience'. One of the largest extra-mural departments in the country, Leeds was headed by Sidney Raybould, a dour econo-mist well known as an administrator and publicist in the field of adult education. Concerned to bring the purpose of the WEA into line with the 'standards' of the University, securing for extra-mural work status and accreditation, Raybould was a staunch advocate of what his itinerant tutors (who travelled throughout the North and West Ridings, teaching four or five tutorial classes, with anywhere from eight to twenty students, who were enrolled in three-year programmes) could bring to the intellectual inadequacies of their students.[11]

Raybould hired Thompson at a time when anti-communism was rife in higher education circles. He could not have been comfortable when, at an early staff meeting, the young Marxist tutor announced that his aim in adult teaching was 'to create revolutionaries'. There were also less rhetorical moments of skirmish, as Thompson and other left-wingers such as J.F.C. Harrison clashed with Raybould and their colleagues over whether the purpose of adult education was to 'elevate' the student to university levels. Thompson and Harrison saw themselves as being true to the original purpose of the WEA: they wanted to offer those blocked from access to higher education by material circumstances the opportunity both to learn *and* to bring their experience to bear on the environment of the classroom. There was no question that Thompson refused any notion of paternalism within the learning experience. He chose adult education precisely because it offered the Morris-like possibility of 'making socialists' at the same time as it opened out into new avenues of learning for himself: 'I went into adult education because it seemed to me to be an area in which I would learn something about industrial England, and teach people who would teach me. Which they did.' 'Give me the chalk, Mr Thompson,' WEA instructor Sheila Rowbotham recalls a student in one class on the history of mining saying before he proceeded to draw a series of intricate diagrams on the board. 'One discovered as much as one taught,' Thompson insisted. And one part of what was learned was, again, a specific tone. Reviewing a study on Methodism and the Durham miners, Thompson closed the book with a curt 'And *fookin'* Amen to that!'

*The* University was never simply a privileged space, and its language and detachment were not always to be elevated above other, class-based, expressions of evaluation. Adult education may well have seemed, for a young Edward Thompson, one of those 'places where no one works for grades or for tenure but for the transformation of society; places where criticism and self-criticism are fierce, but also mutual help and exchange of theoretical and practical knowledge; places that prefigure in some ways the society of the future'. To be sure, by the 1950s adult education was in the throes of change, and its unambiguous class purpose and character, clearer in earlier times, was breaking down with the shifting socioeconomic and ideological contours of British society. Thompson saw this process at work in his extra-mural tutoring, but he nevertheless felt strongly that there was enough class reason left to hold to the original aims of the WEA, in which the experience of workers was valued and drawn upon rather than denied and dismissed. In a 10,000-word paper circulated to colleagues in 1950, he quoted Hardy's *Jude the Obscure*, resisting Raybould's reification of the disinterested superiority of university learning: 'For a moment there fell on Jude a true illumination: that here in the stone yard was a centre of effort as worthy as that dignified by the name of scholarly study within the noblest of the colleges.' Living, Thompson believed, was learning.[12]

It would have been easy to translate this conviction into a passive, receiving encounter with adult education students; polite condescension is often the flip side of paternalism. Thompson refused this as well. Peter Searby's interviews with former students and excavation of Thompson's own annual reports on their tutorial classes provide an illuminating glimpse into the years of Yorkshire teaching. Whatever he was with his superiors and colleagues, Thompson was apparently an extraordinary teacher. Always willing to let his own sympathies be known, choosing topics that reflected his sense of historical relevance (largely, at this time, relating to the Industrial Revolution), he was far more balanced and restrained with students than he was known to be in polemical battle. His own reports, totalling 30,000 words and covering 60 tutorial classes, present, in Searby's words, a 'commentary that is wry, self-critical, pragmatic, and above all generous and enthusiastic'. A sample from a history class in Batley, 1953–4, conveys a great deal:

> This class – part original, part added – has an excellent core to it, of about ten or eleven members, and a further five or six students on the register who blow in and out irregularly, take a vigorous part in discussions, but are not fulfilling stipulated requirements of reading, writing, or attendance. While three of the latter will be taken off the register next year, there seems to be no good reason for excluding any

of them from the meeting room, since everyone likes to see them and they manifestly have no ill effect on the morale or quality of work of the rest. Batley is a small town where everyone knows everyone else: the community sense extends to the W.E.A. and to the class, and is reinforced by it: the most admirable regulations of the most enlightened administrators must bend before the facts of life in Batley. Anyway, how can the tutor exclude the President of the Branch – so busy with his voluntary work for his union, school, chapel, and the W.E.A. itself that he cannot write an exercise when it is required? Class discussions have been extremely vigorous, but one very old member (thundering the table in defence of Gladstone's integrity) has tended always to lead them into the swamp of local reminiscence. Nevertheless, both the tutor and the class feel that this is the kind of thing we have got to expect and put up with, and no one would dream of asking the old gentleman to stop describing his speech at the School Board election of 1877. After all, we cannot have our cake and eat it. If we want academic tidiness, we will not also have the variety of experience and the informal non-vocational spirit to which we give lip-service. Between the Ideal and the Reality falls the shadow of Compromise. And if Compromise be accepted, then Batley is a fairly good tutorial class.

Students taught by Edward Thompson in these years, be they in literature or history classes, were never allowed to be contented with a little. Thompson understood the value of experience and, as the Batley report shows, gave it its due, even when that meant sacrifice. But he expected students to use that experience to reach beyond it. Shakespeare was preferred in English tutorials: 'the distance stimulates application, the in-bred respect keeps philistinism at bay, and it is difficult to graft onto Falstaff a discussion on the Morley local elections'. Reasoned argument and intellectual difference were valued, encouraged by bringing in outside lecturers. 'There is too little rebellion in the class,' Thompson once complained, 'and ... [it] looks as if the whole course of the class might be run without one good earnest row between the students.' Pushing students to write, meticulous in his criticism, Thompson gave inspiring lectures, and his example was cherished for years to come. Dorothy Greenald (to whom *The Making of the English Working Class* would be dedicated) and Peter Thornton, members of Thompson's first 1948–51 Cleckheaton class, remembered that Edward made history come alive for students, and in particular – in Greenald's words – that 'your background wasn't something to be ashamed of'. 'That changed me really,' she said, in what must be the ultimate tribute to any teacher. For Thompson, his years in adult education were also not without their rewards. Writing of one literature class, he stressed that he had 'learnt as much as he ha[d] imparted'. The class found its way 'to work in the spirit so desirable in the WEA – not as tutor and passive audience, but as a group combining various talents and pooling differing knowledge and experience for a common end'.

Years later Thompson would reflect on this theme, drawing it towards his intellectual preoccupation of the mid-1950s, revolutionizing Romanticism. In the Mansbridge Memorial Lecture at Leeds he addressed the uniqueness of adult education which, in refusing the passivity of much teaching, was capable of transforming learning. He saw in the statement of a Goethe character in 1774 a comment on the rigidities of contemporary education: 'Persons of rank tend to keep their cold distance from the common man, as if they fear to lose something by such intimacy.' In contrast to his own father's teaching experience in India, and countered by the Jacobin Romantics of the 1790s, this gulf separating experience and education was impoverishing to both living and learning, as is evident in Wordsworth's *Prelude*:

> When I began to inquire,
> To watch and question those I met, and held
> Familiar talk with them, the lonely roads
> Were schools to me in which I daily read
> With most delight the passions of mankind,
> There saw into the depths of human souls,
> Souls that appear to have no depth at all
> To vulgar eyes. And now convinced at heart
> How little that to which alone we give
> The name of education hath to do
> With real feeling and just sense

Wordsworth's compassion and his capacity to hear 'From mouths of lowly men and of obscure/A tale of honour' would help to steer Thompson through the Marx/Morris encounter, providing, in his own adult education experience, a touchstone to which, one suspects, he could return as he looked with increasing disillusionment on the Stalinism of his own CPGB. 'To strike the balance between intellectual rigour and respect for experience is always difficult,' he acknowledged. He confessed to having himself accommodated those students who valued themselves too complacently:

> My fellow tutors here will, I suspect, take the point: they know, only too well, the student to whom I refer. They may also know the tutor who has made himself accomplice to the giving-up, and who has been happy to accept the moral worth of his students in place of their essays. They may even have seen him, as I have, late in the evening, in the mirror.

But the real balance needed to be redressed in other ways: 'Democracy will realize itself – if it does – in our *whole* society and our *whole* culture: and, for this to happen, the universities need the abrasion of different worlds of experience, in which ideas are brought to the test of life.' Universities as syndicates of experts presented the danger of expropriating 'the people of their identity'. As he lived this awareness in the 1950s, Thompson was also coming to intellectual and political grips with the extent to which Stalinism was crushing the identity of the left.[13]

## II Exit from King Street and the Rise (and Fall) of New Lefts

The Morris volume had occupied Thompson throughout the first half of the 1950s, but his reading in the Romantic tradition was by no means confined to its relationship to Victorian socialism. Nor was it left on the desk. Years later Thompson would equate the positive intellectual and political accomplishments of respected thinkers and writers in the CPGB – many of whom contributed to the *Left Review* (1934–8), and some of whom were actually Morris scholars – with their 'hard moral decisions'. They gave much to the movement of opposition, and the urgencies of their political times sometimes meant 'the death or the suspension of their own creative identity'. This, Thompson claimed, recalled the 'settled tenacity of eighteenth-century dissenters'. Such people, from both the 1790s and the 1930s, kept the idea of social transformation alive.[14] In a 1952 attack on censorship he drew close to John Milton, deploring the 'gross conforming stupidity, a stark and dead congealment of wood and hay and stubble, forced and frozen together', which resulted from the suppression of ideas. Like the seventeenth-century poet he demanded 'liberty to know, to utter and to argue freely according to conscience above all liberty'.[15] Most importantly, it seems, the Morris/Marx encounter was giving way to the Blake/Marx encounter. As an early editorial statement in the *New Reasoner* declared, Thompson now made no apology 'for giving up so large a part of our space to the vision of William Blake and the thought of Karl Marx. We believe that this vision, this theory, influencing the minds and actions of living men and women, are among those human forces which – in the end – ... can keep the bombers grounded and which can make the fruits of men's ingenuity into sources of human enrichment.' The fight remained on the political and industrial ground of traditional Marxist activity, but battles now needed to be fought against those 'whom William Blake denounced in his own strange and forceful way' as those who 'would, if they could, forever depress Mental & Prolong Corporeal War'.[16]

This increasingly intense engagement with Blake and the revolutionary current of Romanticism's moral critique of capitalism as a socioeconomic system was bringing Thompson to a new point of recognition: 'If I devised my own pantheon I would without hesitation place within it the Christian antinomian, William Blake, and I would place him beside Marx.' Drawn to the tenacious persistence of Blake's refusals to accommodate to 'the Beast', Thompson would later sum up the substance of the London craftsman's engagement with the disciplining structures of Church and State:

> I see a firm consistency in a strong antinomian tradition, derived from a 17th-century vocabulary and discourse, which extends in Blake's work from the 1780s (or earlier) to the year of his death. The signatures of this include the radical suspicion of Reason, the repudiation of adulterous relations between Church and State, the vocabulary of the 'Everlasting Gospel' and the 'New Jerusalem', the refusal of any worship entailing self-abasement and professed humility, and above all, the absolute rejection of 'the Moral Law'. ... In discarding the prohibitive Moral Law of 'Thou Shalt Not' Blake could put trust only in an active affirmative 'Thou Shalt Love'.

Thompson now saw Blake's as one of the critical activist tongues which, within the limitations of its time, 'spoke for *humanity*': 'Rent from eternal brotherhood we die and are no more/Man exists by brotherhood and universal love.' Stalinism lacked such a 'moral tongue', anything approximating a brotherhood of love. Blake's visionary genius was to locate the threat to humanity's affirmative potential in the relentless divisive march of acquisitive individualism, a reading somewhat distanced from the conventional academic wisdom:

> We can now see *London* not simply as a terrible *catalogue* of unrelated abuses and suffering; but, rather, as a poem with a clearly conceived, developing emotional logic around the central unifying theme of bourgeois morality. Blake does not only describe the *symptoms*; within the central image which underlies and unites the whole poem, there is the discovery of the *cause*. From the first introduction of the word 'charter'd' Blake never loses hold of this image of buying and selling – not only goods, but of human values, affections and vitalities. The street cries are the cries of people buying and selling, the 'mind forg'd manacles' are manacles of self-interest, childhood (the chimney sweep) is bought and sold, life itself (the soldier) is bought and sold, and to complete the poem, youth, beauty, and love, the *source* of life, is bought and sold in the figure of the diseased harlot. In a series of concrete, unified images of enormous power Blake compresses an indictment of

the acquisitive ethic which divides man from man, leads him into mental and moral captivity, destroys the sources of joy, and brings, as its reward, death.

As Thompson began to chart his way through the political seas of the 1950s, struggling to try to create a new left, he in some ways commenced with Blake, who inspired an antinomianism of refusal that allowed a decisive break from the destructive failures and broken promises of both capitalism and Stalinism. 'The Beast is real,' Thompson would write in 1960, 'but its reality exists within our own conformity and fear. We must acknowledge ourselves in the Beast of history, for only so can we break the spell of fear and reduce it to our own size. And then we must meet it as it is.'[17]

Thompson's disgruntled ambivalence towards the CPGB may well have been longstanding by the mid-1950s, but it was also, at the level of public pronouncement, subdued. The world communist order was somewhat shaken by Stalin's death in 1953, and the next years would witness a series of incidents, beginning with the suppression of an East German revolt, which indicated the destabilizing currents running through official Marxism. The 'elect of King Street' managed to keep overt opposition in check, but seemed largely immune to the message that significant numbers of loyal communists were approaching disillusionment, preparing for a departure. The year 1956 forced the issue away from a Cold War polarization of commitment, pitting capitalism against socialism, into a cauldron of redefinition, in which the fundamental point of identification came to be socialism of what sort, Marxism of what kind, and a Party for what ends, practising what means. First came Khrushchev's February 1956 revelations of Stalin's atrocities which, despite attempts to suppress the speech and confine it to 'secrecy', spread through the Communist Parties of the world and pushed information about repression and coercion further into the public arena. When tanks rolled into Budapest on 4 November 1956, they crushed not only the rebellious anti-

Stalinist aspirations of the Hungarian working class but also the view that official Communist Parties, such as that ensconced in King Street, could be renewed.

Edward and Dorothy Thompson and John Saville were among many shocked and disturbed communists who had nevertheless long believed that a renewal of the Communist Party's moral authority could be achieved, provided that the crisis within the Party was recognized and acted upon by the leadership. This, most emphatically, was not happening. The Thompsons and Saville thus came together to put out a 32-page mimeographed journal which would appear independent of the Party press, but would not reach outside Party circles. Much stress was placed on re-establishing the moral credibility of communism, and the masthead – quoting Marx – proclaimed, with purpose: 'To leave error unrefuted is to encourage intellectual immorality'. King Street wanted no part of it: Thompson and Saville, as editors, were soon instructed to cease publication. They defied the order, suffered suspension and then, with the Hungarian intervention, resigned in protest, 'believing that the Party was now wholly discredited'. The dam had broken: 7,000 members (almost one in five) left the CPGB in 1956, and the old guard at King Street hardened its stance against any and all dissent. Thompson and Saville moved out of the Party – not to abandon working-class revolution, but to build it in new ways. This was the moment of 'socialist humanism' to which Thompson would return again and again in the latter half of the century, a turning point balanced on the two-edged sword of possibility and defeat, directing its political gaze outward to the frustrated aspirations of dissident comrades in Eastern Europe and inward to the state of the communist 'nation' in Great Britain. 'We hope to grow more dangerous as we grow more old,' he wrote, affirming his commitment to the possible.[18]

Within certain circles, this history of 1956 and the implosive rupture of British communism is now well known. As an event it has received consideration; its texts, almost unknown in North America fifteen years ago, are now routinely cited, largely as a consequence of the intellectual furore in the late 1970s and early 1980s around Thompson's *The Poverty of Theory* (1978), where all four essays either grow directly out of or return to the moral imperative of '1956'. Yet in spite of the movement towards encounter with the political writings associated with Thompson's exit from King Street, an interrogation of these works and their relationship to the historicized making of his own thought is largely absent.[19]

We can begin to speak through this silence by excavating some simple genealogies of meaning. Thompson's and Saville's journals of dissident communism, *The Reasoner* and the *New Reasoner*, for instance, took their title from John Bone's publication of the same name, which first appeared in the opening decade of the nineteenth century in an attempt to renew and reinvigorate a flagging Jacobin radicalism. Thompson would later note, in *The Making of the English Working Class*, that 'this honourably named periodical failed through lack of support'. These journals, like Bone's, were attempts to rekindle the dying embers of a spent opposition, posing the critique of Stalinist communism always at the point of its moral decay:

> When we commenced publication, in our duplicated form in 1956, the Communist movement was in a shambles of intellectual disgrace and moral collapse ... we sought to re-habilitate the rational, humane, and libertarian strand within the Communist tradition, with which men of great courage and honour ... have been identified; a tradition which the elect of King Street have brought into shifty disrepute.

While *The Reasoner* and the *New Reasoner* fused many streams of dissident communist thought and sensibility, there is no question that the journals bore the imprint of Thompson's engagement with Blake and Morris, and his insertion of the poetic imagination into the discourse of Marxism. International voices of communist dissent, such as that of the murdered Hungarian

Imre Nagy, echoed throughout the pages of the *New Reasoner*, insistent on the need to create a new, humane socialist morality, in staunch resistance to the depraved Machiavellianism and degenerate Bonapartism of the Stalinist states. They resonated well with Thompson's own – often tortured – settling of moral accounts with his Stalinist past –

> How much more honour then
> To all those dedicated men
> Who saved society
> By rope and calumny!
>
> So giving honour, we
> Who moralise necessity,
> With slats of sophistry erect
> A gibbet of the intellect,
>
> And from its foul and abstract rope
> Suspend all social hope,
> Until with swollen tongue
> Morality herself is hung
>
> In whose distended dedicated eyes
> All honour dies.

– or with his increasingly poetic turn to affirmation of birth and life in the face of Empire's push to devastation and death, captured nicely in 'Mother and Child', written at the time of the Hungarian and Suez crises:

> It is her calm that drives the Emperor mad.
> Why is she looking down? Look to the all-in-one,
> High up aloft ineffable, the abstract drum!
> She smiles, holding within the circle of her arm
> Omens of innocence, a flight of birds,
> Insurgent provinces, revolt within the State.
> Over the bowels of a bull the priests deliberate . . .
> She has held the child too long to take alarm.

And in an action that seemed strikingly reminiscent of his father's stance, Thompson co-authored a 1959 editorial on colonialism that deplored the moral corruption of public life in Great Britain following in the wake of 'the betrayal of human rights and the rule of law' in British-occupied Cyprus. Quoting Mill, he and Saville asked for the kind of 'atonement' E.J. Thompson would have embraced: 'Is there no body of persons willing to redeem the "character of our country"?'[20]

In the eyes and minds of some, we are back to the question of parochial nationalism. This is not, however, where the *New Reasoner* was. Reasoning began as internationalism, the political interrogation of Stalinism commencing with Thompson peering through 'The Smoke of Budapest'. The *New Reasoner*'s ten issues bristled with contact and concern with global events and possibilities – practical, artistic and conceptual. Thompson's lengthy essay 'Socialist Humanism', around which debate centred for months, was primarily a coming to grips with Stalinism *as theory*, but alongside this attempt to reformulate the project of Marxism were accounts of workers' councils in Yugoslavia, discussion of African national congresses, denunciations of phoney state trials in Bulgaria, the reproduction of South African art, letters from America, Thompson's own translation and adaptation of Adam Wazyk's poem 'The Railway Carriage', and documents and debate relating to Gramsci. All this coexisted with attempts to situate historically the experience of the nineteenth-century English working class, the arguments and evidence of *The Making* appearing – like the earlier study of Morris – in a polemical broadside aimed at books that drew Thompson's ire because they dismissed the necessity of a moral judgement of constituted authority, an abdication that managed to go undetected in the 'soggy' notices of *Tribune* and *New Statesman*. What these books – which dealt with the Peterloo Massacre of 1819, in which the Manchester yeomanry violently rode down a reform meeting – failed to do was even to ask the larger questions posed by Peterloo: 'Why has the word echoed ever since in our history? How far was it a defeat, how far a moral victory?' Behind the detached, cautionary noncommitment of such scholarship Thompson detected the key shortcoming of ostensibly objective historiography: 'oppressive class relationships, exploitation, and suffering are *facts* of history and not subjective judgements *upon* history.... True objectivity will lead the historian to the heart of this real human situation; and once he is there, if he is worth his salt, he *will* make judgements and draw conclusions.' After all, this had been done in the past, 'the massacre arous[ing] a hatred among the people.... What a world of savage humour, contempt and confidence is packed into the word itself: "Peterloo!"'[21]

Over the course of the next years Thompson's project of building a new left overshadowed all other aspects of his life. The institutional contours of this contentious period in the history of the British left are reasonably well known. Against the threat of nuclear war the first Campaign for Nuclear Disarmament emerged, with Saville and Thompson throwing themselves into the mobilization, part of a committed core that joined a 140-mile march from Withernsea on the East Yorkshire coast to Liverpool. The *New Reasoner* and *Universities and Left Review* merged to establish the *New Left Review*, where Thompson battled for the minds *and* bodies of the fractured left, writing on revolution and Raymond Williams, bringing to both subjects an insistence on the essential proletarian divide that made an accommodation with reformist labourism or classless culturalism unthinkable. The new journal was to be but a part of the project of left renewal: 'there will be Left Clubs, discussion groups, conferences, educational and propagandist activity'. This, Thompson thought, might well be 'the most serious and sustained attempt in the history of British socialism for those who are actively producing the ideas to also organize their distribution and propagation'. For years he threw himself into this building of a new left, 'making socialists' as well as remaking socialism. He remained true to his commitment to working-class revolution, and was staunch in his rejection of Labour Party reformism; convinced that the primary task of all socialists was to counter the drift to Armageddon, he was ceaseless in his efforts to take Britain out of the 'Natopolitan nuclear alliance'; with Blake and Morris at his back, and a sobering sense of the ways in which historical experience did not always conform to the models of socialist intellectuals, he struggled to instil in the British left an understanding that the much-cherished site of class conflict – *the* point of production – encompassed the industrial environment but reached past it into other locales:

> But the private ownership of the means of production is not a physical act of robbery taking place only at the point of production. It is built-in to our institutions, legal code, customs and possessive morality. When young Tom Mann joined an improvement society at a London engineering works which discussed Shakespeare he began to become an agitator.

The point of production, by the early 1960s, *was* the new left. There and only there was a politics of activism and alternative possible. Historical experience and the failures of orthodox communism and social democratic reformism left Britain 'over-ripe' for revolution, if only left consciousness, theory, and practical activity could catch up with the meanings of the modern world:

> The reasons why capitalism has been left to rot on the bough are complex. First, in the context of dominant imperialism it was possible for liberal reformism (sometimes mistaking itself for 'socialism') to continue to win substantial benefits for the people. Second, the experience of the Russian revolution made the concept of a revolutionary transition – *any* transition – to socialism appear to be synonymous with bloodshed, civil war, censorship, purges, and the rest – a confusion which the apologists of indigenous Communists did a good deal to perpetuate. Third, this experience hardened the doctrines of reformism into dogma, to the point where the British Labour Movement has become largely parasitic upon the capitalist economy, with deep vested interests in its continuance, since all local reforms (whether for more wages or more welfare) are seen as dependent upon its continued health and growth. Finally, the capitalist economy was

given a fresh lease on life in war, post-war recovery, and next-war preparations, while the flagrant corruptions of post-war Communism diminished still further within Britain the desire to consider any revolutionary alternative. So that British people find themselves today, with the assent of orthodox Labour, within the grand alliance of international capitalism, and exposed on every side to the ideology of apathy.

'How much longer can the Labour Movement hold to its defensive positions and still maintain morale?' asked Thompson in obvious anguish. 'Is the aim of socialism to recede for ever in the trivia of circumstances? Are we to remain for ever as exploited, acquisitive men?' In the refusal of this, the final accommodation, Thompson pointed to the need to revive 'the long and tenacious revolutionary tradition of the British commoner':

> It is a dogged, good-humoured, responsible, tradition: yet a revolutionary tradition all the same. From the Leveller corporals ridden down by Cromwell's men at Burford to the weavers massed behind their banners at Peterloo, the struggle for democratic and for social rights has always been intertwined. From the Chartist camp meeting to the dockers' picket line it has expressed itself most naturally in the language of moral revolt. Its weaknesses, its carelessness of theory, we know too well; its strengths, its resilience and steady humanity, we too easily forget. It is a tradition that could leaven the socialist world.

It is perhaps not unfair to say that Thompson's vision of the new left, and the practical creation of the institutions which it desperately needed, rose or fell on his insistence that this 'tradition' be engaged.[22]

It was not; the vision lived, but not at the point of production. The story is well – if incompletely – known. Allegiances drive interpretations and colour the contours of understanding in oppositional hues: the 'Old Guard' – John 'Stonebreaker' 'Sergeant-Major' Saville and the Old Marxist Fraction, the Petty-Humanist Thompsonite Revisionists, and their comrades, Peter Worsley, Mervyn Jones, and others – was banished; a new and energetic crew, headed by Perry Anderson and attuned to theory and the colonial question, assumed the helm of a sinking ship and brought it out of the rough waters of political uncertainty, charting the parochial empiricist English left into the fresh sea of ideas unleashed in Western Marxism's French and Italian rebirth. The sides traded blows in the mid-1960s, and returned to the fray in the later 1970s. Thompson's depiction of events has the virtue not of charitable balance, but of satirical bite:

> Early in 1962, when the affairs of *New Left Review* were in some confusion, the New Left Board invited an able contributor, Perry Anderson, to take over the editorship. We found (as we had hoped) in Comrade Anderson the decision and the intellectual coherence necessary to ensure the review's continuance. More than that, we discovered that we had appointed a veritable Dr. Beeching of the socialist intelligensia. All the uneconomic branch-lines and socio-cultural sidings of the New Left which were, in any case, carrying less and less traffic, were abruptly closed down. The main lines of the review underwent an equally ruthless modernisation. Old Left steam-engines were swept off the tracks; wayside halts ('Commitment', 'What Next for C.N.D.?', 'Women in Love') were boarded up; and the lines were electrified for the speedy traffic from the marxistentialist Left Bank. In less than a year the founders of the review discovered, to their chagrin, that the Board lived on a branch-line which, after vigorous intellectual costing, had been found uneconomical. Finding ourselves redundant we submitted to dissolution.

The 'first' new left was dead as a potent political force, although its ideas and inspirations remained; the 'second' new left had no aspirations to be a mobilizing force, seeing its role as preparatory, cultivating the dying, redundant theoretical garden of British Marxism with the importation of new and exotic species of vegetation, on which the left could dine in order to build up its strength as an organic community of oppositional intellectuals. There was little in this 'second' new left of the vision of Blake, and much of the 'science' of continental Marxist theory. Little was to be learned from a British working class that had long stood captive before imperialism and dogged resistance to Marxist theory. A divide had come.[23]

For the first time in his life, a gulf now separated Edward Thompson from the possibility of engagement. It was an experience of isolation that could have registered in default. He was now *of* a movement that had little place for him, where he could find no space to be *in*. By 1963 he realized that the new left he had worked tirelessly to build was dispersed organizationally and intellectually. 'We failed to implement our original purposes, or even to sustain what cultural apparatus we had,' he recognized. 'Defeats happen,' he said later, alluding to the failure to sustain the momentum of a possible independent left thrown up by 1956: 'It was a precious historical moment, and, in so far as we have lost it, it is an unqualified defeat.' Almost a decade of isolation stretched before him:

What happened was the creation of a New Left that I and my colleagues in England were very active in, at the time of Wright Mills, who was one of our closest colleagues here in the States. And then the transition to a second New Left. At the same time certain intellectual transitions occurred that to my mind were unfortunate. Expressive activity was raised above more rational and open political activity, and simultaneously a highly sophisticated set of Marxisms developed, particularly in Western Europe, which increasingly, it seemed to me, became theological in character – however sophisticated – and therefore broke with the Marxist tradition with which I had been associated. This was followed by a peculiarly tormented period in the late sixties when an intellectual leftist movement existed that was divorced from larger popular movements and that, in some sense, made a virtue of this isolation and did not take measures to communicate with the labor movement and other, larger, popular movements. On the one hand – and surely I don't have to remind you of this in the States – this New Left had elements within it that could be seen at once by a historian as the revolting bourgeoisie doing its own revolting thing – that is, the expressive and irrationalist, self-exalting gestures of style that do not belong to a serious and deeply rooted, rational revolutionary tradition. On the other hand, there was a sense that enough of the causes that this movement was associated with remained causes of the Left, particularly the struggle against the Vietnam War, and, in general, the struggle to democratize the institutions of education. One could certainly not attack or criticize this movement publicly, except within the movement itself – and even this was difficult. So my sense of isolation resulted from the movement's going in a direction that I in many ways deplored and at the same time was, perforce, silent about. I couldn't join the outcry, or the flight from Columbia, or whatever was going on on the Right or in the comfortable social-democratic 'middle'.

Having made his exit from King Street with the intention of continuing the struggle for socialism in a new left, Thompson found himself exiled and voiceless. To be sure, there were others with him, and they would found *The Socialist Register.* Thompson would have outlets for his writing. But this had never, whatever its importance, been enough.[24]

Throughout these years of difficult distance Thompson was sustained by intellectual currents and political commitments that he had forged over twenty years. Many were the product of vigorous acts of refusal. His departure from King Street and its brand of Marxist orthodoxy had helped him to see socialist humanism as counter to Stalinism, which he had come to regard as theory that poisoned practice, governed as it was by anti-intellectualism, moral nihilism, and the denial of the creative agency of human labour and the value of the individual as an agent in historical process. In the mechanical idealism of Stalinism's appropriation of the base/superstructure metaphor, all of humanity's being could be reduced to a mere reflection of *the* economic substance of society, which brought actually existing socialism's world-view in line with that of the reifications and possessive individualism of capitalism and imperialism.

Against the dehumanizing impersonality of these reigning ideologies of East and West, Thompson argued for the need to develop a sense of socialist community, at best; or, in times when this was simply not attainable, at least to acknowledge the lived potential of labouring men and women. He still believed in revolution, but the revolution would not necessarily replicate the Bolshevik experience of 1917. Rather than concentrate on a vanguard party 'seizing power' to create the context in which mass democratic self-activity might take place, the job of revolutionaries was to work everywhere they could – in mines, factories, daycare centres, tenants' associations – to appropriate authority, and sustain workers' and other popular forms of control. 'A break-through at any one of these points', Thompson believed, 'would immediately help in precipitating a diffuse aspiration into a positive movement.' It was a matter of the structures of subordination being assailed by the creative potential and practice of human agency. Stalinism, which was 'socialist theory and practice which [had] lost the ingredient of humanity', was incapable of grasping this or fostering a practice that took this new left perspective into account. In the process it subordinated the moral and imaginative faculties to political and administrative authority, eliminated values from the sphere of political judgement, feared independent thought, encouraged anti-intellectual trends and, finally, personified class experience in ways that belittled its living inner conflicts in a privileging of the lawed unconscious class base over and above the so-called superstructural spheres of consciousness and agency. This was King Street. It was more than a mistake: it could lead directly to death, destruction, immense human suffering, and the obliteration of socialist ideals and visions that were themselves the most cherished foundations of political change. For Thompson the moment of ultimate ironic disappointment came when he looked around at his successors of the 'second' new left, men who now occupied editorial posts on the *New Left Review*, and saw the dark shadow of this same destructive denial cast across the desk of what had once been his own promising point of production.[25]

This must have been more than difficult. Certainly there were private moments of doubt. But Thompson, like others, remained an *example* of resolute commitment. With King Street now closed to even the most languid traffic from Thompson, and with his way to the offices of the ascendant 'second' new left blocked by the virile bodies of a new leadership, those of lesser political integrity and principled commitment might well have made their peace with social democracy and reformism, embracing the Labour Party as the solution to the socio-economic ills of the nation. Stranger turnarounds have occurred on the left. But Thompson was not suited to such a volte-face. In the aftermath of the 1959 Labour defeat at the polls he had written:

> Most of the people at the top of the Labour Party are professional politicians, very much at home in the conventions of capitalist politics. These are a very bad and untrustworthy sort of people. We all know this, but some fetish about 'unity' prevents us from saying it. We should say it now since – being professional politicians and sensing which way the wind blows – some of them may start to try out a leftish 'image' in their speeches. We should not believe them until we see some Aldermaston mud upon their boots. People who proclaim their adherence to principle 'though in muted terms' are people without principle. Such people tell us that we must start to 'fight the next election now'. But we hope that we may never have to fight their kind of election again.

He would not change his mind: in two edited volumes in the 1960s – *Out of Apathy* and the *May Day Manifesto* – he and his collaborators confronted and polemicized against the capitulations of reformism. To be sure, Thompson and his wife Dorothy did apply to join the Labour Party in 1962, but their reasons had little to do with a sense that Labour and its leadership represented a way forward. They were originally rebuffed by 'a high-level screening committee' which 'demanded that we say if we were Marxists or not'. Pressure from their locale mounted within the Labour Party, protesting this ideological exclusion, and the Thompsons were eventually admitted to the Halifax Labour Party. It was little cause for political rejoicing. 'I'm a member of the Labour Party,' Thompson replied to an interviewer's question twenty years later; 'that's just like being a member of the human race. You accept it without enthusiasm.' In one of his last letters to me, eight months before he died,

Edward reported: 'No politics worth mentioning in this country, except that the miners seem once again to have given the Tories a black eye. Without help from Labour, of course,' he snorted, closing the letter with a caustic: 'They are fantastic people!'[26]

It is possible – approaching the century's turn, with the political climate on the left so hostile to Marxism's harder analytic and political edges, with fashion flying so dramatically in the face of class as a central human identity, with pressures to abandon any but the most wilted flowerings of reformism, with revolution just a dirty word fouling the mouths of utopian babes – for this example to be quietly and cutely chastised, as it is by *History Workshop*'s Raphael Samuel, himself once a young member of the Communist Party Historians' Group:

> The weight of the past was particularly apparent in the New Reasoners who were, comparatively speaking, old political hands. Recruited to communism for the most part in the late 1930s or early 1940s, they prided themselves on their 'staying power', having survived the persecutions of the Cold War with their loyalties and beliefs intact. . . . This was especially true of E.P. Thompson, though he had been perhaps the fiercest critic of Stalinism and moved furthest, in his intellectual loyalties, from anything which might be called Marxism. An almost Cossack sense of honour, refusing to yield an inch to enemy attack, and a fierce attachment to the vocation of the intellectual as an oppositionist, made him eager to proclaim himself a 'Communist', interpreting the term not as card-carrying membership of the Party but as commitment to the revolutionary idea.

But there are other, more generous recollections. The novelist Clancy Sigal, a 'rootless socialist American' in the England of the 1950s, has recently expressed his gratitude to 'the people who were running that almost forgotten magazine, *The New Reasoner*, which was absolutely brilliant'. They were part of the energy, the comradeship, and the possibility of the 'first' new left. 'Suddenly the heart of Marxism, which had been stultifying, was broken wide open,' he enthused. 'I thought we were all engaged in a kind of collective endeavour to recapture that essential idealism, freshness, originality of an idea which had been taken away from us by the enemies of promise, by the enemies of socialism.'[27]

At this same point in time, C. Wright Mills classified Thompson as 'a plain Marxist', a communist who had been through the Party but resisted its assimilating grasp. Such plain Marxists 'confronted the unresolved tension in Marx's work – and in history itself: the tension of humanism and determinism, of human freedom and historical necessity'. They worked in 'Marx's own tradition', but recognized the importance of historical specificity. In the political battles of their time, such plain Marxists were most often losers. Yet Mills refused to treat them with the disdain common in contemporary academic circles. These plain Marxists 'confronted the world's problems; they are unable to take the easy ways out'. There would soon be other losers, ensnared in a world problem, also incapable of facile escape, who would come to be associated closely with E.P. Thompson.[28]

# 3

# Making Histories

As the editorial direction of the *New Left Review* shifted in the early-to-mid-1960s, Edward Thompson was putting the finishing touches to the book that would eventually make his name commonplace in academic seminars and statements of historiography. Late in 1962 he spent two weeks on some final research at the British Museum, living in Perry Anderson's London apartment. The two sparred occasionally, debating the virtues of historical and sociological modes of thinking, but they sidestepped the widening political and interpretive gulfs that were now obviously separating the editorial board of the review. For all the apparent harshness of the eventual fallout that drove Thompson away from the journal he had helped to found and into an acidic debate with his new left successors – who, by 1964, were in unchallenged control of the Carlisle Street offices of the *NLR* – there was remarkably little personal animus at the face-to-face level. Anderson recalls the odd 'explosion', but remembers of Thompson: 'his attitude to the youngsters was fundamentally generous, and when the time came he ensured a clear hand-over of the old board to them, without rancour. Whatever his forebodings, he was not possessive.' Years later, when the swords of Anderson, Tom Nairn, and Thompson had crossed and clashed in the pages of *Socialist Register* and *New Left Review*, the two major protagonists bumped into each other in a London pub. Edward was 'good nature itself', recalled Anderson. The indignations of the polemical page were kept separate from the still fraternal impulses of sociability, the hand of experience extended welcomingly to youthful rebels. Thompson was now a personage of stature in the milieu of English radicalism, yet when he finished *The Making of the English Working Class* he was a mere thirty-eight years of age. The book further consolidated his reputation on the left, but it catapulted him into the international world of historical scholarship.[1]

'I am seeking to rescue the poor stockinger, the Luddite cropper, the "obsolete" hand-loom weaver, the "utopian" artisan, and even the deluded follower of Joanna Southcott, from the enormous condescension of posterity', Thompson wrote in the Preface to *The Making of the English Working Class*. I have never before quoted these lines, precisely because they have been reproduced by *everybody* with an interest in the dispossessed and the marginalized. They are undoubtedly the most cited set of words in the making of social history. But it is appropriate to allude to this passage here, for in many ways it captured the essence of Thompson's efforts to remake historical sensitivities. His Morris volume, whatever its value as a rereading of Victorian socialism and the importance of the Romantic critique of capitalism, focused on a figure long recognized as important, however that importance was mistakenly fragmented, its parts isolated and drawn apart rather than integrated and understood in their relationships (arts and craft; poetry; architecture; socialism). In the post-*William Morris* years, Thompson's historical writing turned to the obscure and obscured history of class *experience*: he was increasingly involved in projects, not of Morrisian-like politicization through *reinterpretation*, but of reinterpretation and politicization through *excavation*. This moved from the subject terrain of the Industrial

Revolution, where there was an abundance of comment in antiquarian texts, newspapers, state sources, and established historical writing; from the sympathetic but far from unproblematic commentary of the Hammonds and the Webbs through the dry detachments of the *Economic History Review*; to the work on the eighteenth century, where the writing increasingly turned on closer and closer interrogations of the unmined record of 'plebeian' life and its reciprocal ties to 'patrician' rule.[2]

This historiographic production gave rise to a virtual industry of Thompson comment – some descriptive, much, increasingly, critical.[3] From almost every corner has come the push to assimilate Thompson, be it to sociology or anthropology as academic disciplines, or to the turn to 'new' cultural history.[4] Coincident with the publication of *The Poverty of Theory* a deluge of commentary descended on him, insistent on forcing consideration of the theoretical purity of his method within the context of a historiographic moment of fixation on Marxism's supposedly interpretive structuralist core.[5] Engaging and penetrating critiques of 'experience' as a touchstone of historical analysis appeared in the 1980s, as did a questioning of the selectiveness and perhaps chronologically premature basis of Thompson's understanding of class formation.[6] More recently there has been sustained discussion of the gendered understanding (historical and authorial) of consciousness and class implicit in his *Making*.[7]

This enduring engagement with Thompson's writings suggests their importance. Certainly much can be learned from this literature of critique: about historical process; about the construction of historiography; about the silences and thundering loudness of choice in Thompson's own formulation of what emerges out of the evidence; about the shifting sands of political and intellectual concern in our own time. In their relentless engagement with Thompson *on their own terms*, in which his project is repeatedly scrutinized with a kind of reversereferentiality to what concerns the *critic*, much is gained. But there are also points of loss, and even tendencies to violate matters of political and intellectual substance in a ruthless suppression of interest in WHY *The Making* ended up looking as it did. There has been little enough of this probing curiosity in the manufacture of Thompson comment, which rolls off the academic assembly line with only the most irregular instances of the kind of sabotage that would take analysis back into the confluence of streams that actually structured Thompson's approach.[8]

These streams have already been alluded to here. Thompson's engagement with adult education remained in place as he researched and wrote *The Making* and, earlier, his important revisionist piece on Tom Maguire, socialism, and the Leeds Independent Labour Party. Living in Halifax in the late 1950s, Thompson was now an experienced extra-mural tutor. 'You got to know the members of the classes very well,' he recalled in 1988, 'and also they told you a great deal from their own oral traditions.' Hard up, and cognizant of the need for a text that might reach these student workers, teachers and trade unionists, and the left milieu he was trying to transform, Thompson agreed to a publisher's request to write a history of the British labour movement from 1832 to 1945. He convinced the press to push the chronological beginning point back to 1790, and what became *The Making of the English Working Class* was in fact to be the first chapter of this never-completed survey text. 'I was trying to express the theoretical and philosophical preoccupations of 10 years of extra-mural work,' he noted in 1980, the book being aimed 'at the good extra-mural student'. It was also driven by the political context, where Thompson's creative adaptation of the Blake/Morris courting/marriage of Romanticism and Marxism, his eventual repudiation of Stalinism's destructive denials of human agency, and his efforts to build a new left, all culminated in 'a polemic against abbreviated economistic notations of Marxism' in which 'the creation of the working class was that of a determined process: steam power plus the factory system equals the working class.' Embedded in local sources, oral traditions, and the distinct socialist past of the West Riding, Thompson remembered being largely innocent of academic preoccupations and proprieties as he began the research and writing of *The Making*. 'My material was more likely to come from Batley library than the *Economic History Review.*' And this evidence, in what would be a recurring theme in Thompson's research, overtook him. Far from planning almost a thousand pages on this initial chapter (1790–1832), 'the material took command of me, far more than I ever expected'. Later Thompson would draw this conclusion: 'I would have to say that the historian has got to be listening all the time. ... If he listens, then the material itself will begin to speak through him. And I think this happens.' It would also speak through and to others. Sheila Rowbotham remembers poring over the collections of books assembled by Edward and Dorothy, and how that moved her in the direction of the social and sexual radicalism of Edward Carpenter:

> I must have been about twenty-one when Edward Thompson showed me his 'Homage to Tom Maguire', the account he had written of the emergence of socialism in Leeds. Carpenter appears tangentially in this. He was a friend of Maguire's and of Alf Mattison, who helped Maguire organise the gas workers and was a frequent visitor to Millthorpe. Through Dorothy and Edward Thompson there was a living connection to those early days of West Riding socialism. Among others they had met Alf's wife Florence Mattison, still active in the Leeds labour movement. Edward Thompson started to tell me about that northern socialism, how for a time preoccupation with changing all forms of human relationships had been central in a working-class movement. Somehow the connection had been broken and people like Carpenter drifted away, became slightly cranky and inturned. I didn't really understand what he was saying then but could feel from the way he said it that it was somehow important.

'I think I wrote *The Making of the English Working Class* rather faster than seems probable,' Thompson would tell an interviewer almost three decades later. 'I must have had a lot of energy in those days that I don't have now.' That energy was driven by passions and commitments, feeding off the sources and localized human connections to a past worth recovering. 'History is the memory of a culture,' he claimed later, 'and memory can never be free from passions and commitments. I am not in any sense inhibited by the fact that my own passions and commitments are clear.'[9]

Those passions and commitments drove the form of presentation in *The Making* in specific directions. Irreverent, and unambiguously upholding the case for the human costs paid over the course of the Industrial Revolution, Thompson's book was almost unique in the clarity – not so much of what it was *for*, but of what it stood *against*. Consider the simple matter of concluding sentences for specific chapters: on the field labourers – ' "As for this litel fire," the writer concluded with equable ill-humour, "Don't be alarmed it will be a damd deal wors when we burn down your barn ..." '; on artisans and others – 'A notable victory for Dr. Kay and Mr Plum! [ed.: workhouse administrators] ... 78,536 workhouse inmates. By 1843 the figure had risen to 197,179. The most eloquent testimony to the depths of poverty is in the fact that they were tenanted at all'; on the weavers – 'For those who suffered, this retrospective comfort is cold.' Or this comment on the standard of living and the 'average' working man: 'His own share in the "benefits of economic progress" consisted of more potatoes, a few articles of cotton clothing for his family, soap and candles, some tea and sugar, and a great many articles in the *Economic History Review*.' Against the jaundiced cynicism of R.M. Hartwell, who viewed the experience of child labour against a twentieth-century familiarity with concentration camps to proclaim himself 'comparatively unmoved', Thompson offered words of opposition: 'We may be allowed to reaffirm a more traditional view: that the exploitation of little children, on this scale and with this intensity, was one of the most shameful events in our history.' As he himself pointed out in the case of Cobbett, *tone* matters, and it was the style and persistently charged language of *The Making*, in conjuncture with its emphasis in content on the self-activity of labouring people, that established its enduring political relevance. 'Which argument, which truths?' was scratched into every line of detail, punctuating the *refusal* of complacencies, be they of past or present. Decades later, in a lengthy poem crafted around a historian's sensibilities, Thompson would return to this theme:

> However many the Emperor slew
> The scientific historian
> (While taking note of contradiction)
> Affirms that productive forces grew.

The tone of the book made historical writing and the process and events of history *one*: making history was an interpretive intervention that linked past, present and future; understanding what made history reordered appreciation of these reciprocal chronologies, and opened out into new appreciations of how history could be remade; writing history therefore mattered, as did the living of it, both of which related to its future. This, in part, explains why even critics of Thompson acknowledge that the book 'awoke labour history from its long dogmatic slumbers'.[10]

Because the book is now centrally recognized as a pivotal text within the field of working-class history – and also because I am relatively unconcerned about the particular details of Thompson's argument, as opposed to the way he constructed it, what influences came to bear on that construction, and how his general approach moved the historiography so decisively forward – it is not vitally important to stop and ponder every specific case study developed in *The Making*. This, ironically, has been the strategy of critics, be they Marxist, feminist or mainstream. Yet in the end it matters far less that Thompson's claims *for* the working class of early-nineteenth-century England rest too lightly on an understanding of accumulation and capitalism's uneven march, privilege artisanal debasements and efforts to deflect proletarianization, focus attention on the resisting side of experience – be it the London Corresponding Society or Luddism – and understate accommodation, elevate unnecessarily the question of consciousness to the detriment of an appreciation of socioeconomic structure, reproduce and valorize the masculinist understanding of the politics and workplace meanings of class, and overstate the level of class cohesion in a chronologically premature insistence that the working class was in fact made by 1832, than that the book opened interpretive eyes to a new way of seeing class. *The Making*'s success is not in this or that particular argument, and whether they are, rigidly understood, *right* or *wrong*. Its meaning, rather, and its consequent great achievement, lies in the unmistakable rupture it forced in the historical literature, where class formation could no longer simply be posed, by radicals and reactionaries alike, as a mechanical reflection of economic change.

Those who want to call into question the so-called Thompsonian attraction to aspects of historical process – 'culture' or 'experience' – usually point to legitimate areas of ambiguity. But they, too, miss the fundamental and undeniable analytic edge and advance of Thompson's book: whatever the difficulties in defining such conceptual terms with precision, their utilization in *The Making* allowed entry to whole areas of neglected importance in the lives of workers, areas that could never again be ignored in negotiating the slippery slopes that connect being and consciousness. Moreover, a massive interpretive work such as Thompson's never denied that it selected partially and incompletely from the infinite range of events and processes which, patched together, comprised some kind of quantifiable sum total of class experience. The argument was coloured by West Riding sources, many of the twists and turns needed more research and, upon completion of such inquiry, Thompson was quick to acknowledge that his own admittedly limited project had been surpassed. Yet Thompson's book rightly insisted on generalization, against the fragmenting impulses of a social history which, by the 1990s, would too often measure its maturity in regression into a kind of senile fixation on the particular, denying the very value of integrating experience into an understanding of connections and powerful influences. 'The new social history is becoming', worried Thompson in 1973,

> a series of prints, snapshots, stasis upon stasis. As a gain is registered, in the new dimension of social history, at the same time whole territories of established economic and political history are evacuated. The central concern of history, as a relevant humane study – to generalize and integrate and to attain a comprehension of the full social and cultural process – becomes lost.

*The Making of the English Working Class* refused such evacuations, *assuming* much in the way of economic context, to be sure, recasting the understanding of politics to include the reciprocities of state and class formation.

Reductionist efforts to boil Thompson down to a particular rhetorical flourish – 'the working class made itself as much as it was made' – inevitably caricature the richness of his account. For much of working-class consciousness in this period, as a reading of Thompson will show, was indeed forged from above, in the crucibles of state panic and repression that reach from the Jacobin agitations of the 1790s through the underground threats of the first years of the nineteenth century into Peterloo (1819). Some of the most imaginative passages of Thompson's text emerge out of his exemplary interrogation of the very sources of fear and loathing generated by the state – informers' reports – which allow the judicious historian to get past the self-serving exaggerations of paid spies into the insurrectionary underground that both conservatives and constitutionally inclined Fabians have tended to discount. As the imperatives of capital and the counter-revolutionary panic of the ruling classes expressed themselves, simultaneously, in every corner of life, within the political economy of the Industrial and French Revolutions, the English working class came to consciousness of itself against a dual threat: 'as new techniques and forms of industrial organization advanced, so political and social rights receded'. John Thelwall's *Rights of Nature* (1796) recognized the formative possibility present in this moment of danger: 'Every large workshop and manufactory is a sort of political society, which no act of parliament can silence, and no magistrate disperse.'[11]

'Orphans we are, and bastards of society,' wrote James Morrison in 1834, in a quote that appears on the last page of *The Making of the English Working Class*. 'The tone is not one of resignation,' states Thompson, 'but of pride.' In attending to the history of class formation in ways that looked seriously to the active making of such self-identifications, Thompson's book was obviously related to the politics of his repudiation of Stalinism and articulation of socialist humanism. It drew directly on the Romantic tradition's assault on the formative moment of capitalist consolidation, situating much of the moral authority of antagonism to the Industrial Revolution in the powerful Jacobin indictments of the 1790s, but it acknowledged the failure to forge a common front of poetic and proletarian alternative:

> Such men met Utilitarianism in their daily lives, and they sought to throw it back, not blindly, but with intelligence and moral passion. They fought, not the machine, but the exploitative and oppressive relationships intrinsic to industrial capitalism. In these same years, the great Romantic criticism of Utilitarianism was running its parallel but altogether separate course. After William Blake, no mind was at home in both cultures, nor had the genius to interpret the two traditions to each other. ... Hence these years appear at times to display, not a revolutionary challenge, but a resistance movement, in which both the Romantics and the Radical craftsmen opposed the annunciation of

Acquisitive Man. In the failure of the two traditions to come to a point of juncture, something was lost. How much we cannot be sure, for we are among the losers.

Thus Thompson's history was an attempt to come to grips with the explanatory puzzle of the failure of revolution in nineteenth-century England, and its relationship to more contemporary political failures of the left. But it did so in ways which, however attentive to ideas and immiseration, the capitulations to capital's ideological power and the conflicts of street and workplace, never shunted the subjects aside, their defeats registering only in dismissive marginalization. Instead, Thompson thanked those who were organized in the dead of night, who fell at Peterloo, who hawked the radical press, who did thousands of things and thought thousands of thoughts against the grain of Albion's fatal tree, and stood tall for liberty. In this, as well as in the disciplines of capitalist development, class was made: a happening marked always with the blows of conflict.[12]

*The Making of the English Working Class*, like Thompson's teaching in adult education, was thus constructed on the battleground of class conflict. It was a conscious intervention in the long process of the making of the working class from above that was also an attempt to unmake any realization of class consciousness or identification of class grievance and potential power from below. In a Mansbridge Memorial Lecture at Leeds in the mid-to-late 1960s, Thompson noted:

> The desire to dominate and shape the intellectual and cultural growth of the people towards predetermined and safe ends remains extremely strong right through the Victorian years: and it survives today. . . . From the 1790s, then, one can see the 'march of the intellect', with its mutual improvement societies, its mechanics' institutes, and its Sunday lectures, beginning to move forward: but at the same time, it was leaving behind it the customary experiential culture of the people. . . . The self-educated working man who dedicated his nights and his Sundays to the pursuit of knowledge was also asked at every turn to reject the entire human lore of his childhood and of his fellow workers as uncouth, immoral, ignorant.

At his own point of production, Thompson taught workers themselves that this was not the kind of politico-intellectual trade they need make, just as *The Making* showed that it was not what had necessarily happened historically.[13] By the mid-1960s Thompson's historical understanding of English class experience was relatively firmly grounded – theoretically, historiographically, and in terms of his own considerable immersion in specific source materials. It confirmed, for Thompson, the importance of class, further convincing him of the aridity of the abstract Marxism of the second new left, epitomized by the Anderson–Nairn position that in the class defeats of English society the revolutionary potential of the working class was sacrificed on the altar of a bourgeoisie that failed to win a decisive political victory over the aristocracy in the 1640s, further compromising itself in 1688 and 1832. In Anderson's words, 'a supine bourgeoisie produced a subordinate proletariat'. Yet this did not fit at all with Thompson's own appreciation of the depth of class struggles and the range of working-class resources in nineteenth-century England. He was not starry-eyed in his assessment of the working class, the left, and their respective defeats and shortcomings, particularly with respect to imperialism and a jingoistic nationalism. But the Platonic models of the Anderson–Nairn thesis tidied up all the messiness of class struggles in a kind of tunnel vision that could scope only in the linear sightings of one-dimensional boundaries of hegemony. What this missed, for Thompson, was the extent to which, even in defeat, the working class proceeded to 'warren' capitalist society 'from end to end', building and supporting a network of trade unions, co-operative societies, fraternal associations, and self-help movements. Making histories demanded recognition of this. In a 1973 review of Dyos's and Wolff's *The Victorian City*, Thompson would return to this point:

> This is a city without trade unions, republican clubs, friendly societies, strikes, Reform Bill demonstrations, workingmen's clubs, co-ops,

acclaims for Garibaldi and rough-musicking of General Heinau, female reformers, or any street corner agitators. The poor are in this city, and middle class responses to the poor; but the working class and its movements are not.

This was the academic 'blind spot', the scholastic equivalent of the reification of *the* model evident in the Anderson–Nairn encounter with class. University-ensconced academics, however liberal and humane, were, Thompson suggested, 'alienated from the people as a mass ... deeply skeptical about working-class movements ... impotent in social or political terms'. As a result, there were inevitably gaps of considerable importance in much academic writing:

> Capitalism, class conflict – these are two of the absentees from this book ... we cannot simply set those problems aside, in the interests of a more comfortable seminar. ... What ghost was inside that Victorian machine? What drove the railways and slums here but not there, starved these artists and rewarded those, fueled the ideologies, made the image of 'city' and of 'community' appear as antagonists? ... Those Victorian moralists and literary men who – as many contributors insist – turned their backs on the city, yearned nostalgically for 'nature', allowed protest to petrify in escapism, may still be seen as negative voices. But within their negativity, may also be seen a resistance to utilitarian definitions that sustained values which, transmitted to us, are a major resource for human survival.

Ironically enough, the democratization of education in the 1960s, the mixed academic response to *The Making of the English Working Class*, as well, perhaps, as the book's influence abroad and within the general post-1965 rise of social history, placed Thompson in an increasingly proximate relation to academic research and writing. He had become, through no intention of his own, a historian captivated by research possibilities. Driven by his sources and personal and political circumstances to particular areas where histories could be made in ways that related to the English working class he had long embraced as central to the values and meanings of alternative and possibility, he was moved, step by unanticipated step, in new directions.[14]

In 1965 Edward and Dorothy Thompson moved to the West Midlands, where Edward would become Director of the Centre for the Study of Social History at the newly established University of Warwick; three years later Dorothy would join the History Department of the University of Birmingham. The Centre quickly attracted a number of talented graduate students, many of them from North America, and Edward's drawing power as a thesis supervisor and teacher was accentuated by lively seminars with guest speakers and a resident visiting professor from the United States. Thompson was increasingly drawn into the milieu of History as an academic discipline – in part because his own work had now entered into the professional discourse and was subjected to sometimes searing critique; in part because in training young apprentice historians he was responsible for ensuring that their education took slightly different directions from that with which he had been involved in extra-mural adult education classes through Leeds. Yet the recollections of his academic graduate students from this period do not seem markedly different from those of his Leeds adult learners. Edward's teaching remained marked by its rigour and passion, its fairness in the face of difference, its generosity in sharing ideas and sources. Anna Davin, like Sheila Rowbotham, remembers Thompson's informal sociability alongside this lively and comradely academic environment, drawing attention, as well, to the extent to which Edward stood out 'among teachers and historians as being continually aware that women too were part of history'. And Edward continued to learn from his students, whose labours in the field work of historical reconstruction he regularly acknowledged and supported. If teaching at Warwick did not present the same need to impress upon working-class adult students that their experiences mattered, it led in at least one similar direction: Thompson's students were aware – in the words of Bob Malcolmson and John Rule – that 'Writing history was a life-enhancing activity . . . done with a deep sense of commitment . . . vital to the health of society.' This was something that has stayed with many of them for the remainder of their lives.[15]

At Warwick Thompson's historical work moved back in time: into the eighteenth century. Unlike the Morris volume or the study of the early working class, these eighteenth-century explorations were undertaken against the backdrop of established academic scholarship. There were, in fact, two histories being made in this period.

The first, involving Thompson's pursuit of some themes first elaborated in the discussion of 'community' in *The Making of the English Working Class,* drew him into the customary culture of the plebeian masses. Much of this new research actually overturned assumptions and prejudices buried in undeveloped lines of *The Making,* where Thompson had too easily bought into the very condescension he sought to overcome, accepting at face value the often incomplete and usually 'improving' views of the socially superior, be they novelists, folklorists, or respectable constitutionalist radicals/reformers. Often, Thompson's entry into this material showed him how partial had been his understanding of the available historical evidence. He would later 'confess with shame' that he had written *The Making* without having read John Brand's *Observations on Popular Antiquities* (1777). In his increasingly critical engagement with anthropology, Thompson may – although this is largely conjecture – have been influenced by his father's interest in Indian custom, an interpretation that draws some support from the locale where he chose to present his views on folklore, anthropology and social history: the Indian Historical Congress. What was developing in this period, carrying through into the 1970s, was a close reading of rituals such as the wife sale and rough music, as well as increasing attention to the dispossessed's convictions of common right to the land. These studies, gestured to in general statements on historical method or social history, or presented in edited collections of essays or foreign journals, for the most part started as research projects in this period, but found their way into print only later.

Two lengthy and hugely influential articles, published in *Past & Present*, had more of an immediate impact. 'Time, Work-Discipline and Industrial Capitalism' (1967) and 'The Moral Economy of the English Crowd in the Eighteenth Century' (1971) were carefully formed statements which, more than any other writings, placed Thompson in the forefront of *academic* social history. The first became an undisputed classic, cited routinely around the world as scholars addressed the tensions of peasant, proto-industrial, and early proletarian communities reacting to the disciplines and new work rhythms of capitalist social formations. More controversial was Thompson's discussion of the moral economy of the crowd, which generated an intensive industry of analysis and study. Taken together, these researches and writings all revolved around a reinterpretation of the whole of eighteenth-century society, in which patricians and plebeians were locked in the reciprocal embrace of paternalism, an argument that received an abbreviated airing in the American *Journal of Social History* in 1974. As late as 1992, one of Thompson's students, working in South Africa, remembered this Warwick moment of eighteenth-century discovery: 'In my head I keep hearing Edward Thompson giving his lectures on eighteenth-century paternalism. His voice inspires me still – even in this very different place.' Christopher Hitchens claims that in a police cell in Oxford in 1969 he, Raphael Samuel, and a number of others arrested during a mass demonstration against 'some Tory racist demagogue' had found, to their surprise, that they had all attended 'Edward Thompson's bravura talk on the Enclosure Acts a few weeks previously'. Conscious of a common bond, they found no other topic of conversation. As the chants of opposition outside the cop shop rose and fell, blood congealing on battered faces, Hitchens and his comrades were drawn back into 'a tremendous account of the lost world of the common land and the common people', which Thompson had closed with poetic lines from John Clare. 'All the clichés about bringing history to life had become, for those who listened, vividly and properly true,' Hitchens suggested.[16]

This work, later to form the core essays in *Customs in Common* (1991), was supplemented by other historical writing, most of which broke only lightly from conventional academic proprieties.[17] But the second project of the Warwick period proceeded in ways marked by Thompson's own peculiar engagement with professional historical scholarship.

There seems to have been a co-operative equality linking Thompson and his students throughout this period of the later 1960s. They moved towards the eighteenth-century studies, especially in a collective focus on law and crime, *together*, in a collaborative consultation in which teacher and student shared the excitement of uncertainty as to what would be found. At this time Thompson was balancing a set of creatively destabilizing impulses. In a series of important – and often lengthy – reviews and prefaces he confirmed his continuing interest in the subject of *The Making of the English Working Class*, especially Peterloo; restated his sensitivities to class difference and the politics of making histories in ways that demanded attention to sexuality, gender oppression and rural labour; charted an opening foray into the historiography of crime; and grappled, through engagement with the first instalment of Laslett's Cambridge Group for the History of Population, with an emerging, quantitatively driven 'demographic determinism' that threatened to displace histories concerned with something other than numbers. As early as 1966 Thompson was simultaneously enthusiastic and cautious about the prospect of labour history becoming a 'great testing-ground for historical sociology', embracing the break from traditional confinements as liberation, but insisting that new methodologies must not obliterate older traditions of inquiry, and that the traffic between history and sociology run in two mutually respectful directions.

But if Thompson was increasingly attuned to concerns of academic historians, he was far from overtaken by them, as his Preface to a collection of essays by the American radical historian and 'outsider' Staughton Lynd suggests. Describing himself as a fellow 'objector', Thompson linked himself with Lynd in 'our brotherhood in the shadowy international of revolutionary humanism'. Both, moreover, exhibited the concern with 'actualities' that immersed their thinking in the particular and 'primary discipline of history', that of context. They nevertheless stood apart from both 'the long conservative ascendancy' that denied agency except in its most 'trivialised and personalised expression', and the dual dangers on the left of radical sentimentalism and model-driven Marxist mechanical idealism. The key was context and the 'contradictoriness of culture'; but to 'challenge established positions in this way requires, in the challenger, something of the awkwardness of an Objector'. The meaning of this awkwardness of objection was registered most decisively in the way history was conceived and written, but it also seemed, to many, present in Edward's own physical being. One student remembered his first 'formal' meeting with Thompson:

> The man who greeted me – I mostly remember his wild, prematurely greying hair – was different from any other academic I had observed. He looked ... well, he looked like he had just strolled in from the moors, or returned from a meeting at the pithead. He was intense and energetic and had piercing eyes.[18]

This awkwardness was almost intrinsic to Thompson's method as a teacher, which deliberately blurred the often compartmentalized areas of research and teaching. As he and his students collectively entered into an eighteenth-century world where crime and society overlapped in histories of domination and resistance, they apparently decided to produce a volume of essays. Thompson promised an article-length treatment of the draconian Black Act of 1723, which dramatically extended the number of capital offences. Preliminary research indicated that this was a rash commitment. In the end the chapter grew into Thompson's book *Whigs and Hunters* (1975), and he contributed to the collected essays *Albion's Fatal Tree* (1975), an evocative account of the crime of the anonymous threatening letter. Yet again Thompson was seized by the material, his capacity to listen opening out into an appreciation of long-suppressed and silenced voices. 'One source led me to the next; but, also, one problem led me to another,' he noted, somewhat exasperated. 'What made this exercise more hazardous was that I had neither read nor researched very much on any aspect of social history before 1750,' he continued. 'I was like a parachutist coming down in unknown territory: at first knowing only a few yards of land around me, and gradually extending my explorations in each direction.' Avoiding the actual historical writing in the field until quite late in his researches, Thompson was following his analytic instincts, cultivated over years of adult education teaching and debate on the left. Instead of starting with the conventional academic wisdom, looking first at Walpole and his Court, the Whig architects of the Act, and then – briefly at best – at the people and places subject to this new criminalization, Thompson reversed methodological direction. He began his researches with the Windsor and Hampshire deer forests and episodes of poaching transgression, moving into the shadowy underbrush of the masked hunters and foresters themselves, their networks and often raucous defiance of the King's law, closing with a look at the personnel and politics of administration and interest.

These studies generated immense scholarly concern: they stimulated fruitful debate and the best of intellectual exchange, but they also upset the gentlemanly balance of English eighteenth-century studies, where deference to the grace and goodwill of lordly rule had long been accepted as a part of the curriculum. Disgruntled critics ravaged Thompson's footnotes to find errors of citation, only to commit worse blunders themselves. 'He is rather like a woodman, setting out to do a rigorous hatchet job, and coming back proudly with a couple of twigs and his own severed hand,' Thompson rightly replied to one such conservative challenger. Another saw the publication of Thompson and his students and the odd complementary book in the United States as the thin edge of an ideological wedge, insinuating itself into the fortress of eighteenth-century historiography, bringing the walls down in a tumult of falling interpretive standards, and blasting away the mortar of free criticism. Manipulating this lever was the 'charismatic leader' of a new school, orthodox in its convictions, threatening in its capacity to 'pervert the historiography of eighteenth-century England for a generation'. From his post at a small provincial university, commanding an army of a dozen graduate students, E.P. Thompson had become the combat general of an inter-pretive war over domination of the eighteenth century. In the eyes of a rather traditionalist paranoid academy, he would settle for nothing less than the imposition of 'a Namierism of the Marxist left'.[19]

# 4

# The 1970s:
# Rethinking Marxism,
# Returning to 1956, and the
# Politics of Democracy

Historians, especially those who are comfortable in the confines of academic conservatism, are often the last to look the process of intellectual and political change in the face. No sooner was Thompson's influence as an eighteenth-century historian attacked as 'Marxist' than his own debate with Marxism intensified, drawing him – unplanned, I would argue – into a more critical dialogue with Marxisms that would eventually serve as his own point of departure from Marxism as both theory and practice. But Thompson would never become a crude anti-Marxist and, like his American friend Herbert G. Gutman, he would remain committed to historical materialism precisely because Marxism's conceptualization of how to question the past remained, for him, valid:

> What is left when you clear away the determinist and teleological elements are good questions that direct your attention to critical ways of looking at on-going historical processes. A fundamental contribution of nineteenth- and twentieth-century Marxist thinking is a set of questions having to do with the way in which one examines class relations and how they change, the way in which one examines the institutionalization of power, the way in which one examines popular oppositional movements, the way in which one examines the integration of subordinate or

exploited groups into a social system. These are some of the very useful questions.

'Which arguments, which truths' would always, for Thompson, be answered out of some part of historical materialism, where Marxist concerns could never be *only* a matter of crude dismissal.[1]

Thompson's time at Warwick was destined to be short. Whatever his obvious and admirable merits as a teacher, he always considered himself a *writer*, and as early as 1968 he was growing impatient with the ways in which a university post, with its administrative and teaching responsibilities, seemed to curtail that activity (although, in hindsight, it also stimulated much creative work). In his own words, Thompson's brief tenure at Warwick was commemorated in 'a bulky file full of my own fatuous and long-winded attempts at resignation'. As his children grew up, necessitating less direct parental care, and with Dorothy taking up a teaching position at Birmingham, doors into new possibilities opened, and full-time writing had a pressing allure for Edward.[2]

Thompson would eventually leave Warwick, but not, ironically, before a moment of student rebellion shattered his political isolation and brought him back into the public limelight in ways that may have forced a slightly more charitable reading of the excesses of American-style student rebellion and new left politics. Writing in 1971, Thompson referred to the radicalism of the 1960s as 'more a matter of gesture and style than of practice ... [in which] satire became a means of disguising a general ambivalence of political and social stance'. By no means uncritical in his admiration of youth, he often deplored its indiscipline and indulgence, especially as these related to politics: 'Youth, if left to its own devices, tends to become very hairy, to lie in bed till lunch-time, to miss seminars, to be more concerned with the style rather than the consequence of actions, and to commit various sins of self-righteous political purism and intellectual arrogance.' He deplored left trendiness, especially where it intersected with commercialism: fashion shops named 'Che Guevara' would elicit a Thompson tirade against the trivialization of Third World struggle. Presumably these views were translated, unevenly and awkwardly, into the personal relationships between Edward and his students, perhaps embellished in the relentless gossip that characterizes friendships among students and teachers, especially when teachers do not necessarily cultivate distance and detachment, which Edward did not. But these views probably intruded only lightly, if at all, precisely because the political atmosphere at Warwick, while it was linked to the campus revolts of 1968, remained one of modest disenchantment. Protest was likely to be symbolic (elaborate graffiti) or supportive (endorsement of London School of Economics actions) or directed outward, to a wider, non-university, non-Warwick world (anti-Vietnam War activity).[3]

This changed during the second term of the 1970 academic year, when students, including a number from the Centre for the Study of Social History, occupied the Vice-Chancellor's office and the main building of university administration, the Registry. The sit-in followed three years of protests concerning control of the student building, segregation of the informal space afforded students and staff, and the barren utilitarianism of the learning environment. In the course of this student-led occupation, which was driven by awareness that powerful capitalist interests associated with Rootes Motors Ltd, long a vital player in the funding and governance of Warwick University, were stonewalling on the issue of student buildings and student autonomy, minor discontents opened up into a larger critique of the tight connective links between capitalist industry and academic institutions. This original occupation lasted twenty-four hours. When nothing substantial in the way of change occurred, a second, indefinite occupation, emerging spontaneously out of a mass meeting of students, occurred on

11 February 1970. The militants agreed that there would be no damage to university property, and the secretarial staff vacated their offices, leaving all doors open. Hours later a student, thumbing through a file on 'Student–University Relations' in an unlocked cabinet, came across a disturbing document. Marked 'strictly confidential', it was addressed to the University Vice-Chancellor, indicating that Gilbert Hunt, a Director of Rootes Motors, member of the University Council and Chairman of its Building Committee, had sent his corporate Director of Legal Affairs, accompanied by a security officer, to a meeting of the Coventry Labour Party addressed by Dr David Montgomery, an American working-class historian visiting Warwick's Centre for the Study of Social History for two years. The object of this surveillance was apparently to ascertain if Montgomery's talk provided grounds for prosecution under the 1919 Aliens Restriction Act.

Montgomery had no doubt come to Hunt's attention precisely because he appeared to be a unique blend of academic and activist. He himself had once been a machinist, and his scholarship was distinguished, but he ventured outside universities to establish relations with trade unionists and workers on a regular basis. In Coventry he had advised a group of striking Pakistani workers on the mechanics of securing union recognition, and he regularly spoke to political and trade-union gatherings on matters such as automation. In the eyes of the industrial magnates, he was a man to monitor. Such spying contravened university assurances that no political information was ever kept on faculty/students/staff. It prompted the students to do a larger, disciplined search of other confidential files, and in the process cabinets were carefully opened with a minimum of physical force. Other objectionable material came to light, but the weight of damaging confidential correspondence was hardly overwhelming. The political cat was now out of the proverbial bag, however, with earnest debate sweeping the University about the validity of invading 'private' communications and student assessments.

The University countered with an injunction prohibiting dissemination of such 'illegally' acquired material. Protest raged for weeks, and spread to other universities; there was a demonstration outside Parliament; and trade unionists mounted their own protests against such uses of the University.[4]

Where was Edward Thompson? Whatever unease he may have felt around the need to chart a path of moderation that could result in restoring impartiality to university procedures evaporated before the political necessities of the moment. Melvyn Dubofsky, then Warwick Visiting Professor of Comparative Labour History, recalls Thompson telling those students occupying university property who requested their class to be held that they could be 'either students or revolutionaries'. As long as the occupation was on, classes were off. Thompson was phoned by the student who discovered the incriminating Montgomery file, came to the occupied building to secure the documents, and quickly reproduced and disseminated them to the entire faculty. He challenged the university injunction with a journalistic broadside, was featured prominently in media coverage of the event, and later worked with students to present the history of the Warwick struggle and expose the close relations of power that connected capitalism and higher education at the points of production where ideology and accumulation met.

In a recent article in the *American Historical Review*, Michael D. Bess, in what seems to be an attempt to assimilate Thompson to an uncomplicated liberalism, suggests that Thompson's publication of the 'illegal' Montgomery documents was 'a basic error of judgment'. He rather disingenuously suggests that Thompson, who would later in the 1970s oppose the state using illegally secured information to prosecute dissidents (whom Bess designates 'criminal suspects'), could hardly endorse such use at Warwick. Bess is wrong. There was no error, and Thompson himself would never have conceded that there was, however much he might acknowledge that the case of the

'Warwick files' posed particular dilemmas. But for him the politics *and* the morality of the situation were clear. The students behaved with responsible discipline; they uncovered a document that proved the existence of a deplorable act, and caught the University out in a lie; they looked for more evidence of this kind of wrongdoing, with its *public* implications, and it was only this kind of material that they circulated; they went about their business without making a large matter of the many personal items and issues that must have tumbled out of filing cabinets on to the Vice-Chancellor's carpeted floors and into their range of vision, although they no doubt got an eyeful of the self-important verbosity of their professors.

The politics of conscience demanded a specific course. There must be opposition to the University's complicity in gathering political information on members of the university community: a widening climate of outraged democratic opinion which would *act* to remind the instigators that their surveillance practices were intolerable. This did not mean – in some decontextualized vacuum of absolute liberal values, *à la* Bess – that any and all opening of files was to be commended, or that the defence of constitutionalist political methods was always to be deplored and ridiculed as a sham. But in the much-publicized instance of the Warwick files, Thompson thought the case was clear enough – as it was. To suggest, as Bess does, that students who, virtually by accident (the purpose of the occupation *not* being to rifle through files), came across clear indications of university wrongdoing and made that evidence public are somehow comparable to an ostensibly democratic *state* that utilizes its vast resources and personnel secretly and illegally to gather surveillance on people who have committed no crimes, the better to prosecute them when and if they do, are somehow equatable in their violation of principle, deserving of our condemnation, is actually absurd. 'Only a really subtle and unworldly academic mind', noted Thompson in response to the critics of the early 1970s, could engage in argument such as this.[5]

Thompson's moment of contact with student radicalism was thus one of support rather than hostility. While the Warwick student strike and the resulting turmoil were perhaps not the direct cause of his desire to resign from the Warwick Centre – his reasons were personal – they no doubt hastened and confirmed his exit. Relatively isolated from politics for the better part of a decade, Thompson moved in academic circles from the time of his Warwick appointment in 1965. But he did not move easily and comfortably; he wanted out, and at a moment of rebellion he was with the insurgents – as, indeed, temperamentally he would almost always be. When he left formal teaching in 1970, Thompson took his exit to write. He no doubt had in mind many projects, including a study of Blake, which he would progress through sufficiently to deliver the Alexander Lectures at the University of Toronto in 1978; and finishing the eighteenth-century studies that he had commenced in the mid-1960s. But there was a dual irony in this attempt to move into seemingly ever-widening circles of isolation: from the intense political atmosphere of the late 1950s and early 1960s, where his teaching was centred in adult education; to the largely academic environment of a new university and its Thompson-directed Centre; to the quietudes of the archives, the library, and the study – 'I go back to my desk. If it could fight/Or dream or mate, what other creature would/Sit making marks on paper through the night?'[6] First, the supposed final retreat into writing had been made on the coat-tails of a re-entry into politics, his notoriety during the Warwick days recalling, certainly, his disdain for the sanctimoniousness of much of academic life, and rekindling the fires of appreciation for labour and the unkept press. Second, if Thompson's eye, and a good part of his mind, were on the historical writing that he desired to do, his hand was never quite able to shake free from the necessity of breaking through barriers of political isolation.

For Thompson, the 1970s would, to be sure, encompass a period of research and reflection in fundamentally *historical* questions, but his writing in this field, for the most part, carried old projects through to fruition (as in *Whigs and Hunters*, *Albion's Fatal Tree*, and the essay on rough music or charivari), compressed the beginnings of conceptual and empirical labours into the tight container of a suggestive essay, or offered stimulating insights in important book reviews. This was a period when, apart from his longstanding interest in Blake, he was relentlessly pursuing, against the anthropological discourse and method, a concern with the anthropological subject, insisting on the integrity and worth of the cultural creations and everyday struggles of the poor. Reviews touched down with characteristic flourish on topics such as food riots, transported trade unionists, Eleanor Marx, artisan radicalism in London, and the labour aristocracy. Typical was this injunction on the state of 'family' history late in the decade:

> The history of the 'lower sort of people' between 1500 and 1800 discloses many different familial modes: some may seem to us to be rough, lacking in any foresight, picaresque: others may seem to be cold and bound to elemental needs. But the point of history is not to see their occasions through the mist of our feelings, nor to measure them against the Modern Us. It is first of all to understand the past: to reconstruct those forgotten norms, decode the obsolete rituals, and detect the hidden gestures. Because peasant marriages were arranged out of circumstance and necessity, it does not mean that many families did not learn a profound mutual dependence, a habit of love. ... As a quantitative certainty we – all of us – have more leisure to examine our own feelings than all except a small elite used to have; but it is less certain that, in those days, hearts broke less painfully or lifted with less joy then, than they do now. It annoys me that Professor Stone and Professor Shorter leave their readers to feel so complacent about their own modernity. It annoys me even more that both should indict the poor, on so little evidence, of indifference to their children and of callous complicity in their high rate of mortality.[7]

These ideas and commitments, as well as this annoyance, would figure prominently in what was perhaps the central Thompson writing of the 1970s: that which played itself out in a political duality of interrogating Marxism and demanding democracy.

Early in the decade Thompson saw a revival of 'the pure vitriol of class politics'. It awakened in him an 'enhanced contempt for parliamentarians, and for the parliamentary Labour Party in particular'. In the widespread alienation with what he dubbed 'managerial politics' he glimpsed new possibilities of health for the popular body politic. Struggles of power workers, miners and nurses drew his support, and his marshalling of historical evidence in defence of their beleaguered rights. Reviewing Harold Wilson's self-serving account of the Labour government (1964–70), Thompson bemoaned the book's 'devaluation of the traditions of the labour movement, of politics as a dignified human preoccupation'. He closed his angry denunciation of Wilson with the comment: 'The art of the possible can only be restrained from engrossing the whole universe if the impossible can find ways of breaking back into politics, again and again.'[8] This, I would argue, was what Edward Thompson's *political* project in the 1970s was all about. Against the mechanical idealism of 'modelled' Marxism he proposed the oppositions of historical materialism and human agency, the very same kinds of challenges he would throw journalistically in the face of the debasement of democratic politics.

Thompson's 'Open Letter to Kolakowski' signalled his coming out of isolation, an attempt to clarify where 1956 had gone, and how. Up to this point he stood 'critical and affirmative' to the Marxist tradition, determined to rehabilitate the utopian energies within socialism. He had looked to the Kolakowski of the 1950s for inspiration and guidance, but he saw in the Polish Marxist's writings and views of the early 1970s – and in the places where those thoughts were propounded or published, such as *Encounter* – a disappointing capitulation to the ideological closures of the Cold War. Thompson acknowledged in his discursive discussion that there were different kinds of Marxism, different Marxisms. Yet after thirty years, his allegiance remained 'to the Marxist tradition', *in the singular*:

> We *can*not impose our will upon history in any way we choose. We *ought* not to surrender to its circumstantial logic. We can hope and act only as 'gardeners of our circumstance'. In writing to you I have been, in one way, casting some thirty years of my own private accounts. I have been meditating not only on the meanings of 'history' but on the meanings of people whom I have known and trusted. I have been encountering the paradox that many of those whom 'reality' has proved to be wrong, still seem to me to have been better people than those who were, with a facile and conformist realism, right. I would still wish to justify the aspirations of those whom 'history', at this point in time, appears to have refuted.

Thompson closed his long letter with words of renewal: to internationalism; to common struggle; to the fulfilment of aspiration; to 1956.[9]

A brief year later there were hints that Thompson's re-engagement with Marxism was taking on a new awareness of differentiation. In an important review of an important book, John Foster's *Class Struggle and the Industrial Revolution*, Thompson wrestled with Marxist historical method. He concluded – and strongly so – that Foster's book, for which he had considerable respect, was a statement of 'platonist Marxism': orchestrated around a 'true' or 'correct' model of class organization, consciousness and strategy, it often rode roughshod over the actual ideas, values and motivations of the historical subjects under study, not unlike earlier and more abstract writings on class by Anderson–Nairn. Foster's saving grace was that while his Platonism weakened his understanding of the complexity of consciousness, the scrupulousness of his materialist method ensured that even if his understanding of social being was skewed, it advanced knowledge and placed whole realms of experience within a more precise, quantifiable realm of historical appreciation. This empirical weight had never burdened the writings of Anderson–Nairn.

A similar preoccupation with this Marxist problematic of

being/consciousness animated Thompson's creative re-
engagement with Christopher Caudwell, in whose writings
there was a direct challenge to Platonism and reductionist
idealism. Caudwell, unlike much 'theorizing' in 1970s Marxism,
was not, Thompson insisted, 'retreating into the introverted
security where Marxists speak only to Marxists in a universe of
self-validating texts'. As Thompson resurfaced within Marxist
debate in the 1970s, he rehabilitated the sources of his
longstanding Marxist strength at the same time as he turned
them towards an internal critique of trends in Marxism that he
opposed, from Stalinism to Platonism. Nowhere was this more
apparent than in his revival of Morris, which appeared in 1977
edited away from its earlier complicity with Stalinism, and with
Morris's voices of Romanticism and utopianism speaking loudly
to the needs of Marxism. At this historic juncture Thompson
re-entered the pages of the *New Left Review*, taking up where he
had left off: with the case of Raymond Williams. Twenty-five
years later, with Williams moving more decidedly in the language and interpretive field of force of Marxism, Thompson
was an advocate and a defender, rather than a critic and a
questioner. And it was apparent that he considered himself a
Marxist who was now *back* in the polemical and political fray:

> It may have been thought once, by the Althusserian anti-'humanists,'
> that those of us who acknowledge our continuing relation to the
> transformed Romantic tradition could simply be read out of the
> intellectual Left: we belonged somewhere else. But that attempt has
> failed. We are still here: we do not mean to go. Neither the Left nor
> Marxism can ever belong to any set of people who put up fences and
> proprietary signs; it can belong only to all those who choose to stay in
> that 'terrain' and who mix it with their labour.

With the mention of Althusser came a hint of things to come.[10]

Thompson's 1978 demolition of Althusser, 'The Poverty of
Theory: or an Orrery of Errors', commenced, I am certain, as
his effort to *revive* what was positive in Marxism, but the

consequences of consequences are not always straightforward, and intention, in the maelstrom of historical context, sometimes gets displaced as new directions are taken up. This happens in practice; it can also take place in thought. Reaching back within the Marxist tradition, Thompson drew on Marx's anti-Proudhon polemic, *The Poverty of Philosophy*, for his title, sustained his arguments with wide reading in the texts of classical Marxism and the researches of historical materialism, prefaced his publication with the masthead quote from the *New Reasoner*, Marx's 'To leave error unrefuted is to encourage intellectual immorality', and defended Marxism as a theory and a practice rooted in specific commitments: to the radicalized Enlightenment cause of reason; to the practical process of change; and to the fundamental importance of grasping the meaning of material relations and their historical development. If the credentials were Marxist, the tone was that of Swift. Biting satire, hyperbole, flights of rhetoric, and refusal to let the seemingly squirming subject off the hook of relentless punishment, all made the text unique in the annals of contemporary Marxist criticism.

Counterposing Althusser's *theoretical practice* to the method of historical materialism, Thompson insisted on reclaiming the historical and the materialist *for* Marxism, challenging not this or that flaw in the Althusserian project but the entirety of its premises, arguments, conclusions, and political meanings. The Althusserian orrery was seen as a circular philosophical system that proclaimed itself Marxist, but was in fact an *ideology* that approached *theology* in its idealist distance from any dialogue with an actual historical subject or process. Louis Althusser thus stood as surrogate for the irrationalist degeneration of a Western Marxism encased in the category and divorced from practice or, even, an analytic approach that could explain and integrate human agency into its understanding of the world of conflictual relations, exploitation and oppression:

This mode of thought is *exactly* what has commonly been designated, in the Marxist tradition, as idealism. Such idealism consists, not in the positing or denial of the primacy of an ulterior material world, but in a self-generating conceptual universe which imposes its own ideality upon the phenomena of material and social existence, rather than engaging in continual dialogue with these.

If Althusserian structuralism could be summed up in a few words, Thompson's position was that 'The category has attained to a primacy over its material referent; the conceptual structure hangs above and dominates social being.' In the violence of its mechanical idealism, Althusserianism was the theoretical articulation of excess: in denying agency to the superstructural realm it reified the economic base, which was understood only as static model rather than as relations of change and transformation; what moved this *stasis* was not conscious human activity but the motor of an – again – agencyless category, class struggle (which knew no trade-union organizations, radical agendas, or historic balance of victories and defeats). As a 'retreat into the privacy of a complacent internal discourse', Althusserian structuralism represented a '*dis*engagement from the actual political and intellectual contests of our time'. Because Althusser courted no challenges or contradictions to his model – which for Thompson coincided with the intellectual practice of Stalinism, with which the French philosopher was intimately linked – modes of thought and alternative such as moralism and humanism were ruthlessly suppressed as little more than liberal blows meant to undermine Marxist 'science'. To look at the left in the 1970s through the prism of Althusser, Thompson suggested, was to see that 'Stalinism was the empire, and theoretical practice is the vocabulary'.[11]

Thompson thus stood in a new, schizophrenic relation to a bifurcated tradition, one that now contained, for him, two Marxisms. In 1973 he had been content to proclaim his allegiance to *the* Marxist tradition, albeit as an 'outlaw'; his ground of intellectual and political grasp had shifted with his 1978 inspection of the Althusserian orrery. On the one side of Marxism stood reason, materialism, empirical investigation, open critique, moral concerns, human values, and a dialogue between consciousness and being, past and present; on the other side was arrayed theology, idealism, closure, and blistering denial of history itself and any semblance of agency and choice in its making. This was a divide that could not be bridged:

> I must therefore state without equivocation that I can no longer speak of a single, common Marxist tradition. There are *two* traditions, whose bifurcation and disengagement from each other has been slow, and whose final declaration of irreconcilable antagonism was delayed – as an historical event – until 1956. . . . Between theology and reason there can be no room left for negotiation.

Reading Althusser, therefore, sharpened Thompson's sense of that place of choice *within* Marxism. He had always located his choice, as a stand of opposition, outside Marxism, *against* capitalism. This he would not change. But he now faced the realization that for him a second front had appeared inside what had long been his tradition of allegiance. Against Marxisms of the Althusserian, Stalinist stripe, Thompson now declared 'unrelenting intellectual war'.[12]

Yet 'The Poverty of Theory' remained a Marxist text. Thompson entered the Althusserian orrery a Marxist and he left it a Marxist. This must be said, whatever one's disagreements with Thompson's text. His tenacity was striking. When Conor Cruise O'Brien used the pages of the *Observer* to propagate the view that Marxism was little more than a contagious hate, destroying the Labour Party, Thompson rose to Marxism's public defence. Whatever the 'crisis' of Marxism, however many crimes were committed by Stalinist regimes in the name of Marxism, this did not negate Marxism's historical contribution and potential. Thompson saw in O'Brien's article the rancour of the *grande peur*, 'a psycho-social class spasm of irrationality', the first victim of which was always reason, the end result 'an "abyss" in which the humane restraints of our society would not survive'.[13] Through two decades of intense engagement with the Marxist left, often culminating in disappointment, if not defeat, Thompson had returned to rethink Marxism and resuscitate it in the face of the perceived suffocating dangers of theoretical absolutism and abstentionism from actual socialist practice, and to defend it against the ugly face of reaction. Within a matter of a few short years, however, this longstanding commitment to Marxism would soften, weaken and, ultimately, fade quietly away. Why? An answer lies in the context of the late 1970s, where a series of related developments – political and intellectual – converged.

As Thompson re-engaged with Marxism, he was also earning his living from his writing, shoring up his insecure income in this area with teaching stints and public lectures in North America (University of Pittsburgh and Rutgers in 1976; University of Toronto in 1978; Brown in 1980). Alongside his letter to Kolakowski and the Althusserian polemic – the Thompson of socialist humanism and 1956 – appeared a journalistic Thompson, concerned with 'the state of the nation'. Writing regularly for *New Society*, with other pieces appearing in newspapers from the *Observer* to the *New York Times* and magazines such as *New Statesman*, Thompson took on an increasingly public face. While Marxism and socialist values figured in this consciously constructed popular appeal to reaffirm democratic rights, curtail the incursions of a state draped in cloaks of secrecy and clandestine acts, bent on perverting traditions of popular justice, and recultivate a Liberty Tree long overshadowed by the Tree of Money, these writings drew less on the heritage of 1956 than they did on the tradition of 'the freeborn Englishman'.

In tone and substance, Thompson's public interventions of the 1970s turned towards Cobbett and Paine in an effort to stimulate resistance to a very old set of Corruptions proceeding in new, 'modernized' directions. Quoting Yeats, he asked: 'What if the Church and the State/Are the mob that howls at the door!' Carrying his views on the rule of law – first voiced against an overly mechanistic model-driven Marxism in the concluding pages of *Whigs and Hunters* – into more public forums, Thompson defended the traditions of the English commoner, especially the right to trial by jury. This had become an inconvenience to the state which, by 1977, 'quietly mugged' seven centuries of legal tradition, unleashing a set of discounting, vetting, and tampering innovations. 'Modernizing authority finds democratic practice to be inconvenient,' concluded Thompson. 'It can manage us better in the dark, where it has put all our rights.' Such 'miscreants . . . seeking to undo the rule of law' were expressing their 'contempt for the people of [the] country', 'tearing down the structures of the past', and hoping to inculcate 'amnesia'. Against this 'approaching . . . state of anarchy, or arbitrary and unaccountable administrative rule', Thompson offered a stream of refusals. He was playing an old role, that of radical dissenter, out to the end. One commentator, under the title 'Thompson and Liberty!', insisted that Thompson had become 'the best political essayist today in the tradition of Swift, Hazlitt, Cobbett and Orwell'.[14]

None of this repudiated Marxism. But it did mark a departure, as Perry Anderson has suggested, in emphasis and political understanding. Thompson's journalism of the 1970s turned on defensive tactics, leaving the wider strategy for socialist transformation in abeyance. As he indicated in a 1979 interview, Thompson thought the horizon of political possibility was shrinking, with the last decades of the twentieth century turning inevitably on 'control of a very powerful State machine'. Opposition to this democracy had to be demanded, and in Thompson's view there was obviously no better ammunition to fire at the architects of the new 'statism' than arrows from the past, drawn out of a quiver full of the history of democratic constraints on power's prerogatives.[15]

So Thompson's essentially *political* writing – it is necessary to say essentially, for his political and historical texts were never distinguished by rigid separation – of the 1970s was Janus-faced. In one direction Marxism and 1956 came into focus; in another loomed the politics of democracy, and calling to order notions of freedom and rights within a bourgeois state. Had context made this possible, I suspect that Edward Thompson could have negotiated these diverging politics. With time he might well have constructed a convergence. But in his view the climate and the political space did not allow this.

An avalanche of Marxist criticism came down on Thompson's head in the aftermath of *The Poverty of Theory*. This *reaction* (response is too tame a description) was no kinder and no more fraternal than the original anti-Althusser polemic. Edward could have expected nothing less. Regardless of the content of this body of commentary, the form was a deluge of antagonism. It hardened the fragmentations within what Thompson perceived as the two Marxisms, but it did so in ways that made any dialogue almost impossible. Thompson's rhetoric of an uncompromising war, of exposing and driving out the Althusserian error, was replied to in the pages of almost every left press and journal, the flood of criticism inundating a wide array of academic disciplines (history, sociology, political science, literary criticism). Some of this came to a head in the legendary encounter at St Paul's Church, where a 1979 History Workshop gathering of more than a thousand witnessed the digging in of position and the subsequent blazing battle: theoretical practice in one corner; historical materialism in the other. Perry Anderson watched from the pews. In the damp cold of that dilapidated religious edifice Thompson 'rose like some wrathful divine to warn the congregation once more of the dangers of Gallican dogma. . . . Disputation followed, before a rapt, shivering audience.' According to Raphael Samuel, Thompson 'proceeded on a demolition job on his critics which caused evident personal pain and discomfort to many of those present'. Delivered with his usual polemical arsenal of 'maximum theatrical force', the result was 'that subsequent discussion was impossible. The aftermath of the . . . fusillade hung like a pall of smoke over the rest of the conference.'

This smoke remained for years, and to this day there are those who will still choke on it. Outside a small circle of old Reasoners, the blame is almost universally attributed to Edward: he had violated the fundamentals of fraternity; his tone, *this time*, had gone too far. Perhaps. But those who think in such ways should consider not only what was at stake – which was considerable in both intellectual and political terms – but also contexts, then and now. Many former Althusserians who called Thompson to task for the 'violence' of his polemic, insisting on the need for a quieter, more caring discourse of differentiation, have now – in the anti-Marxist stampede of the late 1980s and early 1990s – attributed to Althusser the very crimes Thompson pilloried. But they neglect to mention where they, and Thompson, were in the late 1970s and before. Finally, there is the important issue of the material resources of the combatants. Thompson had allies, to be sure, but for the most part he was alone. An independent writer of limited and insecure income, with no research assistants, secretaries, or connections to granting agencies and university largesse, faced an *army* of – for the most part – professional academics. When you fight on this kind of terrain, where your opponent can draw on so much more, how are the lines of fraternity to be drawn? In the end, they were faint indeed.

When it was all over and done with, Edward, I suspect, had had enough. His engagement with Marxism, now of decades' duration, was over. As he closed his book on Althusser, and theoretical Marxism closed its many lavishly funded, elegantly bound books on him, Thompson was irrevocably distanced from Marxism for the first time in his adult life. He would never attack it, turning his words into State Department bullets, but he put aside his own lengthy relationship to it. In 1980 he wrote to me from Brown University, perhaps using me as a conduit to apologize to people whom he thought I would know in Toronto:

'I'm afraid I *did* misbehave myself when a man rang me from Toronto from some Marxist Institute and asked me if I would be interested in going up there to talk about "the present state of Marxism": I told him that subject bored me out of my mind, and he seemed a little hurt.'[16]

The final straw pushing Thompson off the Marxist ledge he occupied in the 1970s would not, however, come from 'theory' and its debates. This should come as no surprise, for Thompson was always a Marxist of words *and* deeds. It would be the necessity to act in opposition that increasingly moved him to boredom with Marxism as theory. For the furore around the Thompson/Althusser clash happened precisely when, in Thompson's view, a renewed arms race threatened global annihilation. Making peace became more important than making history; making a space for survival was far more of a political necessity than making Marxism human; 1956 would mean little if the year 2000 never happened.

# 5

# Making Peace

Thompson's audience, be it academic or political, had never, since 1956, been negligible, but it had not been large. Referring to the first new left and the original Campaign for Nuclear Disarmament, he once noted that it was difficult to appreciate 'how few we were, how limited our resources, how difficult it was to keep a journal, a London office, and a few Left Clubs in being'. By 1981 this had changed. He stood before rallies of 250,000; he spoke to the world. At a massive gathering in Trafalgar Square he waited for the crowd to quieten down and then, into the hush of thousands, he spoke the politics of a past he had long laboured to translate to the present: 'Against the kingdom of the beast, we witnesses shall rise.' Left-wing cynics winced at the 'millennialism' of the presentation, but then looked up at Thompson with renewed interest as they heard snippets of sentences from those around them. 'Say what?' asked one protester, confused as to the meaning and ancestry of this obviously antiquated language. 'Blake, you idiot,' replied his companion with irritation, '*William* Blake.' A peace movement of colossal proportions, partly inspired and initiated by Thompson, made him, in the early-to-mid 1980s, a figure with an immense public profile. Polls placed him high in the ranks of the most admired, trailing only the 'first women' of the nation: Thatcher, Queen Elizabeth, and the Queen Mother.[1]

Thompson's protests for peace reached back decades and encompassed opposition to the Korean War, support for the World Peace Council's Stockholm Appeal to outlaw nuclear weapons, and dogged resistance to the imperial crusades of Britain, France, and others in Malaya, Cyprus, Kenya, Algeria, and British Guiana, all dutifully backed by the Cold War's respectable social democrats in the Labour Party. This was a deep history, not without resonance in his own family. Edward John Thompson's 'Commentary' reached back to the century's first 'great war':

> These shall be thy missionaries, Peace!
> These, though they may not run, shall hobble before thee.
>
> Tremulous, agued, starved, and agony dazed,
> These by their foolishness shall save the nations.
>
> Yea, if War ever gets his bowler hat,
> The world shall owe their eloquence great thanks!

Thompson's direct circle of Yorkshire peace comrades turfed out of Labour included eighty-year-old veteran Florence Mattison, whose Leeds remembrances included ILP anti-Boer War rallies and music-hall riots where the 'unpatriotic' were tossed from the gallery into the pit. With the exodus of Thompson and others from the Communist Party in 1956, much of this energy was transferred to the late 1950s/early 1960s Campaign for Nuclear Disarmament, but not without attending to a series of complex political entanglements that tied up the work of protesting for peace in endless ideological knots. In all this work *class* interests necessarily took a back seat to *human* issues of survival, but the two were never as easily dichotomized as it might superficially seem. The link related directly to Thompson's longstanding refusal to see the English working class as somehow inferior to other superior class models. Reviewing two works on the history of the peace movement in Britain, he took one author to task for reproducing the Orwellian caricature of the xenophobia of English labour:

> In a reasonably long life I have not observed that the working class of Other Nations (for example, the French) is to be noted for its internationalism as contrasted with our own ... it is very much the fashion these days to take the Orwell view, especially among Leftist intellectuals who *wish* to see the working class as racist, chauvinist, and (if male) sexist. I am pissed off with this stereotyping which obscures contrary evidence from view.[2]

Thompson's peace campaigns of the 1980s, then, while definitely altering the terrain of his relationship to Marxism, hardly constituted a wholesale abandonment of his long-standing commitments.[3] Late in 1979, his journalistic writing came out of questions of jury tampering and the secret state, and into what he called 'the doomsday consensus'. It was announced in November that Britain was to be the favoured recipient of some 160 NATO Cruise missiles, armed with nuclear warheads. This announcement was followed with the usual leaks of 'official secrets', and the conventional media replied by literally constructing acceptance of the state's assertions of its intention to house the new weapons, which would remain in the control of United States forces. Without a ripple of debate in Parliament, the British people were being presented with a *fait accompli*. Thompson pointed out that the deployment of Cruise missiles in Britain, scheduled for 1983, served distinct purposes: to localize nuclear war within a particular 'theatre' – primarily Western and Eastern Europe and Great Britain; to stifle dissent in an 'Official-Secrecy-cum-Prepackaged-Official-Information' double-speak that allowed citizen involvement only within the constructed oppositional boundaries of patriotic consensus and treason. While voices of protest against the new NATO initiatives rose throughout Europe, from Holland to Italy, *nothing* had been heard from

Britain. Thompson saw the British people 'publicly shamed', the 'breath in the lungs of British democracy' stale and seemingly spent. When, within a matter of weeks, NATO ratified its plans for nuclear escalation, and the Soviet Union invaded Afghanistan, it was clear to him that the Cold War's militaristic guard dogs were now unleashed, running hawkish in a soon-to-be-out-of-control set of reciprocal provocations. Thompson called for protests in the name of human survival; stopping the nuclear warheads was a common cause that linked the people of East and West. Against the 'hawkish interest groups and ideological jamming' of the Cold War's frozen imperviousness to rationality, the only hope for humanity lay in the 'internal exile' of dissidence.[4]

Within a matter of months Thompson was at the centre of a new politics of European Nuclear Disarmament, or END. Working with the Bertrand Russell Peace Foundation and a revived CND, he replied to a short letter in *The Times* late in January 1980 from Oxford's Chichelle Professor of the History of War, M.E. Howard. The letter bought into the British state's assumptions that the 'modernized' weapons scheduled to be housed at Lakenheath, Upper Heyford, and Scunthorpe were necessary, and that it was possible to speak, in a post-Hiroshima age, of deterrence and 'limited' nuclear 'strikes'. What Howard objected to was the total lack of any serious civil defence policy, which left the British people insecure and enemy forces certain of their capacity to create the utmost social, economic and political turbulence through a nuclear targeting of specific weapons-holding sites. Thompson's pamphlet, *Protest and Survive*, opposed this logic, insisting on the need to break out of the 'deep structure of the Cold War'. It sought to stop the destructive march of deterrence thinking before the deployment of Cruise missiles convinced many in the war machines of East and West that 'limited' war could indeed be fought in a European theatre, with the Soviet and American authors of destruction free to peer down on the spectacle without having the disruption of nuclear 'strikes' against their own elevated seats.

To do this required *refusals*: of the belligerent and aggressive content of the policies and practices of the capitalist West; of the reactionary response of the ostensibly communist bloc; of the right of bureaucratized, ossified structures of unaccountable militaristic might to have their fingers on the buttons of nuclear arsenals, while the people remained uninformed and manipulated with misinformation, a language of degenerative placation, and the rigid political categories of Cold War ideology. 'Three decades of "deterrence", of mutual fear, mystery, and state-endorsed stagnant hostility,' wrote Thompson, 'have backed up into our culture and ideology. Information has been numbed, language and values have been fouled, by the postures and expectations of the "deterrent" state.' The solution was not that of Professor Howard. 'We must throw whatever resources still exist in human culture across the path of this degenerative logic,' continued Thompson, his message of resistance to a 'normality' that had been allowed to spawn 'hideous cultural abnormalities' drawing yet again on the poetic interpretive power of Blake:

> And mutual fear brings peace;
> Till the selfish loves increase.
> Then Cruelty knits a snare,
> And spreads his baits with care ...
>
> Soon spreads the dismal shade
> Of mystery over his head;
> And the Catterpiller and Fly
> Feed on the Mystery.
>
> And it bears the fruit of Deceit,
> Ruddy and sweet to eat;
> And the Raven his nest has made
> In its thickest shade.

In the contorted face of this kind of threat, a policy of civil defence was little more than capitulation and appeasement. 'We must protest if we are to survive,' thundered Thompson. He drafted a much-publicized Appeal for 'A Nuclear Free Europe', which became, after input from his wife Dorothy and countless others, the programmatic statement of END. First announced at a special press conference in the House of Commons on 28 April 1980, and in four other European capitals, the appeal received massive European support, reaching across a wide swath of opinion and through numerous long-established political identities. Against the logic of deterrence, Thompson called for a counter-logic of nuclear disarmament. 'It would be nicer to have a quiet life. But they are not going to let us have that,' he argued. 'Which end is it to be?'[5]

Thompson moved quickly to the organizational core of the new anti-nuclear mobilization: he was soon on the National Council of CND, occupied a Vice-Presidential chair, and was a founder member of the more recently established END. But it was as a publicist and campaigner that he came constantly before the British and European peoples. Between 1980 and 1982 he was never far from battling the logic of deterrence: he reviewed the literature on the nuclear age extensively; penned countless letters of protest to newspaper editors and journals; was interviewed repeatedly on television and the radio; and, most significantly, spoke at hundreds of meetings, rallies and tours. 'I am scarcely at home for more than two days on end, and have had to stop my own historical work completely,' he wrote to me in June 1980. Three years later it was no better. 'You can't imagine how hectic everything here is just now,' Dorothy commented in 1983. Thompson's own estimate was that he appeared to give speeches at public forums of one sort or another roughly ten times a month for an entire two-year period, covering the length and breadth of Great Britain and touching down in fourteen other countries including Canada, the United States, Iceland and Greece. One such appearance was at an Oxford debate with Professor Howard and others.

Paul Flather described the 'duel':

> Thompson, silver white hair flying, lean and hungry, all fire and brimstone ... once guru of the New Left, now in self-imposed exile in Worcester ... 'left his desk' last year to rouse popular conscience to the imminent dangers of nuclear war. ... Howard, quieter, less used to the hurly burly of polemical argument, but none the less digging into his ground ... matched against the polemical equivalent of Bjørn Borg on the Centre Court ... [gratified] that he, as the other gladiator, was at least assured of immortality, 'preserved for posterity as the dim professor plucked from deserved obscurity' by the formidable Thompson. ... The real difference between Howard and Thompson comes in the language and framework each man adopts: military parlance leads to deterrence, Marxist roots lead to populist approaches.

Thompson was now selling newspapers. He was also overwhelmed with responsibilities; his personal correspondence was often handled by his fellow anti-nuclear advocate, Eveline King; and most letters were responded to with an apologetic 'quite overwhelmed here with work so please excuse this brief acknowledgement'. But the peace efforts were paying dividends. *Protest and Survive* sold 50,000 copies in less than a year, and when it reappeared in the company of other anti-nuclear arms essays as a Penguin Special, 36,000 books were sold in the same period. Protest rallies surged into the millions across Western Europe (Thompson himself estimated that not since 1848 had demonstrations been so endemic to society and mass action so popular), discontent with the arms race swelled behind the Iron Curtain, and polls showed that anywhere from 25 to 68 per cent of the populations of given West European countries opposed the basing of new American nuclear missiles.[6]

Thompson's notoriety as END's unofficial spokesperson and the leading theoretician of the new disarmament movement fed on itself. One informal poll conducted by *The Times* ranked him the second most influential British intellectual in the post-World War II period, A.J.P. Taylor being the first. In August 1981 the British Broadcasting Corporation suggested that Thompson give the prestigious Dimbleby Lecture, which usually commanded an audience of several million. The proposal was withdrawn on the insistence of the BBC's director-general, Sir Ian Trethowan, who pleaded that the talk would have been too controversial (translation: there would have been a price to pay for airing it). Eventually presented in the Worcester City Guildhall on 26 November 1981 as a kind of unofficial Dimbleby Lecture (the BBC decided to forgo the talk entirely for the year), Thompson's remarks were preceded by two months of intense media attention, and received widespread dissemination in the form of newspaper articles and interviews, a published pamphlet entitled *Beyond the Cold War: NOT the Dimbleby Lecture*, and a core statement in a collection of his own disarmament essays. Calling for an end to the addiction and habit of the Cold War, Thompson, reaching back to the language of his brother, argued: 'There must be that kind of spirit abroad in Europe once more. But this time it must arise, not in the wake of war and repression, but before these take place. Five minutes afterwards, and it will be too late.' The enemy 'other' was an ideological perversion humanity could no longer afford. 'Humankind must at last grow up,' he concluded. 'We must recognise that the Other is ourselves.'

A sequel to *Protest and Survive* appeared in the middle of the 1983 general election under the title *The Defence of Britain*. It was packaged as a nineteenth-century political tract, presented, in a manner reminiscent of Cobbett, as 'Published for the Defence of the Common People of this Nation'. Like other of Thompson's writings of this period it argued for the 'third way', active neutrality in the arms race, with no support given to either ideological side of the Cold War. Again the notoriety grew, especially as Thompson railed against 'the war of Margaret Thatcher's face', leaning into the potent patriotic 'Rule Britannia' tide of the embarrassingly one-sided Falkland Islands war with words of condemnation. Few wanted to hear of 'imperial atavisms' in this moment of supposed national glory and nostalgic militarism. For Thompson the lessons of the Falklands were clear: 'it tells us all that we need to know about the behaviour of great persons of state, and the way in which, around some other issue, in some other year, we may drift into World War III'.[7]

The politics of peace in the nuclear age thus turned, for Thompson, primarily on breaking the ideological chains of Cold War allegiance. Proliferating nuclear armaments were fuelled by the adversarial blocs themselves as NATO's hawks fed the hawks of the Warsaw Pact: the process was one of reciprocity. Throughout the mid-1980s he campaigned tirelessly for this 'double exposure' of the reciprocal responsibilities of East and West. Largely because of Thompson's prodding, END twinned what so many anti-nuclear arms protesters had obscured and denied: a powerful Western disarmament movement had to connect up with the exiled and incarcerated voices of Eastern European and Soviet dissidence, creating a space for dialogue around disarmament by stopping Western weapons, and freeing up and supporting like-minded people behind the Iron Curtain, who could then wage the struggle for peace within their own societies. Mass public protests against nuclear arms build-up in the West would be complemented by support for Poland's Solidarity, Czechoslovakia's Charter 77, and other dissident groups, calls for conventional arms reductions within the Eastern bloc, propagandizing around issues of human rights, and efforts to solidify cultural ties across the gulf that cut Europe with the knife of Cold War division. This, of course, brought the wrath of Natopolitan generals and Soviet bears down on Thompson's head, which was presented on various ideological platters to partisan audiences of the conventional 'Only Two Sides' schools.[8]

Indicative of END's and Thompson's politics of autonomous peace activism in Eastern Europe were dialogues with the non-Soviet-aligned disarmament forces in Hungary in 1982. Invited to Budapest by the Peace Group for Dialogue, Thompson met young dissidents who were separate from the established Hungarian National Peace Council, but able to negotiate a sensitive – if difficult – space for oppositional discourses within the established forums of 'actually existing socialist' culture. Thompson found 'the political and ideological climate' of Hungary 'altogether less centralised and repressive' than other East European regimes, such as Ceaușescu's Romania, but he appreciated the sensitivities of the local terrain, which dictated that peace activists chart a course of independence and inter-action with the official Peace Council *and* Western forces such as END and CND. In Budapest he met both sides, but respectfully insisted that his hosts were the unofficial advocates of an independent peace movement. Rather than give his public lecture under the auspices of the National Peace Council, which offered him their premises to speak before an invited audience, Thompson felt obliged to insist that while he would be honoured to speak, he could take up the invitation only if he could also address publicly those non-aligned hosts who had originally asked him to Budapest. This proved impos-sible, and Thompson's talk was delivered in a private apartment, at two hours' notice, to a gathering of approximately eighty people.

Quick to stress that this was not some 'cold war drama', in which the freedoms of the West are extolled and the restrictions of the East bemoaned, Thompson pointed out that even in ostensibly democratic political economies such as Britain, his views created unease within circles of authority to the extent that public lectures and forums were sometimes proposed and promised, only to be withdrawn. What stood out in his Hungar-ian journey was not that it was a 'dramatic or furtive event' but, rather, that it was a perfectly '*normal*' one, where procedures and politics followed a reasonable course within a context of understood limitations. What mattered, for Thompson, was the end result: 'It is normal and right that peace people in every part of Europe should find each other and enter into dialogue.' In his lecture, called 'The "Normalisation" of Europe', Thompson reiterated this basic need for dialogue: 'We have to act as citizens of a healed continent. We have to act as if the Cold War is already at an end. It is a responsibility to be here. There is an artificial ideological chasm across our continent, and voices cannot always be heard across it.' The politics of nuclear disarmament involved more than simply absolutist rejection of the irrational strategy of deterrence, tending as it did to annihilation. It also reached inevitably towards a critique of the deep structures of the authoritarian state, both East and West. Quoting Blake – 'The strongest poison ever known/Came from Caesar's laurel crown' – Thompson pointed to the link between the arms race and the 'secret state':

> I used to jest at our peace meetings that the only growth area of the British economy today is telephone-tapping. Now we have had the Falklands War, and the growth area is building replacements for sunken battleships. If the present Cold War – or adversary posture of the two blocs – is protracted for a further 20 years, it will not inevitably lead to the final holocaust, although it will probably do so: but it will, very certainly, give rise to two profoundly distorted economies and damaged cultures – to two opposed warlike societies, ruled by leaders who are intolerant security-minded persons: and hence to a diminution of every citizen's freedom and right as against the demands of the rival armed states. ... I am not talking about the *intentions* of leaders, on your side or on mine. To predict the course of history from the intentions of individual leaders is futile. I am indicating a deep process, quite beyond the intentions of individuals, by which the overfat military establishments of one side continually feed and further fatten the other.

Pledging himself and END and CND to the vigorous support of all fellow European workers for peace, Thompson was nevertheless adamant that when and if differences between East and West came up, as they inevitably would, they must be settled by the activists themselves, in their own locales. But there must be support, and talk, and trust. What was at stake was nothing less than the creation of a 'new Europe which renounces all recourse to the weapons of barbarism, and which permits controversy about social systems and ideologies to be contested only by normal political and cultural means'. Seemingly a small demand, such a position opened out into the cause of human preservation and a politics of dissidence capable of beginning the wholesale restructuring of both East and West.[9]

Such a stand also reintroduced the issues of nuclear disarmament and the peace movement to those on the left unaligned with the Soviet Union. Once pivotal in the politics of the first British new left, nuclear arms and the question of global peace had fallen by the wayside with the modifications of East–West Cold War posturing occasioned by Khrushchev's quest for détente, the popular demand for peace arising out of brushes with nuclear catastrophe such as the Cuban Missile Crisis, and the tilt in left approaches to war and peace occasioned by the anti-imperialist struggles of the 1960s. Thompson reintroduced these themes in the pages of *New Left Review* with an original formulation of the nuclear-arms-driven Cold War logic of exterminism and the Marxist left's immobilism:

> exterminism can only be confronted by the broadest possible popular alliance: that is, by every affirmative resource in our culture. Secondary differences must be subordinated to the human ecological imperative. The immobilism sometimes found on the Marxist Left is founded on a great error: that theoretical rigour, or throwing oneself into a 'revolutionary' posture, is the end of politics. The end of politics is to act, and to act *with effect*. Those voices which pipe, in shrill tones of militancy, that 'the Bomb' (which they have not looked behind) is 'a class question'; that we must get back to the dramas of confrontation and spurn the contamination of Christians, neutralists, pacifists and other class enemies – these voices are only a falsetto descant in the choir of exterminism.

*The Poverty of Theory* must have been close at hand as these words were written. In the politics of mobilization, Thompson saw not only the necessity of survival but also the desire of possibility, 'a new space for politics'. 'Within the threatening shadow of

*137*

exterminist crisis,' he concluded, 'European consciousness is alerted, and a moment of opportunity appears.' There was a vigorous response to this lecture, one that brought into question Thompson's own views, addressed the extent to which Europe was indeed the weak link in the Cold War, suggested the need to attend more directly to the struggles of the Third World if *socialism* was to capture the rising consciousness of oppositional politics, and challenged some of his assessment of the role of the Soviet Union in the arms race. Thompson responded with notable restraint and openness. He had written in the pages of *New Left Review* to encourage discussion and debate, not polemically to terminate it. 'I will not fight for the category of "exterminism",' he wrote, 'provided that the problem it indicates is not tidied away.' An end of an epoch had come. A new discourse was being made. But the point, as ever, was to interpret the world so that it could be *changed* and, in the context of the 1980s, *saved*: 'We cannot write our recipes at leisure in the drawing-room and pass them on to the servants' hall (although some try to do that still): we must improvise our recipes as we sweat before the kitchen fires.' Thinking and doing were mutually related undertakings. Left-wing intellectuals, 'the couriers who must take the first message across the frontiers of ideologies', had the responsibility to cultivate the new internationalism.[10]

This, in effect, was what Thompson was doing for much of the early 1980s. It did not bring immediate or easy results, and the NATO missiles were in place on schedule in 1984. The situation actually worsened in March 1983, with Reagan's Strategic Defence Initiative (SDI), the tragically ludicrous proposal, driven by the rapacious military–industrial–academic complex, that came to be known as Star Wars. Centred on the proclaimed possibility of creating an impermeable shield of ballistic missile defence, anti-satellite weapons and laser research, the pie in the sky of Star Wars was a fleeting, but immensely threatening, moment of nuclear neurosis. It spoke directly to what Thompson had long addressed as the degenerative logic of deterrence. Space-based death rays were said to be 'the longest "big stick" in history', and one that would ensure 'unilateral control of outer space and consequent domination of the earth'. The very Reaganite notion that the nuclear militarization of outer space would prevent nuclear war, that more and more ominous weapons would secure a truly secure peace, was itself confirmation that any semblance of political morality in the nuclear age had long since succumbed to the blindness of ideology incarcerated in its own self-referentiality and the hundreds of billions of dollars that were up for grabs in the race for SDI largesse. 'When a trillion dollars is waved at the U.S. aerospace industry,' wrote a group of scientists in a letter to the *Wall Street Journal*, 'the project in question will rapidly acquire a life of its own.' Thompson tried to counter this 'life' with more writing and research, increasingly detailed in its explorations of the technologies, budgets, and corporate connections behind the large lie of Star Wars. The powerful and heady mix of American isolationism, technological solutions, material avarice and ideological ossification threatened a new atmospheric annihilation. It was a 'terrifying signal of our human predicament'. 'There will never be an impermeable shield against nuclear evil,' he concluded. Star Wars, the logical extension of deterrence dementia, was no protection against holocaust and chaos. The only barrier known to humanity was, to be sure, 'pitifully weak ... as full of holes as a sieve', but the continuity of civilization depended on it, not on the 'zap' of SDI. Human conscience was the only hope, Thompson concluded, and it was 'time to put it in repair'.[11]

Fortunately, and somewhat ironically, the madness of the moment had – in terms of escalating technologies of nuclear destruction – reached its zenith with Star Wars. By the mid-1980s the hot flashes of technological and ideological outburst associated with the last half-decade had cooled and subdued considerably. One part of this process was external to the peace movement, associated with Soviet and American internal developments. Barely capable of keeping its crumbling 'empire' together in the 1980s, the Soviet ruling caste was noticeably inept at subduing rebellious Pathan tribesmen in Afghanistan, had militarily to cuff the insurgent Poles, and seemed understandably preoccupied with holding out against the clamour of internal political dissent and growing popular discontent with the material chaos of everyday life. The writing was on the Soviet wall, and it spelled collapse, however shocking the rapidity of the final demise would prove. It was hard even to regard the Soviets as much of a 'superpower' any more. They looked increasingly unlikely to challenge America to a nuclear standoff. Meanwhile, the United States turned its bellicose countenance in the direction of 'counter-terrorism' – bombing Libya in 1986 – and expanding its nineteenth-century imperial vision of Manifest Destiny to the Middle East, with a pre-emptive conventional warfare strike against Iraq's Saddam Hussein. It was all bad enough, but the escalating logic of exterminism, threatening global destruction, seemed to have been held partially in check.

Thompson by no means vacated the cause of peace. He was central in protesting the US raids on Libya, and in 1991 he would ponder the predicament of a peace movement faced with the Gulf War, writing to me:

> I am confused about the Gulf also (the press sometimes rings me still). I can't with any conscience cry enthusiastically 'Hands Off Saddam Hussein', since he is a prime bastard, and a bloody one: worse than Galtieri or Noriega or other creatures of the CIA. But the sight of the world's most advanced military technologies unleashing thousands of tons of high explosives on Iraq – and the sound of bought radio commentators assuring us that the brave-hearted Americans and British (And Canadian. Isn't it delightful to be brothers in arms?) will *never* allow a single ton to fall on a civilian sickens me. I think this war is of the pattern of the future, when the bits of the Third World involved turn out often to be Very Nasty, and we must find a strategy for war resistance less simplistic (and perhaps sometimes more revolutionary) than 'Hands Off'.

END issued 'An International Citizens' Appeal for Peace and Democracy in the Middle East', calling for peace, democracy, and the right of national self-determination. Citing an appalling list of Hussein's crimes, the Appeal was nevertheless staunch in its insistence that 'Democracy and self-determination can never be imposed through war and violence.' Thompson signed the statement, aware that it contained inner contradictions, not yet perhaps quite sure in his own mind of the more revolutionary strategy of war resistance that the complexities of the Middle East in the 1990s demanded. So the issue of war and peace continued to be uppermost in his mind, well into the 1990s.

Nevertheless, by 1985 his *total* immersion in the peace movement and its cause of nuclear disarmament was easing. He and Dorothy went to China in April, and Edward was struggling, with difficulty, to reacquaint himself with the discipline of historical research and writing. 'I MUST use the next twelve months to try and reactivate myself as a (writing) historian,' he wrote, in obvious frustration. 'Here the peace movement is into quieter times, but polls (whatever they are worth?) oddly show a huge surge towards us: most strongly after Chernobyl. People are less activist, but if they are changing their minds it is our way,' he commented in September 1986. Two months later, Edward and Dorothy were finalizing plans to spend a teaching semester at Queen's University, Canada, in 1988. They were still deeply involved with END, and the stress of raising money for the cause and organizing events such as book sales and fairs pressed on them both as they prepared to cross the Atlantic to teach. Hoping (in vain) to have *Customs in Common* in press by that time, Thompson was open to all kinds of suggestions about what he would lecture on and the kinds of seminars he could teach. He was adamant on only one point: 'What I will not do is "teach" my views on the 57 varieties of "Marxism", which', he added, 'tend to make me cross.' After *The Poverty of Theory* and after half a decade of intense political campaigning, in which the end had been to heal the gaping wound separating East and

West, Thompson had little patience left for what he regarded as 'doctrinaire absolutisms', be they Marxist or anti-Marxist.[12]

Thompson had always believed that politics was about bodies; they needed to be placed *against* what threatened them. He had done this, giving intellectual and political leadership, in the campaign to break from the orthodox rigidities of the ideologies of the Cold War. However much he was at his desk, he was also in the streets, and not always as a keynote speaker. He was a proud observer and car driver when Greenham Common was surrounded by 40,000 women; he was 'lugged around' by police when, with thousands of other CNDers, he sat down in Oxford Street in protest against the bombing of Tripoli; he was not far from any effort to make peace in the years 1980–86, in spirit *or* in body. With the publication of *Protest and Survive*, he passed from being 'a private citizen and free-lance writer and historian into being a famous (or infamous) Public Person, "Professor" (which I am not) E.P. Thompson, on call at any hour of the day and sometimes night for the service of a huge, untidy, sometimes quarrelsome but always high-spirited and dedicated movement arising in every part of the globe which is called "the peace movement".' Years later, when he could go back to his gardens, both metaphorical and real, his body had been through a lot. Whether our bodies had been saved by his commitment and sacrifice is not a question that can easily be answered. But they had made a difference and Thompson left our world, in 1993, a safer place than he entered it, in 1979–80, with his urgent call to protest in order to survive.[13]

# 6

# A Return to Roots:

# Cultures/Internationalisms

Thompson's last years were years of labouring against the clock. He knew he had so much to do, and the hands of time were moving against him. What he wrote in the late 1980s and early 1990s must be placed firmly in this context. No doubt there are medical explanations for Edward's failing health, but the extent to which his intense giving of himself, which included constant wear and tear on his person (flying here and there, eating inadequately, sleeping irregularly, bent over the desk into the early hours of the morning, preparing for the public lectures that took so much energy), weakened his constitution is undeniable. Thompson himself attributed the beginnings of his health problems to 'some bug' he came back from a conference in New Delhi with, which landed him in hospital for much of the winter of 1987.[1] Across my desk are scattered pictures from the early and late 1980s, images of an unmistakable physical deterioration. Even in sickness he remained a man who could muster energy for his work and for his friendships, but what had come easily and naturally in the late 1970s was an effort ten years later.

At this time he was battling against colitis, worn down by the prescribed steroids but hopeful that his rate of improvement would accelerate. At Queen's University in Kingston, Canada, in 1988 he threw himself into his teaching and public lectures with gusto, but he was obviously run down and, his immune system weakened, highly susceptible. After a Sunday outing to the Kingston harness track with Dorothy, myself, and my five-year-old daughter Beth, with whom Edward was in close playful contact, Beth came down with a dose of chickenpox; a week later Edward was afflicted with a bad case of shingles. Things worsened in 1989–90, when Edward and Dorothy were at the Rutgers Centre for Historical Analysis. Hospitalized for one malady, Edward had a brush with what he was convinced was Legionnaire's Disease. When I visited the Thompsons in New Jersey shortly afterwards, he was on prescribed oxygen and so frail that he could barely get the roast to the table. On his return to England, his back gave out and he suffered loss of much of the use of his lungs. He continued to cherish improvement, the chances for increased work and small labours in the garden, and the freedom it would afford those, such as Dorothy and his sons and daughter, who were now caring for him. Well into 1991 he went into a tailspin. 'Dorothy has pulled me through the latest illness,' he wrote, alluding to how it 'was much worse than any before – I was more than three weeks unconscious and in intensive care'. Afterwards he improved enough to have a large and pleasant family Christmas, but 'collapsed in exhaustion at the end of it'. He was 'a semi-invalid, full of drugs'. Two bouts of viral pneumonia had pretty much done in his lungs, and he was plagued with sudden and debilitating fevers. There were neurological problems and loss of memory. Eventually he would suffer heart problems as well. But he took some good-humoured solace in his physician's comment: 'I evidently must have some mission in the world still, since I have narrowly escaped death twice.' And, sick as he was, he didn't give in, but again offered his refusals.[2]

In these years he battled back into his historical writing on the eighteenth century. He felt insecure about his knowledge of eighteenth-century demographic, economic, industrial and social history, deciding that he could not tackle teaching a graduate seminar at Queen's around 'Customs in Common' in 1988. Instead he opted for working through the 1790s, where he had sufficient grasp of the primary materials 'that whatever duffer I prove to be on current scholarship [the students] are bound to spend some time in useful primary stuff'. There was no need for such reticence. Thompson's lectures on themes in the social history of eighteenth-century England were superb, although he would later uncharitably regard some of them as 'muddled' and 'old hat'. He found the literature on the moral economy of the crowd, in particular, overwhelming, and had to abandon an initial attempt to redraft the essay on food riots in the light of subsequent scholarship, opting to append a hundred-page historiographic essay to his original statement. In the end, the final published version of *Customs in Common* was something of a scholarly landmark, bringing Thompson's views on eighteenth-century England into clearer focus. But it was not the book it would have been had he completed it as the momentum of his research and thought on the subject peaked, just before his full-time entry into anti-nuclear politics. Lacking a conclusion and insufficiently integrating the discrete discussions of ritual and custom, the text, whatever its substantial merits, suffered from the years it had spent in the bottom drawer of Thompson's desk. Thompson chafed against some of the revisionist scholarship on the eighteenth century and good-naturedly joked about other work, which he admired: 'I have been very impressed by Nick [Rogers's] *Whigs and Cities*,' he wrote to me in 1991. 'Indeed some of it is so good that I feel quite cross. It will make my *C in C* into a yawn and some of its interpretive arguments either preempt or improve upon my own. GRRRRR!' This only made the job of preparing the manuscript for publication, under the adverse conditions of ill-health (at this point his back had seized up and he walked in pain, with the aid of a stick), trying. 'I can sit at my desk, type, etc., and the proofs of *C in C* are promised next week. I am a bit bored with the book, and fear that readers will be also.' He was perhaps his own harshest critic, and he was glad to be getting back to Blake.[3]

The final publication of *Customs in Common* could not help but be something of an intellectual anticlimax. Some of its parts had been more than twenty-five years in the making, and had themselves, in previous published versions, opened scholarly eyes to new ways of seeing – as the unrevised chapter on 'Time, Work-Discipline and Industrial Capitalism' most certainly did – or given rise to entire new fields of study – as had the essay on the moral economy of the crowd – so it was understandable, perhaps, that the academic community would expect the book containing these particular statements to offer an interpretive *tour de force* around which an entirely new conception of eighteenth-century England could turn. Instead, *Customs in Common*, researched over almost three decades, put together in the aftermath of a long departure from academic concerns, and returned to in the difficulties of ill-health, opted for a more limited purpose. Thompson presents his essays on a slowly turning spit, where the reader can both observe and savour the oscillations of eighteenth-century power, in which new disciplines of patrician authority and appropriation are in perpetual clash with plebeian notions of customary rights, which can actually congeal in a particular culture, uniquely traditional and, in the face of incursions of the elite, rebellious. A long and powerful chapter, 'Custom, Law, and Common Right', addresses the popular meaning of local common right usages and their place in constraining the legal codification of property as 'possessive individualism'. For the commoners' poet, John Clare, this was the essence of freedom:

> Unbounded freedom ruled the wandering scene
> Nor fence of ownership crept in between
> To hide the prospect of the following eye
> Its only bondage was the circling sky.

The estrangement and displacement attendant upon the patrician victory over common right was the historical preface to 'the making of the English working class'. Solidarities that Thompson celebrated in his 1963 book could now be seen not only in terms of heroic struggles and positive accomplishments, but also as the exacting of a particular price: 'Common right, which was in lax terms coterminous with settlement, was *local* right, and hence was also a power to exclude strangers. Enclosure, in taking the commons away from the poor, made them strangers in their own land.' If custom and the plebeian masses were indeed the losers, as they were, Thompson's intention was to establish that the model of human nature that was willed to us in this defeat was not an accomplished fact of being, but a constructed historical outcome whose consequences, in our time, have now perhaps reached the point where processes of social devastation and ecological catastrophe demand a new accounting:

> As capitalism (or 'the market') made over human nature and human need, so political economy and its revolutionary antagonist came to suppose that this economic man was for all time. We stand at the end of a century when this must now be called in doubt. We shall not ever return to pre-capitalist human nature, yet a reminder of its alternative needs, expectations and codes may renew our sense of our nature's range of possibilities. Could it even prepare us for a time when both capitalist and state communist needs and expectations may decompose, and human nature may be made over in a new form?

As was typical of Thompson, his histories always spoke to his understanding of a project of political renewal and possibility. Introduced in this manner, the eighteenth-century sale of a wife or the rough musicking of a culture of alternative stand in political relation to the meanings of various 'moments' in Thompson's own development: 1956; the writing of working-class history; the repudiation of idealized, model-driven, 'lawed' conceptual frameworks such as the Althusserian orrery; the destructive divides of a Cold War fracturing of East/West; the threatening material overdrive of bloated 'need' that pressures the contemporary discourse of North/South difference.[4]

In the late 1980s, as he struggled to put together the eighteenth-century essays, Thompson was drawn to questions of 'need'; ironcially, this led him to questions of dearth and the North/South relation that helped to precipitate him into an exploration of his father's place at the 'interface' of Indian and British cultures. 'The best work on food and famine recently is all done by Indians, as one might expect,' he wrote in 1988. His father's papers had gathered dust for years in the Thompsons' Wick Episcopi attic. Pressed to participate in the Tagore conference and festival held in London in 1986, celebrating the 125th anniversary of the Indian poet's birth, Thompson explored Edward John Thompson's archives, which included 120 letters and postcards from Rabindranath Tagore. Yet again, the material seized Thompson, and he was soon embarked on a study of his father's relationship with Tagore. The resulting book, which appeared shortly before Edward's death in 1993, was 'unbidden and unplanned'. It offers a unique perspective on Tagore, the cultural side of Indian nationalism, and the ways in which a 'friend of India' such as Edward John Thompson charted his way personally and politically through the maze of relationships and rituals that marked the literary path of Indian–British understanding. The mapping of this journey in 'Alien Homage' reveals the tortured misunderstandings that accompanied Edward John Thompson's personal interface with the poet of Bengal – some of them of Tagore's making, some of them a result of his missionary friend's failures to grasp what was happening and what was at stake in the meeting of minds East and West. For E.P. Thompson, however, the Thompson–Tagore relationship was a metaphor for the larger difficulties and possibilities of internationalism. Fresh from his global campaigns for nuclear disarmament, Thompson's internationalism was highly receptive to rethinking the particular and the general within all cross-cultural exchanges, and he perhaps gravitated to an appreciation of the interface of cultures that a leftist sensibility to imperialist distortions had long misunderstood and dismissed smugly.[5]

The overlapping concerns of eighteenth-century customary culture, and the 'interface' of 'nations' caught in the web of imperialist authorities and negotiated possibilities, found further expression in Thompson's late-1980s fascination with the case of Sampson Occum, a Native American who led an eighteenth-century struggle to reclaim land alienated from customary aboriginal use rights in the displacements of revolutionary America. Intrigued by the legal, cultural and economic ramifications of Occum's persistent challenges to British and American understandings of property, Edward was drawn into the contemporary struggle of aboriginal peoples around the hotly contested issue of 1980s land claims. In April 1988 this was the subject he chose to address in his Herbert G. Gutman Memorial Lecture at the New York Public Library. After that lecture Edward, Dorothy and I drove north, through upstate New York, visiting Brothertown, where Occum's people eventually settled.

Thompson's last years were thus filled with projects and discoveries, linked to his intellectual and family past, but bound together in common analytic and political concerns. His own material needs pressed constantly on him, however, and with Dorothy's retirement and the weight of writing yet to be completed resting heavily on his mind, Thompson looked for paid employment to ease his financial constraints. In 1988 he wrote to me with boyish enthusiasm: 'Oh, and did I tell you that I've got another JOB? A Simon Research Fellowship at Manchester from Oct to June, with a proper salary: duties are mainly being at Manchester for most of most weeks and giving odd lectures and seminars.' After being shut out of the academic establishment for so long, he was actually surprised to land such posts. The Manchester fellowship was followed by another stint in the United States, Edward and Dorothy taking up a teaching offer from Rutgers University. And into the 1990s some of Edward's published essays and short introductions to book reprints were undoubtedly undertaken, in part, with financial considerations in mind. His last years were a self-imposed and, one suspects, pressured commitment to finish up a series of writing projects. After *Customs in Common* appeared in 1991, there was the Tagore–Thompson manuscript to clean up (a complicated matter made more cumbersome by an unorganized archive, letters gone astray, and other difficulties). Immersed in his subject, he named the Thompsons' new cat Rabindranath Tigger. Finally, there remained the book on Blake, so vital to Thompson's own self-conception and a study on which he had laboured since the 1960s and before. His last letters to me summarized his projects and their status: 'My Blake is going through press, the Tagore shd appear any day, and I must now turn to My Mohegans,' he wrote early in 1993, just months before his death. Dorothy confirmed the point late in 1992: 'Edward's health is holding up and even improving a bit the last few weeks. Blake and Tagore are finished and he is muttering about Sampson Occum.'[6]

Thompson's eighteenth-century studies and the book on Blake were awaited with much anticipation in certain fairly wide circles. The Tagore and Sampson Occum research was largely unknown and unexpected, except in specific academic quarters. Other writing that appeared in the late 1980s was equally unanticipated – Thompson drew on a 1985 visit to China and his decades-old opposition to nuclear weapons to fashion statements in poetry and fictional prose. Both writings are centrally concerned with power and its abuses, with despotism and destruction, with challenge and resistance, with language and its capacities to tyrannize *and* liberate.

In 'Powers and Names', inspired by a reading of the historian Szuma Chien, Thompson addresses constituted authority, stating bluntly: 'You have the power to name: Naming gives power over all', but he follows with a rebellious query: 'But who will name the power to name?' Interestingly, this was a theme that Thompson's father, Edward John, had explored in 'A Wind of Question', which ended with the stanza:

> So men will speak, and so
> Will through their homes a wind of question blow,
> And clamour of tongues awake
> Along Earth's ways, an hour, ere friends forget
> That Conrad's sun has set.
> But Thou, that little heed
> Of men's wild words and wilder thoughts dost take,
> Behold Thy servants jealous for Thy sake!
> And, lo, how love dare duty's bounds exceed!
> Yea, Conrad asks, made bold;
> 'What thing is this, hereafter told,
> That thou, a King, should'st unto service call
> Thy sons, ye leave amid dark ways to perish,
> Unhelped to stray and fall
> For all Thy Name that in their death they cherish?'

Speech, art and spirituality combined in acts of social construction not unlike those imagined by postmodernist theory. Thompson continued 'Powers and Names' with:

> And Chi his son hereditary
> Owner of all under Heaven, he and his family
> In perpetuity. From that ancestral power
> Sprouted the state:
> Armies invented slavery: astronomy
> Led the stars captive through the calendar:
> Taxes invented the poor.

But knowledge, as interpreted by the scholars, proved to be something less than power:

> Says the Grand Historian:
> It was a great mistake
> To tutor power, for when
> The law at last was learned

From legalist or mystic
By the Emperor of Chin
He ordered the imperial rule
Of benevolence to begin:
He buried the scholars alive
And the *Book of Songs* was burned.

Centuries of exploitation ensued:

Heaven's mandate swarmed the land like locusts:
Taxation's inquisition racked the rocks and holes
Exacting the confession of their surplus.
The peasants hacked at famine with their hoes
And stirred the dirt to flower
A hundred million hoes held up the vault of power.

Against this historical record of structured human containment, Thompson posed the question of resistance and its sources of strength, of necessity and desire:

Or was it propped up by the arch of awe
Whose proper name is self-expropriation?
If so, materialism turns a somersault:
We are the subjects of our own negation
And exploitation's basis floats
On the cold surface of our confiscated thought.

Past and present blurred as humanity's cause fused the ancient despotisms and dynasties with themes of ultimate contemporary destructiveness in 'the rectification of names':

Whose needs are the material habitus
From which the goddesses and dragons came,
Whose archers will shoot down the nuclear fire,
Whose nameless pillars are imagination's flames,
Whose arcane oracles proclaim
The rectification of the human name.

For all history there is but one 'charm against evil':

*152*

Throw the forbidden places open.
Let the dragons and the lions play.
Let us swallow the worm of power
And the name pass away.

As Thompson would later write: 'At certain moments history turns on a hinge of new ideas.' Those ideas and the corresponding acts of resistance are humankind's hope. In these late 1980s lines of internationally inspired verse, Thompson was conveying the lessons of his life: 'We learn, for neither the first nor the last time, that it is a terribly long and thankless task to try to influence the course of history by little movements "from below". Yet such minority positions, through most of recorded human history, have been the only honourable places to be; nor do they always fail in the long run.'[7]

More pessimistic, but of a piece with the poetic vision of 'Powers and Names', is a misunderstood futuristic Swiftian satire concerned, again, with what Perry Anderson neatly decodes as 'the alien gaze of an incorporeal reason fall[ing] – too late – on the world of property and authority and war, as it moves towards nuclear destruction'. Thompson's first and only novel, *The Sykaos Papers*, was fifteen years in the writing. It fused his longstanding concerns with history and disarmament in an account of the voyage to Earth (Sykaos) of Oi Paz, a poet-explorer dispatched from Oitar, a perfectly programmed computer-like social formation threatened with environmental collapse, to determine the suitability of colonizing the alien globe. Oi Paz is quickly made into an international celebrity, 'exploited' by a promotional huckster and painfully but brusquely introduced to the capitalist essentials of Western existence: commodification and alienation. Oi Paz soon grasped the meaning of life on earth, where 'property is the rule ... "money" is its messenger'. He was also prophetic about earth's destiny: 'Your species will end itself in nuclear war. Soon. It will not be your choice.' The bureaucratized war machines of East and West take over, incarcerating Oi Paz and importing academics to decipher him. One such scientist is the anthropologist Helena Sage, who eventually connects with Oi Paz, conceiving a child – christened, appropriately, Adam, later to be dubbed Ho Mo. As the superpowers follow their logic of exterminism, blowing up Planet Earth, Adam escapes to an Oitarian-outfitted moon, where he becomes the first rebel of a new intergalactic order. 'There is nothing in the universe ... which is not cross-grained, contradictory, divided against itself, awkward, and at odds,' declares this rebellious figure in opposition to Oitarian authority. He was speaking of historical process, but he was also speaking to Edward Thompson's life, to his *example*.[8]

# 7

# The Awkwardness of
# Antinomian Antithesis

'Thompson had a streak of perversity in him, of contrariety,' remarked Edward about his father. It was something of a family trait. *The Sykaos Papers*, perhaps the single richest elaboration of E.P. Thompson's refusals, stands as an imaginative drawing together of much that he opposed, illuminated against the background of poetic insight, earthy sensuality, raw humour, and ill-fated struggle for human betterment and survival that ordered his attachments and governed his political activism for decades. Against the bureaucratized, militarized 'blocs' of East and West, whose languages and technologies of repression and restraint threaten to overwhelm humanity in an ultimate fatal folly of nuclear annihilation, Thompson places voices of reason, sensitivities of poetic creativity, the sexuality of a smile. His attraction to the Romantic critique of capitalism translated through linguistic slippages that congeal Milton and Blake with contemporary idioms of erotic desire, Thompson probes the promise of humanity even as he details its derailment. In his historical writing, he always developed arguments that balanced structure and agency, necessity and desire, determination and freedom. The balance tilted towards the possible, accentuating the ways in which human consciousness opened out into

OBJECTIONS AND OPPOSITIONS

alternatives and resistance. But in his fictionalized, futuristic satire the thrust is more pessimistic, and as Benjamin DeMott suggested in the *New York Times Book Review*, *The Sykaos Papers* 'focuses provocatively on narrowed consciousness' and its human costs. Thompson's values remain anti-capitalistic, his distaste for the self-important followers of academic fashion, the bought professoriate, and the cash-craving scientists of destruction unleashed in passages of scathing wit. Oi Paz is treated to a lecture from Margaret Thatcher, appropriately studded with rhetorical gestures to the virtues of the *free* market, a culture of *incentive*, and the *dynamism* of unfettered economic growth. He is proposed as 'Distinguished Extraterrestrial Boeing Professor in perpetuity at the Edward Teller Center for Astro-Behavioral Studies'. It is not enough.

> Clouds roll back the sun
> And brown dust stains the blue air of memory
> In which a word stirs: it is 'mortality'.
> Oi Paz rises to deliver sentence
> On that programmeless uncollegiate species –
> A flux of uncured egos,
> Beasts without rule or roll,
> Deserving discard and self-deadline . . .

For Helena Sage, her last will and testament is a Thompsonian act of refusal:

> I go out, leaving Curses upon Power and Abstract Enmities and Public Lies.
>   I go out through the gate of my flesh, carrying with me, like a basket of flowers, my memories of love and of friendships and natural joys.
>   Accepting the Knowledge of Good and Evil
>   Sorry that the Good lost out (it was a near thing)
>   RENOUNCING MY CONSCIOUSNESS NOT AT ALL
>   REFUSING THE LEAST TRIBUTE TO THE RULE OF NIHIL

Such a statement of antithesis is central to understanding Thompson's powerful fusion of past and present, the authority of his historiographic production and his insistence on forging politics out of specific oppositions and objections.[1]

'To write old history afresh', Thompson once wrote, 'cannot be done without un-writing other people's history.' The statement can be read in many ways. To rewrite the history of the English working class, for instance, it was necessary not only to rewrite the history of the Hammonds and Hartwell, of Francis Place, Susan Thistlewood and Joanna Southcott, but also of Oliver the Spy and William Pitt. For Thompson, making history was not so much an undertaking of objectivity (although he was simultaneously imaginative and scrupulous in his handling of evidence) as an act of *objecting*, of *refusing*, of *opposing*. This, too, was how he made his politics (against the grains of convention, left *and* right) and – yes – *his* theory, which emerged and re-emerged out of the continuous and confrontational dialogue of idea and actuality, concept and evidence.[2]

As Thompson argued in his letter to Kolakowski, and as his friend Christopher Hill insightfully emphasized in his obituary upon Thompson's death, standing this ground of refusal and objection was no easy matter. It was an awkward business. There was little stability to be found in this oppositional niche, where forces of incorporation and barriers to serious communication of principle were so thorny. '[I]f one is not to be pressed through the grid into the universal mish-mash of the received assumptions of the intellectual culture,' Thompson said, '[o]ne must strain at every turn in one's thought to resist the assumption that what one observes and what one is is in the very course of nature.' And this was doubly so when one faced into the winds of right and left, all the while resisting the comfort of the centre. This often left Thompson, as he himself acknowledged, out on his own lonely ledge. 'How do you react to the circus which used to be the USSR? They always were pretty thin socialists, at any time after about 1921 anyway,' he wrote to me in 1991. But he found little politically to cheer about in the actual implosion of the Stalinist state: 'These great "free market" converts on the other side piss me off: they just won't listen, won't get into a dialogue, think they know it all. About 1,000 miles to the right of Galbraith. I don't intend to bend my pen for them.' Nor was there more congenial space on the broad Western left: 'I am also pissed off with those of my erstwhile lefty colleagues who think that nationalism is such a lovely thing – Baltic, Georgian, even Croat!!!'[3]

His refuge, perhaps, was in poetry and laughter, which he embraced as foundations of 'human civilization'. Thompson turned to them continuously, deflecting his awkwardness – his fears and his angers – with pleas for imagination and conscience or, if these were irretrievably backed up into the bowels of ideological constipation, barbs of irreverence and ridicule. He disliked lack of a sense of humour, and considered such deficiency a failing in certain fields of historical research, where temperamental incapacity to grasp how laughter, mockery or irony could have been used to extend and deepen meaning could handcuff analysis in the wrist-lock of an overly deferential embrace of propriety. His own personal correspondence was peppered with light moments of mockery – some directed at his correspondent, others at himself. 'Daughter Kate and son Ben will be coming in series to keep an eye on their old dad, in case he falls out of an apple tree. Which he is quite likely to do,' he wrote, with reference to his own health. When some valuable eighteenth-century books were lost in postal transit from Canada to England, he offered a 'political' explanation: 'Instituted high level enquiries about loss ages ago but have now accepted fatalistic resignation, knowing all is due to high level organisation of postal workers t.u. with Bryan Palmer's blessing.'[4]

A measure of his awkwardness was Thompson's alienation from the academic milieu he nevertheless spent much of his time and writing within. He deplored 'the modish subjectivism and idealism now so current'. Amazed at 'the unabashed regurgitation of laissez-faire apologies for the market' that swamped eighteenth-century studies in his absence, he was amused by the rise of an Empire of Discourse: a 'mobile academic chat-show, self-admiring gossip circus moving from King's College Cambridge . . . to Washington DC to Bellagio . . . which I suppose has some interest but which never touches down and which is the current form of idealism.' While by the mid-1980s he had long since moved off anything resembling 'class politics', he could not bear to see the postured cleverness of the university 'intellectual' marshalled against the idea and historical embeddedness of class.[5]

Indeed, 'the enormous pomp and propriety of the self-important academic' always put Thompson's back up in awkward antipathy. This was a significant part of the importance of *tone* to Thompson who, after all, grew up in the shadow of Oxford. As early as 1961 he was moved to opposition in a review of Williams's *The Long Revolution*, noting the way in which a disengaged language detached ideas and arguments not only from socialism but from people themselves:

> I sometimes imagine this medium (and it is the church-going solemnity of the procession which provokes me to irreverence) as an elderly gentlewoman and near relative of Mr. Eliot, so distinguished as to have become an institution: The Tradition. There she sits, with that white starched affair on her head, knitting definitions without thought of recognition or reward (some of them will be parcelled up and sent to the Victims of Industry) – and in her presence *how one must watch one's Language!* The first brash word, the least suspicion of laughter or polemic in her presence, and The Tradition might drop a stitch and have to start knitting all those definitions over again. ... But The Tradition has not been like this at all: Burke abused, Cobbett inveighed, Arnold was capable of malicious insinuation, Carlyle, Ruskin, and D.H. Lawrence, in their middle years, listened to no one. This may be regrettable: but I cannot see that the communication of anger, indignation, or even malice, is any less *genuine.* What is evident here is a concealed preference – in the name of 'genuine communication' – for the language of the academy.

That language and that stand Thompson saw, at times, as

carrying overtones which were 'actively offensive'. Those who felt the bite of his counter-tone often imagined themselves to have been bloodied in abuse. This, too, was part of the cause of his awkward 'otherness', yet it was also a large factor in his greatness as a historian and a polemicist, where his *refusals* were always registered in ways that separated him out from the passive propriety of the academic crowd.[6]

Of all species, *Academicus superciliosus* was his least favoured:

> He is inflated with self-esteem and perpetually self-congratulatory as to the high vocation of the university teacher; but he knows almost nothing about any other vocation, and he will lie down and let himself be walked over if anyone enters from the outer world who has money or power or even a tough line in realist talk. . . . He can scurry furiously . . . around in his committees, like a white mouse running in a wheel, while his master is carrying him, cage and all, to be sold at the local pet shop. These people annoy me a good deal. . . . Academic freedom is forever on their lips, and is forever disregarded in their actions. They are the last people to whom it can be safely entrusted, since the present moment is never the opportune moment to stand and fight. Show them the last ditch for the defence of liberty, and they will walk backwards into the sea, complaining that the ditch is very ill dug, that they cannot possibly be asked to defend it alongside such a ragged and seditious-looking set of fellows, and, in any case, it would surely be better to write out a tactful remonstrance and present it, on inscribed vellum, to the enemy.

Nor did *Academicus superciliosus* think any better of 'Professor' Thompson. When I attempted to drum up support for a 1980s visit to Queen's University by Edward and Dorothy, I thought there would be enthusiastic welcome in some quarters for Thompson's work on Blake. I sent off tapes of a lecture he had delivered at Brown University, anticipating a warm response. I got some heat:

> Thompson's approach might hold some interest for the historian, but I doubt whether even the literary historian could afford much sympathy for its methodology. Thompson clearly revels in being curmudgeonly in this respect and aligns himself with the traditions of

19th century scholarship. He freights his texts with so much historical evidence, and with such an exclusiveness, that it would appear that he assumes a work of literature is primarily and even solely a confluence of historical currents. ... The approach brings him closer to the literary approach of writers like Hippolyte Taine, whose influence did outlast the 19th century, but not by much. It is, moreover, somewhat cranky and unproductive. His delivery is often maddeningly digressive, turning aside to plod interminably after the slightest digression. ... And it is, for all its melodramatics, largely boring because it is so centrifugal, undermining the authority and centrality of the text for any excuse to digress into peripheral matters.

My own *Academicus superciliosus* closed his book on Thompson with a polite gesture to collegial sensibilities and a final burst of critical bravado: 'I hope you won't be offended by my account, but I do find the performance in its arch-conservative crankiness somewhat eccentric and antediluvian.'[7]

Thompson's study of Blake, which represented decades of research and thought, appeared posthumously in autumn 1993. It is a remarkable book, and one that explains much about Edward Thompson and the hostility of his scholastic critics, as well as about William Blake. Concerned to situate Blake in terms of an antinomian tradition reaching back to the seventeenth-century ranting impulse of dissent, the book is a careful exercise in creative exploration, an education in the influences that worked on Blake and the milieu of London Dissent, where experience and textual learning rubbed against one another in ways that produced faiths, fragmentations and frictions. Thompson looks to Blake's family and to associations – not of sect-like churches and scriptural works, but of images and rhetorics of faith, of antinomian impulses that saw in all proclamations of Moral Law the oppressive confinements of priests and powerful authorities 'Who make up a Heaven of our misery'. Against the weight of such proclamations of Law pushed the opposition of dissent – Ranters, Quakers, Fifth Monarchists, Muggletonians – which, as early as 1650, was being described in a language of levelling: 'they maintain that God is essentially in every creature, and that there is as much of God in one creature, as in another, though he doth not manifest himself so much in one as in another'. This loose tradition of thought and faith wafted through the seventeenth century and into the early years of the eighteenth, carrying 'an unsettling and potentially subversive' tone linked tenuously to unbridled sexuality and the pursuit of worldly pleasures. Gatherings such as the Sweet Singers of Israel were noticed in 1706 as 'very poetically given, turning all into Rhime, and singing all their Worship. They meet in an Ale-house and eat, drink and smoak. ... They hold that there is no Sin in them: that Eating and Drinking and Society is bles'd: That Death and Hell are a terror only to those that fear it.' In his quest to relate this mood and religious movement of enthusiasm to Blake, Thompson located the last Muggletonian, uncovering in the process the Muggletonian Archive, suggesting that Blake's mother, Catherine, and her first husband had possibly been followers of Ludowick Muggleton.

This exploration of antinomianism comprises more than half of Thompson's discussion in *Witness Against the Beast*, the book closing with Blake's images – of the New Jerusalem, of the divine human of Swedenborgian discourse, of innocence and experience, of London – and their meaning. Arguing that Blake's vision was in direct opposition to the governance of man, to the uncontrolled rule of the Beast and the Whore (the state and priestcraft), Thompson lays continual stress on the intensity of Blake's faith in the liberation of human nature, a vast unrealized potential of alternative, repressed by Moral Law. Convinced that Blake never compromised his vision of hope with 'the least sign of submission to "Satan's Kingdom"', Thompson applauds Blake's refusal of 'the least complicity with the kingdom of the Beast'. It is a refusal as characteristic of Thompson himself as it was of Blake, the kind of refusal that Thompson saw too little of in certain quarters inhabited by *Academicus superciliosus*. Thompson's willingness to read Blake against the decontextualized canonical grain – to see his prose as both beautiful and powerful because of its historicized message, rather than in spite of it – drew the ire of scholastic criticism, as did so much of his writing. Thompson, for his part, saw in such petulance 'the uncreative mediocrity of these latter days and also, perhaps, . . . the encroaching Thatcherism of the upwardly-mobile historical mind'. This was what he lived with in his awkward placement: now in the academic circle, now out of it.[8]

For Thompson, Blake was 'the last and greatest antinomian', founder of an obscure sect of which, only partly in jest, Thompson was willing to acknowledge membership: 'the Muggletonian Marxists'. Indeed, in tracing the lineage of Blake's antinomianism back in time, through swirling streams of dissent, Thompson's own objections and oppositions take on a clarity and a coherence that are easily missed in glosses on the discontinuities of his histories and politics. Perry Anderson's 'Diary' comment on *Witness Against the Beast* in the *London Review of Books* understands this, I think, but muddies the issue with a scholasticism that is unfortunate in its inability to refrain from scoring yet another polemical hit. To argue, as Anderson does, that 'readers who recall rolling thunder against the obscurity of Parisian marxism may be allowed a smile as they wrestle with the mysteries of the divine influx and the two seeds, the dispersal v. the unity of the godhead, painstakingly expounded here', is to bypass what is surely the main point. It does not matters so much that Blake perhaps faltered in moments of political condescension, could turn inward in fear of persecution, mocked those with whom he should have shown a sterner solidarity, or refrained from acting publicly as a consequence of a self-isolating strand of the Muggletonian penchant for withdrawal. This, to be sure, is the point where the personal is not quite political enough, and Anderson is characteristically acute in exposing these shortcomings. But doing so speaks too faintly to what, in the interface of Blake and Edward Palmer Thompson, matters. For centuries there have been those willing to proclaim 'the Moral Law'. The proclamations have differed dramatically over time, but metaphorically they are the fruit of similiar seed. To follow that 'Moral Law' and succumb to its dictates – instead of to a rational, humane interrogation of them, in which reason is complemented by the affirmatives of (in the language of Blake) Mercy, Pity, Peace and Love – has been the order of much political economy and culture from the time of the seventeenth-century revolutions.

Capitalist and Stalinist, academic ideologue and Cold War warrior, like their predecessors from Mr Worldly Wiseman of John Bunyan's *Pilgrim's Progress* to Edmund Burke, have always been adept at elaborating *law's* course. Antinomianism objects and opposes, insisting that 'by the deeds of the Law no man living can be rid of his Burden', and that 'if the path of *Legality* be taken, then it leads on to formalism, carnal policy, opportunism and, finally, to a mere simpering *Civility*'. 'I like these Muggletonians,' declares Thompson in the middle of *Witness Against the Beast*, 'but it is clear that they were not among history's winners.' With Marx he believed that 'To leave error unrefuted is to encourage intellectual immorality.' The impulse to rant and rebel, to object and oppose, was, throughout history, the space Thompson chose to recover and revere, to connect across centuries and countries and through many struggles; just as it was, in his own politics of dissent, the place he chose to be. As he noted in one of his last comments on the non-aligned peace movements' contribution to the ending of the Cold War, 'Ends and Histories', such traditions emerge from defeat as the only honourable political practice, and even at the point of seeming failure they leave a legacy, and occasionally much more than that, which makes victory possible.

World War II and the internationalism of the left's resistance to fascism, Morris and the Romantic critique of capitalism, 1956, the new left, the writing of working-class history, debates within Marxism, the non-aligned peace movements of East and

West, common right and customary culture versus the disciplines and possessive individualism of the eighteenth-century market, Oi Paz, and rethinking the interface of cultures via Tagore and Thompson or Sampson Occum, are not, after all, moments of easy victory. But they all stood, in one way or another, against the Moral Law. They made no compromises with the legalisms of their own time, interpretively or politically; and they never spiralled downward in the *Civility* which, in its simpering hypocrisy, Thompson always associated with the worst of *Academicus superciliosus*. In these histories and politics, as in Blake, there is a vision of possibility and potential, and a form of presentation that reinforces the content. These forms and contents do not aim to please either Moral Law or its advocates, be they in the seminar room or the corridors of state power. Anderson's 'Diary' ends on a personal note, and one which – as its author, to his credit, must have appreciated – reflected back on him with an ironic twist. Speaking of Edward's oppositional stand, Anderson concluded:

> Whatever shape his ideas might have taken, they would have been uncovenanted. He was not in a mood to settle. *A Life of Dissent* is the affecting film Tariq Ali made of Edward and Dorothy Thompson earlier this year, recently reshown. While it was being shot, there was talk of mutual acquaintances. 'What's Perry up to these days?' he enquired. Tariq mentioned something I'd written on conservatism in this paper. 'Yes, I know,' Edward replied. 'Oakeshott was a scoundrel. Tell him to stiffen his tone.'

Against the beast, wherever it might be, Thompson looked for those who would rise up in objection and opposition. He expected it of others. He could do no less.[9]

I know I have offered too many pages here, and I know, quite acutely, that they are likely to be dismissed, as have other pages I have written on Thompson, as 'hagiographic'. Thompson himself thought my 1980 book on him 'too uncritical perhaps?'. I have written these pages in what I tried to make Thompson's terms, rather than mine. My own criticisms seem rather unimportant at the moment. There will be others to do this kind of much-needed work. They should attend, however, to Thompson's own *history*, which this comment has pointed towards, and which the factory management of the Thompson academic industry has been lax in coaxing into production. They may find explanations and resonances in Thompson's past with those areas where legitimate difference arises out of his historical and political writings. The treatment of the Irish in *The Making of the English Working Class*, and Thompson's brief contemporary comment on 'terrorism', the current Irish malaise, and 'British imperialism', for instance, may benefit from engagement with Thompson's father's experience as a 'friend of India'. It is only a perhaps. More than one thoughtful scholar has suggested that Thompson's chapter on Methodism owed much in its creatively explosive anger to the tensions of his own upbringing. But there are other long-overgrown interpretive paths to walk. No doubt this criticism will be 'benevolent', in the complex eighteenth-century senses of the word that Thompson discussed with respect to the wobbling Jacobin William Goodwin, who carried the virtues and vices of an early enlightened intelligensia.[10]

I have looked at Thompson with my own sense of benevolence. It has not been as easy as some will assume. But it is now there to be considered, as, in many ways, Thompson considered others:

> If many of the ... young people had in fact got socialism 'inside of them', then something of its quality – the hostility to Grundyism, the warm espousal of sex equality, the rich internationalism – owed much to [him.] It is time that this forgotten 'provincial' was admitted to first-class citizenship of history. . . .

> He didn't ask for intellectual allegiance, nor did he respect those who offered it too readily. His work provoked a critical admiration. We had come to assume his presence – definitions, provocations, exhortations – as a fixed point in the intellectual night-sky. His star stood above the

ideological no-man's land between the orthodox emplacements of West and East, flashing urgent humanist messages. If we couldn't always follow it, we always stopped to take bearings.

> You do not fall within
> Our frames of reference. Transfixed by promises
> Pledged to the poor in the high Andea pastures;
> The crowd in Santiago; the clasped-hand of the metal-worker;
> The earnest village schoolmistress, searching your face:
> These brought their treaties. You signed them with your life

[He] was right. But that did him no kind of good. Come 1956 and all that, and surely [he] was at last liberated, freed from the Stalinist shackles, in touch once again with the new and ebullient radicalism of the 1960s, in accord with an audience once more? Well, no. That wasn't how it was.

Maguire, Wright Mills, Allende, McGrath – awkward examples all; men, dead or largely lost from our sights, whom Thompson brought back to us with his words, reintroducing values that they espoused, enlarging and sustaining them in our present.[11]

'In the end we also will be dead,' wrote Thompson, 'and our own lives will lie inert within the finished process, our intentions assimilated within a past event which we never intended.' All that could be hoped for was that 'the men and women of the future will reach back to us, will affirm and renew our meanings, and make our history intelligible within their own present tense'. Extending this humanity its own agency, Thompson declared: 'They alone will have the power to select from the many meanings offered by our quarrelling present, and to transmute some part of our process into their progress.'[12] This we can, awkwardly, try to do. We have, after all, your *example*. Homage to you, Edward Thompson. In your objections and oppositions you gave us so much of what we need.

# Notes

## Preface

1. Bryan D. Palmer, *The Making of E.P. Thompson: Marxism, Humanism, and History* (Toronto 1981).

2. There is something of this personal history in A.M. Givertz and Marcus Klee, 'Historicizing Thompson: An Interview with Bryan Palmer', *left history*, 1 (Fall 1993), 111–20.

3. E.P. Thompson, *The Poverty of Theory and Other Essays* (London 1978), iv.

4. See, for instance, E.P. Thompson, 'Homage to Tom Maguire', in Asa Briggs and John Saville, eds, *Essays in Labour History* (London 1960), 276–316; 'Remembering C. Wright Mills', in E.P. Thompson, *The Heavy Dancers* (London 1985), 261–74; 'Homage to Thomas McGrath', *TriQuarterly*, 70 (Fall 1987), 106–57.

5. E.P. Thompson, 'An Open Letter to Leszek Kolakowski', in *The Poverty of Theory and Other Essays*, 183.

6. E.P. Thompson, 'Agency and Choice', *New Reasoner*, 4 (Summer 1958), 106.

7. Thompson, 'McGrath', 115.

8. See E.P. Thompson, *The Sykaos Papers: Being an Account of the Voyages of the Poet Oi Paz . . .* (New York 1988).

9. Thompson, 'The Poverty of Theory; or, an Orrery of Errors', in *The Poverty of Theory and Other Essays*, 238.

10. E.P. Thompson, *The Making of the English Working Class* (Harmondsworth 1968), 12.

11. Thompson, 'An Open Letter to Leszek Kolakowski', 186. For another brief comment on Thompson and opposition/objection, see Michael Merrill, 'E.P. Thompson: In Solidarity', *Radical History Review*, 58 (Winter 1994), 152–6.

12. E.P. Thompson, 'The Politics of Theory', in Raphael Samuel, ed., *People's*

*History and Socialist Theory* (London 1981), 396; E.P. Thompson, 'Wordsworth's Crisis', *London Review of Books* (8 December 1988), 3–6.

13. Thompson, 'McGrath', 108.

14. E.P. Thompson, *Witness Against the Beast: William Blake and the Moral Law* (New York 1993), 229.

15. E.P. Thompson, 'Ends and Histories', in Mary Kaldor, ed., *Europe from Below: An East–West Dialogue* (London 1991), 24.

# Introduction

1. Perry Anderson, *Arguments within English Marxism* (London 1980), 1; Anna Davin, 'Memories of E.P. Thompson', *Radical Historians Newsletter*, 69 (November 1993), 16.

2. In a review of *Customs in Common* (1991) in *The Independent on Sunday*, 5 January 1992, 26, Linda Colley noted that the English tradition of making iconoclasts and dissidents 'national possessions' in their old age was almost certainly not going to overtake Thompson, who would continue to draw antagonism precisely because of his commitment to protest and irreverent mockery of established authority, both academic and political.

3. On the academic response to the Morris volume, see E.P. Thompson, 'Postscript', in *William Morris: Romantic to Revolutionary* (New York 1977), esp. 768–71; *Times Literary Supplement*, 15 July 1955, 391; Edmund Penning-Rowsell, 'The Remodelling of Morris', *Times Literary Supplement*, 11 August 1978, 913–14. On the more extensive and engaged commentary on the *The Making of the English Working Class*, see Thompson's reply to his critics in E.P. Thompson, 'Postscript', *The Making of the English Working Class* (Harmondsworth 1968), 916–39; my own comments on and citations of various reviews in Bryan D. Palmer, *The Making of E.P. Thompson: Marxism, Humanism, and History* (Toronto 1980), esp. 65–7, 78; F.K. Donnelly, 'Ideology and Early English Working-Class History', *Social History*, 2 (May 1976), 219–38; Gertrude Himmelfarb, 'A Tract of Secret History', *The New Republic*, 150 (11 April 1964), 24–6; 'Enter the Cloth Cap', *Economist*, 210 (February 1964), 622; John Gross, 'Hard Times', *New York Review of Books*, 2 (16 April 1964), 8–10; Herman Ausubel, 'The Common Man as Hero', *New York Times Book Review* (26 April 1964), 44; J.D. Chambers, 'Making of the English Working Class', *History*, (1 June 1966), 183–9; R. Currie and R.M. Hartwell, 'The Making of the English Working Class?', in Hartwell, *The Industrial Revolution and Economic Growth* (London 1971), 361–76. A unique review is Tom Nairn, 'The English Working Class', in Robin Blackburn, ed., *Ideology in Social Science: Readings in Critical Social Theory* (New York 1973), 187–206, which originally appeared in *New Left Review*. Hobsbawm's comment is in 'Obituaries: E.P. Thompson', *The Independent*, 30 August 1993. Place as 'the White Man's Trusty Nigger' appears in *The Making of the English Working Class* (New York 1963), 155, but in the 1968 edition this has been altered to 'the White Man's Uncle Tom' (170). For the eighteenth-century studies note, especially, J.C.D. Clark, 'The Namierism of the Left', *Cambridge Review*, 22 October 1976; Lawrence Stone, 'Whigs, Marxists and Poachers', *New York Review of Books*, 23 (5 February 1976), 25–7. Other statements include Keith Thomas, 'Folk Law', *New Statesman*, 90 (10 October

1975), 443–5; George Rudé, 'Poachers and Protesters', *Times Literary Supplement*, 30 January 1976, 104. Thompson has replied to critics of *Whigs and Hunters* in 'Postscript', *Whigs and Hunters: The Origins of the Black Act* (London 1977), 301–11. Finally, note the response to 'The War of Thatcher's Face', *The Times*, 29 April 1982, acknowledged in E.P. Thompson, *Zero Option* (London 1982), 197–8; Roger Scruton, *Thinkers of the New Left* (London 1985), 10–19, 212, an account characterized by a cavalier disregard for accuracy and a breezy insubstantial style, typified in the following biographical note: 'Thompson is no longer connected with any university, and in recent years has given his time, and some of his considerable wealth, to the Campaign for Nuclear Disarmament, upon whose platforms he appears regularly, his white hair blowing romantically about his leonine features.' Thompson was personally miffed at the reference to his 'considerable wealth', which he has never really had. He told me it prompted him to look up his tax returns, which confirmed a rather less than modest personal income.

4. For representative obituaries, see W.L. Webb, 'A Thoroughly English Dissident', and Christopher Hill, 'From the Awkward School', *The Guardian*, 30 August 1993; E.J. Hobsbawm and Mary Kaldor, 'E.P. Thompson', *The Independent*, 30 August 1993; 'Obituaries: E.P. Thompson', *Daily Telegraph*, 30 August 1993; 'Obituaries: E.P. Thompson', *The Times*, 30 August 1993; Neal Ascherson, 'E.P. Thompson: Defender of the Faithful Few', *The Independent*, 5 September 1993; Greg Kealey, 'E.P. Thompson: More than a Historian', *Evening Telegram* (St John's), 5 September 1993; Rick Salutin, 'E.P. Thompson: Ornery and Humane', *Globe*, 10 September 1993; Fred Inglis, 'Thompson Invictus', *The Nation* (20 September 1993), 265–8; Michael Kazin, 'The Last Socialist', *Washington Post*, 19 September 1993; Sheila Rowbotham, 'E.P. Thompson: A Life of Radical Dissent', and Boyd Tonkin, 'Stay Angry', in *New Society*, 3 September 1993, 14–15, 41; Bryan Palmer, 'E.P. Thompson: In Memoriam', *In These Times* (20 September–3 October 1993), 34–5; Harvey J. Kaye, 'E.P. Thompson, Historian and Radical', American Historical Association, *Perspectives* (November 1993), 19; Deborah Valenze and Peter Weiler, 'Edward Palmer Thompson (1924–1993)', and Anna Davin, 'Memories of E.P. Thompson', *Radical Historians Newsletter*, 69 (November 1993), 11–16; Robin Blackburn, 'Edward Thompson and the New Left', Penelope Corfield, 'E.P. Thompson, the Historian: An Appreciation', and Peter Linebaugh, 'From the Upper West Side to Wick Episcopi', *New Left Review*, 201 (September/October 1993), 3–25. Among the large memorials were 'Remembering E.P. Thompson: A Celebration', Logan Hall, Institute of Education, London, 7 November 1993; the Nation Institute-sponsored Memorial at the Ethical Culture Society, New York, 12 December 1993; and 'Edward P. Thompson, 1924–1993: An Appreciation of His Life and Work', American Historical Association Convention, San Francisco, 8 January 1994. There were other 'memorials' as well: at York University (Toronto), the Newbury Library (Chicago), the 1994 meetings of the Organization of American Historians, and elsewhere.

5. See E.P. Thompson, ed., *Warwick University Ltd: Industry, Management, and the Universities* (Harmondsworth 1970), esp. 153–5.

6. See, for example, E.P. Thompson, 'Socialist Humanism: An Epistle to the Philistines', *New Reasoner: A Quarterly Journal of Socialist Humanism*, 1 (Summer 1957), 105–43; Thompson, 'An Open Letter to Leszek Kolakowski', in E.P. Thompson, *The Poverty of Theory and Other Essays* (London 1978), 92–192.

7. Thompson, 'Letter to Kolakowski', 186.

8.  John Saville and E.P. Thompson, 'Editorial', *New Reasoner*, 3 (Winter 1957–8), 1–4; Blake quote in Thompson, *William Morris: Romantic to Revolutionary*, 126, and again in Thompson, 'Socialist Humanism: An Epistle to the Philistines', 125; Rowbotham, 'Thompson: A Life of Radical Dissent', 15. Note also the discussion in Michael Francis McShane, ' "History and Hope": E.P. Thompson and *The Making of the English Working Class*', PhD dissertation, McMaster University, 1990, esp. 30–69. Raphael Samuel discusses the general place of liberal dissent, radical Nonconformity and, suggestively, Methodism, in the religious making of communist intellectuals in 'British Marxist Historians, 1880–1980: Part One', *New Left Review*, 120 (March–April 1980), esp. 42–55, as does Rodney Hilton, 'Christopher Hill: Some Reminiscences', in Donald Pennington and Keith Thomas, eds, *Puritans and Revolutionaries: Essays in Seventeenth-Century History presented to Christopher Hill* (Oxford 1977), 7. 'I'm a Methodist, what's your heresy?' was Hill's recollection of an ironic introduction common among communist historians of the Popular Front period.

9.  Thompson, 'The Place Called Choice', in Thompson, *The Heavy Dancers* (London 1985), 247–60; Rick Salutin and Theatre Passe Muraille, *1837: William Lyon Mackenzie and the Canadian Revolution – A History/A Play* (Toronto 1976), 264; William Morris, *A Dream of John Ball* (New York n.d.), 19–20 and Frederick Engels, 'Ludwig Feuerbach and the End of Classical German Philosophy', in Karl Marx and Frederick Engels, *Selected Works* (Moscow 1968), 623, both quoted without citation in Thompson, *Morris*, 722; and Thompson, 'Agency and Choice', *New Reasoner*, 4 (Summer 1958), 106.

10. Anderson, *Arguments*, 1.

11. Note E.P. Thompson, 'Outside the Whale', in *The Poverty of Theory and Other Essays*, 1–34; Thompson, 'Disenchantment or Default? A Lay Sermon', in Conor Cruise O'Brien and W.D. Vanech, eds, *Power and Consciousness* (New York 1969), 149–81.

12. Thompson, 'Letter to Kolakowski', 101, 182; Thompson, 'My Study', and 'The Place Called Choice', in *The Heavy Dancers*, 338–9, 259–60. Gertrude Himmelfarb has castigated Thompson, among others, for not writing the history of communism, offering comment on Stalinism's crimes. See Himmelfarb, ' "The Group": British Marxist Historians', in Himmelfarb, *The New History: Critical Essays and Reappraisals* (Cambridge 1987), 70–93. Thompson, in fact, has offered more comment on this issue than any other member of the Communist Party of Great Britain's Historians' Group, much of his writing in issues of *The New Reasoner* constituting such a critique of Stalinism. Himmelfarb obviously prefers academic publication, but Thompson has answered this challenge in his 'Letter to Kolakowski', 182: 'You will have noticed, if you have followed my footnotes, that my criticisms of socialist reality have always been made in socialist journals.'

13. This is not easily documented, for much of it remains less on the printed page and more in the atmosphere of discussion. Still, note E.J. Hobsbawm's *Independent* obituary, which mentions Thompson's 'star quality', his 'unconvincing' 'persona of a traditional English country gentleman of the Radical left', his 'fluctuating moods', 'an uncertain relation to organisations and organisation men', the 'occasional hit-and-miss quality in the excursions of his powerful and imaginative intellect into theory', his 'rolling, intuitive course, moving with the winds and currents of private and political currents'. 'A lone wolf of the Left', Hobsbawm's Thompson failed adequately to 'plan his life's work', but he had the gifts of genius, and for this his 'admirers forgave him

much. ... His friends forgave him everything.' Hobsbawm's review of *The Making*, 'Organised Orphans', *New Statesman*, 66 (29 November 1963), 787–8, identified Thompson as 'a historian of striking gifts, though hampered by a lack of self-criticism from which this book also suffers'. No doubt much of this relates to the quite different choices that marked each historian's relation to 1956 and the Communist Party.

# Chapter 1

1. See Perry Anderson, 'Socialism and Pseudo-Empiricism: The Myths of Edward Thompson', *New Left Review*, 35 (January–February 1966), 33–5; Tom Nairn, *The Break-Up of Britain* (London 1981), 303–4. Olive branches include Anderson, *Arguments within English Marxism*, although the chapter on 'Internationalism' (131–56) casts the discussion of socialist internationalism in entirely theoretical terms and avoids engagement with the internationalist origins of Thompson's imagination; 'E.P. Thompson: Interview', in MARHO, *Visions of History: Interviews* (New York 1983), 17. On 'Englishness', see Harvey J. Kaye, 'E.P. Thompson, the British Marxist Historical Tradition and the Contemporary Crisis', in Kaye, *The Education of Desire: Marxists and the Writing of History* (London 1992), 98–115, and the obituaries by W.L. Webb, *Guardian*, 30 August 1993; E.J. Hobsbawm, *The Independent*, 30 August 1993; Neal Ascherson, 'E.P. Thompson: Defender of the Faithful Few', *The Independent*, 5 September 1993; and on awkwardness, the obituary by Christopher Hill, 'From the Awkward School', *Guardian*, 30 August 1993, as well as much in Thompson, *The Poverty of Theory and Other Essays* (London 1978), esp. iii–iv, 109–10. The passage on causes lost that could be won in Asia or Africa is, of course, from Thompson, *The Making of the English Working Class* (Harmondsworth 1968), 13, and it was often attacked in academic reviews. See, for instance, John Gross, 'Hard Times', *New York Review of Books*, 2 (16 April 1964), 8–10; J.D. Chambers, 'Making of the English Working Class', *History*, 1 (June 1966), 188.

2. Anderson, 'Socialism and Pseudo-Empiricism', 26, which cites Thompson, 'William Morris and the Moral Issues To-Day', *Arena*, 2 (June/July 1951), 25–30.

3. Henry Harris Jessup, *Fifty-Three Years in Syria*, 2 vols (New York 1910), I, 16, 233. Thompson's brother Frank read Lincoln's Second Inaugural two weeks before being parachuted into Yugoslavia in 1944, considering it, within the context of its times, 'one of the most remarkable speeches in human history'. See Freeman Dyson, *Disturbing the Universe* (New York 1979), 43.

4. Jessup, *Fifty-Three Years in Syria*, II, esp. 570–71, 581–2, 767–8. I cannot agree with Thompson's reading of *Fifty-Three Years in Syria*: 'there were Americans in those days who did not regard the Islamic world as being made up of "wogs", "gooks" or targets for bombardment'. See Thompson, 'Letter to Americans', in Thompson and Mary Kaldor, eds, *Mad Dogs: The US Raids on Libya* (London 1986), 11; Thompson, 'An Open Letter to Uncle Sam', *Observer*, 27 April 1986. Note Edward W. Said, *Orientalism* (New York 1979).

5. On Methodist missionary women in a slightly earlier period see, for instance, Leslie Flemming, ed., *Women's Work for Women: Missionaries and Social Change in Asia* (Boulder, CO 1989); Ruth Compton Brouwer, *New Women for God: Canadian Presbyterian Women and India Missions, 1876–1914* (Toronto 1990);

Rosemary R. Gagan, *A Sensitive Independence: Canadian Methodist Women Missionaries in Canada and the Orient, 1881–1925* (Montreal 1992).

6. See, for instance, the views of M.K. Gandhi, *Christian Missions: Their Place in India* (Ahmedabad 1941).

7. The above paragraph draws on Webb, 'A Througly English Dissident', *Guardian*, 30 August 1993; Thompson, 'America's Europe: A Hobbit Among Gandalfs', *The Nation* (24 January 1981), 68–72; Thompson, 'Letter to Americans', in Thompson and Kaldor, eds, *Mad Dogs: The US Raids on Libya*, 11–15; Thompson, 'Homage to Thomas McGrath', *TriQuarterly*, 70 (Fall 1987), 117; 'E.P. Thompson: Interview', *Visions of History*, 11. On the New York City of the Popular Front era, see Maurice Isserman, *Which Side Were You On? The American Communist Party during the Second World War* (Middletown, CT 1982); Martin Bauml Duberman, *Paul Robeson: A Biography* (New York 1989).

8. This paragraph draws on H.M. Margoliouth, 'Thompson, Edward John (1886–1946)', in L.G. Wickham and E.T. Williams, eds, *Dictionary of National Biography* (Oxford 1959), 879–80; E.P. Thompson, *'Alien Homage': Edward Thompson and Rabindranath Tagore* (Delhi 1993), esp. 10–12, 62, 103; and for the specific lines of verse, Edward Thompson, 'Olive Groves: Ludd, Palestine, 1927', in *Crusader's Coast* (London 1929), 192. A most useful and sensitive account of Edward John Thompson is Sumit Sarkar, 'Afterword', in Edward John Thompson, *The Other Side of the Medal* (New Delhi 1989), 83–126. On missionaries, see C.P. Williams, ' "Not Quite Gentlemen": An Examination of "middling Class" Protestant Missionaries from Britian, *c.* 1856–1900', *Journal of Ecclesiastical History*, 31 (1980), 301–15. For Edward John Thompson's critical comments on the state of poetry in this period, see *Cock Robin's Decease: An Irregular Inquest* (London 1928).

9. See, especially, E.P. Thompson, *'Alien Homage'*, 1–12, 118–19. Tagore would figure forcefully, and roughly, in Thompson's life. I will address this relationship with respect to E.P. Thompson's analysis of it at the end of this book. Note also E.P. Thompson and E.J. Thompson, 'Memories of Tagore', *London Review of Books*, 22 May 1986, 18–19.

10. E.P. Thompson, *'Alien Homage'*, 2, 8, 9; Sakar, 'Afterword', *The Other Side of the Medal*, 92; Edward John Thompson, *Crusader's Coast*, 98–9, although the entire volume is a statement on Thompson's affection for the geography and wildlife of the 'East'; Edward J. Thompson, 'Dear Earth of Flowers', in *Poems: 1902–1925* (London 1926), 15.

11. E.P. Thompson, *'Alien Homage'*, 22, 28, 71–3; Edward John Thompson, *Crusader's Coast*, 95, 117, 189–91; Edward John Thompson, 'Spring, 1916', 'Remembrance', 'Royal Audience', in *Poems: 1902–1925*, 16, 218–19, 47–8.

12. See Sarkar, 'Afterword', *The Other Side of the Medal*, 93–4; E.P. Thompson, *'Alien Homage'*, 1–26, 89; Amit Chaudhuri, 'Bankura's Englishman' (review of *'Alien Homage'*), *London Review of Books*, 15 (September 1993), 10–11; E.J. Thompson, 'An Old Woman', 'Lepers', and 'I Have Sought a City', *Poems: 1902–1925*, 40–41, 51; E.J. Thompson, *Crusader's Coast*, 103.

13. The major source for the above paragraph is E.P Thompson, *'Alien Homage'*, with direct quotes from 72, 85. See, as well, Sarkar, 'Afterword', *The Other Side of the Medal*, 93–5.

14. The above two paragraphs draw upon K. Mukherjee, 'In Memoriam: Professor Edward Thompson', and Kalidas Nag, 'Introduction', in Edward J. Thompson

and Kalidas Nag, eds, *Rabindranath Tagore: His Life and Work* (Calcutta 1948), 92–5, xii–xiv; Edward Thompson, *Rabindranath Tagore* (1925), 3; Webb, 'A Thoroughly English Dissident'; E.P. Thompson, 'C.L.R. James at 80', back cover of *Urgent Tasks: Journal of the Revolutionary Left*, 12 (Summer 1981); and, for context, C.L.R. James, *Beyond a Boundary* (New York 1983); Edward Thompson, *The Reconstruction of India* (London 1930), esp. 11, 130–36, 258, 276, 302; Edward Thompson and G.T. Garratt, *Rise and Fulfilment of British Rule in India* (London 1934), esp. 447–59; 'E.P. Thompson: Interview', *Visions of History*, 11; E.P. Thompson, '*Alien Homage*', esp. 32, 85; Margoliouth, 'Thompson, Edward John', *DNB*, 879–80; Edward John Thompson, *A History of India* (London 1927). The most useful concise overall statement on Edward John Thompson is Sarkar, 'Afterword', *The Other Side of the Medal*, 83–126, but see also Benita Parry, *Delusions and Discoveries: Studies on India in the British Imagination, 1880–1930* (Berkeley and Los Angeles 1972), 164–202. There is also considerable comment on Thompson's India-focused fiction in Allen J. Greenberger, *The British Image of India: A Study in the Literature of Imperialism, 1880–1960* (London 1969).

15. Quotes and references in the above paragraphs come from: Freeman Dyson, *Disturbing the Universe*, 35, referring to Frank Thompson; Edward J. Thompson, 'This Sword of Verse', *100 Poems* (London 1944), 19; Thompson, *Reconstruction of India*, 256; Parry, *Delusions and Discoveries*, esp. 182–200; Thompson, *Suttee: A Historical and Philosophical Enquiry into the Hindu Rite of Widow-Burning* (Boston, MA 1928); Thompson, *The Life of Charles, Lord Metcalfe* (London 1937); Thompson, *Sir Walter Raleigh: The Last of the Elizabethans* (London 1935); Thompson and Garratt, *Rise and Fulfilment of British Rule in India*, 170; Thompson, *Robert Bridges, 1844–1930* (Oxford 1944); Stowers Johnson, *Agents Extraordinary* (London 1975), 16–17; Webb, 'A Thoroughly English Dissident'; Edward Thompson to Nehru, 30 October 1936, in Jawaharlal Nehru, *A Bunch of Old Letters: Written Mostly to Jawaharlal Nehru and some written by him* (London 1960), 209; E.P. Thompson, 'The Nehru Tradition', in Thompson, *Writing by Candlelight* (London 1980), esp. 142. For discussion of the poetry/politics dichotomy, introduced by Margoliouth, 'Thompson, Edward John', *DNB*, 879–80, a view challenged by Theodosia Thompson, see Sarkar, 'Afterword', *The Other Side of the Medal*, 106, 119. Sarkar tempers much of Parry's argument, as does E.P. Thompson, '*Alien Homage*'. On poetry and classicism, which figured prominently in the youth of Edward John Thompson and his eldest son, William Frank Thompson, see E.J. Thompson, *The Thracian Stranger* (London, 1929); E.J. Thompson, *Cock Robin's Decease*. For the most accessible basic collection of poetry, see Edward John Thompson, *The Collected Poems of Edward Thompson* (London, 1930).

16. Amit Chaudhuri, 'Bankura's Englishman', *London Review of Books*, 15 (September 1993), 10–11. For Thompson's statement on modelling himself after his father, see Penelope Corfield, 'University of London Interviews with Historians: E.P. Thompson'.

17. The above paragraphs draw upon E.P. Thompson, '*Alien Homage*', esp. 104–5; Sarkar, 'Afterword', *The Other Side of the Medal*, esp. 82, 87–9, 97–100, 108–9, 111, 114–19; Reginald Reynolds, *The White Sahibs in India: British Imperialism From the Days of the John Company to Date* (New York 1937), 42; Parry, *Delusions and Discoveries*, 164–202, esp. 166; Edward Thompson, *These Men Thy Friends* (New York 1928), 17; Michael Edwardes, *The Last Years of British India* (London 1963), 16; Thompson, *Atonement* (London 1924); Nehru, *A Bunch of Old Letters*, esp. 209–11, 311; Edward Thompson, *The Making of the Indian Princes* (London

1943), esp. v, 287. For E.P. Thompson's statements on Methodism, see *The Making of the English Working Class* (Harmondsworth 1968), pp. 385–420.

18. In the above two paragraphs, quotes are from Edward Thompson, *The Other Side of the Medal* (New Delhi 1989) and Sarkar's 'Afterword', 4, 6, 75, 87–8; E.P. Thompson, 'Alien Homage', 89; Edward Thompson, *The Other Side of the Medal* (London 1925) and a December 1925 letter are drawn from Parry, *Delusions and Discoveries*, 176–7; Edward W. Said, *Culture and Imperialism* (New York 1993), 206–7. For discussions of the representation of the 1857 Mutiny, see Ralph J. Crane, *Inventing India: A History of India in English-Language Fiction* (London 1992), 11–54; and the older G.T. Garratt, *An Indian Commentary* (New York 1928), 116–17. Nehru presents some critical commentary on *The Other Side of the Medal* in *Toward Freedom: The Autobiography of Jawaharlal Nehru* (Boston, MA 1961), 49–50. For a reference to 'apologists for imperialism', referring to Thompson and Garratt, *Rise and Fulfilment of British Rule in India* (1934), see the Communist Party's R. Palme Dutt, *India To-Day* (London 1940), 245; and Dutt, *The Problem of India* (New York 1943), 41. Non-communist support for oppositional nationalism in India is outlined in Reginald Reynolds, *The White Sahibs in India*, which appeared in 1937 with a preface by Nehru.

19. This paragraph draws on Thompson, 'The Nehru Tradition', in *Writing by Candlelight*, 135–48. See also Edward Thompson, *Enlist India for Freedom!* (London 1942); Sarkar, 'Afterword', *The Other Side of the Medal*, 106, 114.

20. Thompson quoted this passage from Marx's writing on India in the 1850s in E.P. Thompson, 'Socialist Humanism: An Epistle to the Philistines', *New Reasoner*, 1 (Summer 1957), 143. This citation and Marx's position on Britain's conquest of India as 'the annihilation of old Asiatic society, and the laying of the material foundations of Western society in Asia' would have drawn an ambivalent response from Thompson's father, but he would probably have appreciated a part of this destructive/constructive paradigm. The full quote is from Marx, 'The Future Results of the British Rule in India', *New York Daily Tribune*, 8 August 1853, in Karl Marx, *Surveys From Exile* (Harmondsworth 1973), 325:

> Bourgeois industry and commerce create these material conditions of a new world in the same way as geological revolutions have created the surface of the earth. When a great social revolution shall have mastered the results of the bourgeois epoch, the market of the world and the modern powers of production, and subjected them to the common control of the most advanced peoples, then only will human progress cease to resemble that hideoous pagan idol, who would not drink the nectar but from the skulls of the slain.

For useful – if not entirely congruent – discussions, see V.G. Kiernan, *Marxism and Imperialism* (London 1974); Anthony Brewer, *Marxist Theories of Imperialism: A Critical Survey* (London 1980); Bill Warren, *Imperialism: Pioneer of Capitalism* (London 1980); Said, *Orientalism*. India was a formative experience for a number of members of the Communist Party of Great Britain's Historians' Group (Kiernan, Saville, Pearce). See E.J. Hobsbawm, 'The Historians' Group of the Communist Party', in Maurice Cornforth, ed., *Rebels and Their Causes: Essays in Honour of A.L. Morton* (London 1978), 24. Note Dorothy Thompson interview with Sheila Rowbotham, 'The Personal and the Political', *New Left Review*, 200 (July–August 1993), 94: 'That India had got its freedom was one of the great triumphs in our lifetime, and yet these antagonisms have led to thousands of people being killed today and yesterday.'

21. E.P. Thompson, *'Alien Homage': Rabindranath Tagore and Edward Thompson* (Oxford 1993), and two reviews: Amit Chaudhuri, 'Bankura's Englishman', 10–11, and the more abbreviated (and patronizing) Raleigh Trevelyan, 'Twain Meeting?', *Times Literary Supplement*, 24 September 1993, 34. See also E.P. Thompson and E.J. Thompson, 'Memories of Tagore', *London Review of Books*, 22 May 1986, 18–19. Tagore scholarship is voluminous, although not without its silences and failures to probe available sources, including those generated in the Thompson–Tagore relationship. See, as an introduction, Mary M. Lago, *Rabindranath Tagore* (Boston 1976); Mary Lago and Ronald Warwick, eds, *Rabindranath Tagore: Perspectives in Time* (London 1989); Probhat Kumar Mukherji, *Life of Tagore* (New Delhi 1975); K.S. Ramaswami Sastri, *Sir Rabindranath Tagore: His Life Personality and Genius* (Delhi 1988); Mohit Chakrabarti, *Rabindranath Tagore: Diverse Dimensions* (New Delhi 1990).

22. Thompson, *100 Poems*; Thompson, *The Making of the Indian Princes*, 264–5; and the comment on this passage in Jawaharlal Nehru, *The Discovery of India* (New York 1946), 286–7, in which Nehru argues:

> The two Englands live side by side, influencing each other, and cannot be separated; nor could one of them come to India forgetting completely the other. Yet in every leading action one plays the leading role, dominating the other, and it was inevitable that the wrong England should play that role in India and should come in contact with and encourage the wrong India in the process.

23. 'E.P. Thompson: Interview', *Visions of History*, 19; E.P. Thompson, 'Caudwell', in Ralph Miliband and John Saville, eds, *Socialist Register 1977* (London 1977), 228–76; Webb, 'A Thoroughly English Dissident'; Johnson, *Agents Extraordinary*, 17 and 31, which notes that Edward sent Frank a copy of Caudwell's *Studies in a Dying Culture* (1938) for Christmas 1942.

24. On Frank Thompson, see Murray Hogben, 'E.P. Thompson, Historian, Peace Activist', *Whig Standard Magazine*, 4 June 1988; Dyson, 'The Blood of a Poet', *Disturbing the Universe*, 33–7; Hobsbawm, 'E.P. Thompson: Obituary', *The Independent*, 30 August 1993; Johnson, *Agents Extraordinary*, 16–24; Peter Scott, 'Voluntary Exile from History's Mainstream', *Times Higher Education Supplement*, 27 June 1980, 7. The lines of verse relating to Spain refer to the young Marxist critic who went to his death fighting fascism in the Spanish Civil War, Christopher Caudwell, and come from R.F. Willets, 'Homage to Christopher Caudwell', *Envoi*, 15 (1962), cited in E.P. Thompson, 'Caudwell', *Socialist Register, 1977* (London 1977), 272.

25. 'E.P. Thompson: Interview', *Visions of History*, 11; Sarkar, 'Afterword', *The Other Side of the Medal*, 114; E.P. Thompson, *'Alien Homage'*, 105.

26. I have drawn on Johnson, *Agents Extraordinary*, although it sometimes lapses into a patronizing tone. Also Dyson, *Disturbing the Universe*, 37.

27. Thompson, 'The Secret State within the State', *New Statesman* (10 November 1978), 618, drawing on P. Auty and R. Clogg, *British Policy Towards Wartime Resistance in Yugoslavia and Greece* (London 1975), 221–8.

28. Dyson, *Disturbing the Universe*, esp. 37–8; Johnson, *Agents Extraordinary*, esp. 167–8; E.P. Thompson, 'The Secret State within the State', 616; T.J. Thompson and E.P. Thompson, eds, *There is a Spirit in Europe: a Memoir of Frank Thompson* (London 1947), 20–21, quoted in Thompson, 'Letter to Kolakowski', 160. Note Edward John Thompson's poetic comments on war prisoners in 'And Sitting Down, They Watched Him There', and 'Prisoners of War: Damascus,

1918–19', in *The Thracian Stranger*, 102–3.

29. The above draws on various pieces in E.P. Thompson, *The Heavy Dancers*, 169–246, most especially 'The Liberation of Perugia', 'Overture to Cassino', 'Cassino: Coda', and 'Mr Attlee and the Gadarene Swine'. Note also Thompson, 'The Secret State within the State', esp. 618; Fred Inglis, 'Thompson Invictus', *The Nation* (20 September 1993), 265. Thompson's first published prose would be a short story, 'Drava Bridge', which centred on the experience of World War II. First appearing in *Our Time* (December 1945), it was later reprinted in the American Marxist journal *New Masses*. It appears in *The Heavy Dancers*, 231–7. See also E.P. Thompson, 'Homage to Thomas McGrath', *TriQuarterly*, 70 (Fall 1987), 116–17. For Thompson's father's war verse, see Edward John Thompson, *Poems: 1902–1925*, 16; *The Thracian Stranger*, 102–3.

30. Thompson, 'The Secret State within the State', 618; Dyson, *Disturbing the Universe*, 39.

31. Bryan D. Palmer, *The Making of E.P. Thompson: Marxism, Humanism, and History* (Toronto 1980), 33–4; 'E.P. Thompson: Interview', *Visions of History*, 12; E.P. Thompson, *The Railway: An Adventure in Construction* (London 1948), esp. viii, x, 3, 24; Thompson, 'An Open Letter to Kolakowski', 160; Thompson, 'America and the War Movement', in *The Heavy Dancers*, 42; Webb, 'A Thoroughly English Dissident'; Dorothy Thompson interviewed by Sheila Rowbotham, 'The Personal and the Political', *New Left Review*, 200 (July–August 1993), 94–5. Thompson's comment on 'The Railway' was in response to my attempt to track down the pamphlet he edited on the experience. At the point when it was written I had met Edward once and corresponded once. He was helpful, but impatient, and not at all convinced that I was the proper person even to be thinking about such matters. He later relented, softened, and grew supportive. Thompson to Palmer, 18 June 1978.

32. This paragraph draws upon 'E.P. Thompson: Interview', *Visions of History*, 12; Thompson, 'Homage to Thomas McGrath', 116; E.P. Thompson, *The Fascist Threat to Britain* (London 1947), 16; E.P. Thompson, 'Response to Tony Benn', in Ken Coates and Fred Singleton, eds, *The Just Society* (Nottingham 1977), 36–7; Thompson, 'The Secret State within the State', 618; Neal Ascherson, 'E.P. Thompson: Defender of the Faithful Few', *Independent on Sunday*, 5 September 1993; Thompson, 'Mr Attlee and the Gadarene Swine', in *The Heavy Dancers*, esp. 243. The sergeant major in India was John Saville. See Tariq Ali, *Street Fighting Years: An Autobiography of the Sixties* (London 1987), 71. Hobsbawm's *Independent* obituary, 30 August 1993, comments: 'Tradition and loyalty, within and outside the family, were important to Edward Thompson.' Terry Eagleton has identified the importance of 'metaphor, image, poetry' to Thompson in a review of *The Poverty of Theory* (1978) in Eagleton, 'The Poetry of E.P. Thompson', *Literature and History*, 5 (Autumn 1979), 139, but he then fails to explore these areas adequately. It comes as something of a shock to see historians of imperialism attributing Thompson's comments on the British Empire in the aftermath of the Falklands War as striking 'a new note in his work'. See Ben Shephard, 'Showbiz Imperialism: The Case of Peter Lobengula', in John M. Mackenzie, ed., *Imperialism and Popular Culture* (Manchester 1986), 94.

# Chapter 2

1. Thompson, *The Fascist Threat to Britain*, 5. The words on the post-war communist culture of contacts and friends actually come from Dorothy Thompson, but they could just as easily be Edward's. Dorothy Thompson, 'The Personal and the Political', 90–91.

2. The above paragraphs draw on Dorothy Thompson, unpublished typescript of an 'Introduction' to a collection of her published essays forthcoming with Verso, 1993, under the title *Outsiders*; Dorothy Thompson interview, 'The Public and the Private', 87–100; Amy Friedman, 'A Woman to Admire', *Whig-Standard Magazine*, 4 June 1988; and Richard Hoggart, 'Death of a Tireless and True Radical', *Observer*, 29 August 1993. Of course there are those who consider that Dorothy was exploited by Edward. For particularly offensive statements, to which Dorothy Thompson replies with restrained intelligence in her 'Introduction', see Marion Glastonbury, 'The Best Kept Secret – How Working Class Women Live and What They Know', *Women's Studies International Quarterly*, 2 (1979), 29; Dale Spender, *The Writing or the Sex? or why you don't have to read women's writing to know it's no good* (New York 1989), 142, 146. I once heard a feminist historian in the United States castigate the gender-specific language of the preface of *The Making of the English Working Class*, and then add, for good measure, that Dorothy was the only one in the family ever to have held 'a real job'. Apart from the untruth of this statement, it reeks of complacent elitism, implicitly defining jobs of real worth as university posts, and it panders to the very gender stereotypes one would think feminists should be opposing, implying that men *should* be the breadwinners, and households where women earn an income and men assume other responsibilities (some paid, some unpaid) are somehow dubious. All these matters are addressed thoughtfully in Dorothy Thompson, 'The Public and the Private'. On the communist milieu, see John Saville, 'May Day, 1937', in Asa Briggs and John Saville, eds, *Essays in Labour History, 1918–1939* (London 1977), 232–84. For a later new left and Edward's and Dorothy's importance, see David Widgery, 'Foreword', in Widgery, ed., *The Left in Britain, 1956–1968* (Harmondsworth 1976), esp. 14–15.

3. E.P. Thompson, *The Railway*, 20–21; Hobsbawm, 'The Historians' Group of the Communist Party', 25; Christopher Hill, 'Foreword', in Harvey J. Kaye, *The Education of Desire: Marxists and the Writing of History* (London 1992), ix–x; 'E.P. Thompson: Interview', *Visions of History*, 13; Dorothy Thompson, 'Introduction', *Outsiders*; Peter Searby, Robert W. Malcolmson and John Rule, 'Edward Thompson as a Teacher: Yorkshire and Warwick', in Malcolmson and Rule, eds, *Protest and Survival: Essays for E.P. Thompson* (London 1993); Peter Scott, 'Voluntary Exile from History's Mainstream', *Times Higher Education Supplement*, 27 June 1980, 7.

4. Hobsbawm, 'The Historians' Group of the Communist Party', 28; Bill Schwarz, ' "The People" in History: The Communist Party Historians' Group, 1946–1956', in *Making Histories: Studies in History-Writing and Politics* (London 1990), 44–95; Thompson, 'William Morris and the Moral Issues of To-Day', *Arena*, 2 (June–July 1951), 27; 'E.P. Thompson: Interview', *Visions of History*, 13; Dorothy Thompson, 'Introduction', *Outsiders*; Michael D. Bess, 'E.P. Thompson: The Historian as Activist', *American Historical Review*, 98 (February 1993), 20–21; Searby *et al.*, 'Edward Thompson as a Teacher', in *Protest and Survival*; Scott, 'Voluntary Exile', 7; E.P. Thompson, *William Morris* (1977), 769;

Thompson, 'Romanticism, Moralism, and Utopianism: The Case of William Morris', *New Left Review*, 99 (September–October 1976), 84; Thompson, 'The Massacre of the Innocents', adapted from 'On the Liberation of Seoul', *Arena* (1951), in *Infant and Emperor: Poems for Christmas* (London 1983), 12; Thompson, 'Caudwell', 273, n15, where the problematic phrase 'Jungle Marxism' appears.

5. Thompson, *The Fascist Threat to Britain*, 15; Searby *et al.*, 'Edward Thompson as a Teacher', *Protest and Survival*; Thompson, 'William Morris and the Moral Issues To-Day', *Arena*, 2 (June–July 1951), 27, 29; and, for a forceful statement on the reciprocities of collective Marxist scholarship: 'E.P. Thompson: Interview', *Visions of History*, 22. 'Literature' is almost absent from Stuart Macintyre's discussion of 'Literature and Education', in *A Proletarian Science: Marxism in Britain, 1917–1933* (London 1980), 66–90.

6. 'E.P. Thompson: Interview', *Visions of History*, 13; Scott, 'Voluntary Exile', 7; Thompson, *William Morris* (1977), 810; Thompson, 'Romanticism, Utopianism, and Moralism', 83–111. The importance of Morris was early alluded to in Anderson, *Arguments within English Marxism*; Palmer, *The Making of E.P. Thompson*, 36–40; John Goode, 'E.P. Thompson and "the Significance of Literature"', in Harvey J. Kaye and Keith McClelland, eds, *E.P. Thompson: Critical Perspectives* (Philadelphia 1990), 183–203. It is necessary to dissent from the overly schematic commentary on Morris/Thompson which, perhaps, owed much to the debate around *The Poverty of Theory*. See Richard Johnson, 'Three Problematics: Elements of a Theory of Working-Class Culture', in John Clarke, Chas Critcher and Richard Johnson, eds, *Working-Class Culture: Studies in History and Theory* (London 1979), esp. 213–14; Gregor McLennan, 'E.P. Thompson and the Discipline of Historical Context', in *Making Histories: Studies in History-Writing and Politics* (London 1982), 108. More offensive, perhaps, is the depoliticized scholasticism of Michael D. Bess, 'E.P. Thompson: The Historian as Activist', 21, which manages to avoid the Cold War context of Thompson's mid-1950s defence of Morris in Stalinist terms. The most thoroughgoing discussion of Thompson and Morris is Michael Francis McShane, ' "History and Hope": E.P. Thompson and *The Making of the English Working Class*', PhD thesis, McMaster University, 1990, 70–103.

7. Thompson, *William Morris* (1977), 1, 273, 699–700, 714, 809; Thompson, 'Romanticism, Utopianism, and Moralism', esp. 90, 109; Edward Thompson, *The Communism of William Morris: A Lecture Given on 4 May 1959 in the Hall of the Art Workers' Guild* (London 1965), esp. 1, 11; Thompson, 'Disenchantment or Default: A Lay Sermon', in Conor Cruise O'Brien and William Dean Vanech, eds, *Power and Consciousness* (London 1969), 149–82, esp. 175–6; Edward J. Thompson, *Rabindranath Tagore: His Life and Work* (1948), 94, 84; Edward John Thompson, *The Thracian Stranger*; Johnson, *Agents Extraordinary*, 24; and, on Blake, and his form, E.P. Thompson, 'Blake's Tone', *London Review of Books* (28 January 1993), 12–13; Thompson, 'London', in Michael Phillips, ed., *Interpreting Blake* (London 1978), 1–31.

8. Thompson, *Poverty of Theory*, esp. 247–62; Michael Merrill, 'An Interview with E.P. Thompson', *Radical History Review*, 3 (Fall 1976), 23–4; 'E.P. Thompson: Interview', *Visions of History*, 22; Thompson, *William Morris* (1977), 729, 786, 806; Thompson, *The Communism of William Morris*, esp. 8, 18–19; Thompson, 'William Morris and the Moral Issues To-Day', 30. For a different reading, see Anderson, *Arguments within English Marxism*, esp. 157–75. The verse is from Tom McGrath, quoted by Thompson in 'Disenchantment or Default', 180–81.

9. Many sources comment on the relationship between Thompson's 1955 and 1977 studies of Morris, looking at what Thompson himself refers to as 'casuistries explaining away what one should have repudiated in the character of Stalinism' (Thompson, *William Morris* [1977], 769, 806; Merrill, 'An Interview with E.P. Thompson', 10, 23). See, for instance, Palmer, *Making of E.P. Thompson*, 36–40; McShane, '"History and Hope": E.P. Thompson and *The Making of the English Working Class*', 93–6; Anderson, *Arguments within English Marxism*, esp. 171–2; McLennan, 'E.P. Thompson and the Discipline of Historical Context', *Making Histories*, 108.

10. Thompson, 'William Morris and the Moral Issues To-Day', 27, 30.

11. Much of what follows in this section draws on Peter Searby's discussion of Thompson's Yorkshire years in adult education in Peter Searby, Robert W. Malcolmson and John Rule, 'Edward Thompson as a Teacher', in Malcolmson and Rule, eds, *Protest and Survival*, pp. 1–17. I am extremely grateful to Professors Searby and Malcolmson for making this manuscript available to me. Searby has done important work in the Leeds Archives, and interviewed a number of Thompson's students. See also Roger T. Fieldhouse, *Adult Education and the Cold War: Liberal Values Under Siege, 1946–1951* (Leeds 1985); J.F.C. Harrison, *Learning and Living, 1790–1960* (London 1961).

12. Thompson, *William Morris* (1977), 366–426; 'E.P. Thompson: Interview', *Visions of History*, 13, 23; Dorothy Thompson, 'The Personal and the Political', 91; Rowbotham, 'E.P. Thompson: A Life of Radical Dissent', 14; Hogben, 'E.P. Thompson', *Whig-Standard*, 9; E.P. Thompson, 'On History, Sociology, and Historical Relevance', *British Journal of Sociology*, 27 (1976), 396, 402. The Hardy quote, from Thompson's paper 'Against University Standards', appears in Searby, 'Thompson as a Teacher', in Malcolmson and Rule, eds, *Protest and Survival*, p. 5. Certainly communists were present in adult education, but statements of revolutionary intentions could not but have exacerbated latent tensions. See Roger Fieldhouse, 'Oxford and Adult Education', in W. John Morgan and Peter Preston, eds, *Raymond Williams: Politics, Education, Letters* (New York 1993); John McIlroy and Sallie Westwood, eds, *Border Country: Raymond Williams in Adult Education* (Leicester 1993).

13. E.P. Thompson, *Education and Experience: Fifth Mansbridge Memorial Lecture* (Leeds 1968), esp. 1, 2, 6, 18, 22–3. On Thompson's father, Indian education, and connection with ordinary people, see Chaudhuri, 'Bankura's Englishman'; and Thompson and Thompson, 'Memories of Tagore'. See also the later reflections on Wordsworth in a review of Roe's *Wordsworth and Coleridge*, E.P. Thompson, 'Wordsworth's Crisis', *London Review of Books*, 10 (8 December 1988), 3–6.

14. [E.P. Thompson], 'Organizing the Left', *Times Literary Supplement*, 19 February 1971, 203–4.

15. Milton is quoted in E.P. Thompson, *The Struggle for a Free Press* (London 1952), 8, and this quote would resurface in a series of writings: 'Winter Wheat in Omsk', *World News*, 3 (30 June 1956), 408–9 (Thompson's first public criticism of the Communist Party); 'Revolution Again! Or Shut Your Ears and Run', *New Left Review*, 6 (November–December 1960), 20 (Thompson's reply to critics of the book he edited in 1960, *Out of Apathy*); and as the last unacknowledged line in 'Postscript', *Whigs and Hunters: The Origin of the Black Act* (London 1977), 311. Part of this I reconstructed myself (Palmer, *Making of E.P. Thompson*, 53), but I was also guided by McShane, '"History and Hope": E.P. Thompson and *The Making of the English Working Class*', 137.

16. Thompson and Saville, 'Editorial', *New Reasoner: A Quarterly Journal of Socialist Humanism*, 2 (Winter 1957–8), 1–4. The next issue also carried a lengthy piece that made the Marx/Blake encounter explicit: Kenneth Muir, 'Marx's Conversion to Communism', *New Reasoner*, 3 (1957–8), 57–64.

17. Thompson, 'Open Letter to Kolakowski', 106; Thompson, 'Socialist Humanism', 124–5; Thompson, 'The New Left', *New Reasoner*, 9 (Summer 1959), 1; Thompson, 'Winter Wheat in Omsk', 408, quoted in McShane, ' "History and Hope" ': E.P. Thompson and *The Making of the English Working Class*', 141. Thompson's actual written commentary on Blake has been limited, but his four-decade engagement with the radical craftsman culminated in the late-1993, posthumous publication of *Witness Against the Beast: William Blake and the Moral Law*. A preview was offered in Thompson, 'London', in Phillips, ed., *Interpreting Blake*, 5–31, which develops ideas that first surfaced in *New Reasoner*, 3 (1957–8), esp. 68; and a series of lectures in North America, which included the distinguished Alexander Lectures at the University of Toronto (1978), public lectures on Blake at Brown University (the last of which, given on 5 November 1980, was taped and graciously provided to me by Paul Buhle), and a series of talks given to Thompson's seminars at Queen's University over the winter term, 1988. See also Thompson, 'Blake's Tone', a review of Jon Mee's *Dangerous Enthusiasm: William Blake and the Cutlure of Radicalism in the 1790s* (1992), which appeared in *London Review of Books*, 28 January 1993, 12–13; and Heather Glen, *Vision and Disenchantment: Blake's Songs and Wordsworth's Lyrical Ballads* (Cambridge 1983). The final quote on the Beast is from E.P. Thompson, 'Outside the Whale', in Thompson, ed., *Out of Apathy* (London 1960), 191, reprinted in *The Poverty of Theory*, 32.

18. See, among many possible sources, John Saville, 'The XXth Congress and the British Communist Party', Malcolm MacEwen, 'The Day the Party Had to Stop', Margot Heinemann, '1956 and the Communist Party'; Mervyn Jones, 'Days of Tragedy and Farce', all in Ralph Miliband and John Saville, eds, *The Socialist Register, 1976* (London 1976), 1–57, 67–88; Ralph Miliband, 'John Saville: A Presentation', in David E. Martin and David Rubenstein, eds, *Ideology and the Labour Movement* (London 1979), esp. 24–7; Neal Wood, *Communism and the British Intellectuals* (New York 1959), 182–213; Dorothy Thompson, 'Introduction', *Outsiders*; Kate Soper, 'Socialist Humanism', in Harvey J. Kaye and Keith McClelland, eds, *E.P. Thompson: Critical Perspectives* (Philadelphia 1992), 204–32; Palmer, *Making of E.P. Thompson*, 45–63; David Widgery, ed., *The Left in Britain, 1956–1968*, 19–72. The Thompson quote is from 'Editorial', *New Reasoner*, 10 (Autumn 1959), 7–8. John Saville has recently returned to this issue in 'Edward Thompson, The Communist Party, and 1956', in *The Socialist Register, 1993* (London 1993), pp. 1–13.

19. As late as 1976, Thompson was able to refer in a United States interview to 'a side of my writing that is less known in the United States, which is a very distinctly political engagement': 'E.P. Thompson: Interview', *Visions of History*, 10. This changed. Thompson's *The Poverty of Theory* was composed of four essays. 'Outside the Whale', first published in 1960, was an attempt to address the drift to complicity among once committed intellectuals (with an emphasis on Auden and Orwell), insisting that 'socialist humanism' had to define ways of using existing human strengths and values to 'break simultaneously with the pessimism of the old world and the authoritarianism of the new'. 'The Peculiarities of the English', a polemic against the *New Left Review*'s Perry Anderson and Tom Nairn, offered strong refusals of what Thompson conceived of as the second new left's ruthless theoretical tidiness, in which bolts

were 'being shot against experience and enquiry'. Against this, Thompson declared: 'there are some of us who will man the stations of 1956 again'. 'An Open Letter to Kolakowski' refers to 'the moment of common aspiration: "1956"', while 'The Poverty of Theory: or, an Orrery of Errors' declares: 'My dues to "1956" have now been paid in full.'

20. Thompson, *The Making of the English Working Class* (Harmondsworth 1968), 497; Palmer, *Making of E.P. Thompson*, 25–6; Thompson, 'In Praise of Hangmen', in 'Open Letter to Kolakowski', 131–2; 'Imre Nagy: Murdered, June 1958', *New Reasoner*, 5 (Summer 1958), 88; 'Editorial', *New Reasoner*, 7 (Winter 1958–9), 11; Imre Nagy, *On Communism: In Defence of the New Course* (London 1956), 49, 43, cited in McShane, ' "History and Hope": E.P. Thompson and *The Making of the English Working Class*', 147; Thompson, 'Mother and Child', in *Infant and Emperor*, 10. Thompson's desires and frustrations around poetry are the subject of some comment in the 1956 Saville–Thompson correspondence, touched on in Saville, 'The XXth Congress and the British Communist Party', 18–19.

21. On international themes see, for a brief selection only: Thompson, 'Through the Smoke of Budapest', *The Reasoner*, 3 (November 1956, supplement), 1–7, reproduced in Widgery, ed., *The Left in Britain*, 66–72; *New Reasoner*, 2 (Autumn 1957), esp. 56–64, 99–102; 3 (Winter 1957–8), 87–93; 4 (Spring 1958), 107–13; 6 (Autumn 1958), 32–4; 7 (Winter 1957–8), 1–11; 9 (Summer 1959), 141–4. Thompson's major statements were: 'Socialist Humanism: An Epistle to the Philistines', *New Reasoner*, 1 (Summer 1957), 105–43; 'God and King and Law', 3, (Winter 1957–8), 69–86; 'Agency and Choice: A Reply to Criticism', 5 (Summer 1958), 89–106; 'The New Left', 9 (Summer 1959), 1–17; 'An Psessay in Ephology', 10 (Autumn 1959), 1–8. For responses to Thompson, many replied to in his 'Agency and Choice', see Harry Hanson, 'An Open Letter to Edward Thompson', Charles Taylor, 'Marxism and Humanism', *New Reasoner*, 2 (Autumn 1957), 79–98; Jack Lindsay and John St John, 'Socialist Humanism', Tim Enright, 'Materialism or Eclecticism', 3 (1957–8), 94–112; and, in some senses, Alasdair MacIntyre, 'Notes from the Moral Wilderness, I', 7 (Winter 1958–9), 90–100; 'Notes from the Moral Wilderness, II', 8 (Spring 1959), 89–98. There were those on the Trotskyist side of the debate who were excluded, complaining that 'Pre-Khrushchev anti-Stalinists are too "dogmatic", too fond of raising questions of principle to be permitted to rub shoulders with William Blake, Harry Hanson, and Korni Zilliacus.' See Peter Fryer, 'Lenin as Philosopher', *Labour Review*, 2 (September–October 1957), 136–47; 'Rejected by the *New Reasoner*', *Labour Review*, 3 (May–June–July 1958), 92–3; 'An Unreasonable Reasoner', *Labour Review*, 3 (March–April 1958), 34–6.

22. See, for instance, E.P. Thompson, 'The New Left', *New Reasoner*, 9 (Summer 1959), 1–17; Thompson, 'A Psessay in Ephology', ibid., 10 (Autumn 1959), 1–8; Thompson, 'Nato, Neutralism, and Survival', *Universities and Left Review*, 4 (Spring 1958), 49–51; Thompson, 'At the Point of Decay', and 'Revolution', in Thompson, *Out of Apathy*, 3–18, 287–308, esp. quoted passages on 10–11, 15, 308; and the following articles from the *New Left Review*: 'The Long Revolution, I', 9 (May–June 1961), 24–33; 'The Long Revolution, II', 10 (July–August 1961), 34–9; 'The Point of Production', 1 (January–February 1960), 68–70; 'Comments on Revolution', 4 (July–August 1960), 3–11; 'Countermarching to Armageddon', 4 (July–August 1960), 62–4; 'Revolution Again! or Shut Your Ears and Run', 6 (November–December 1960), 18–31. See also Thompson, 'Remembering C. Wright Mills', in *The Heavy Dancers*, 261–74; McShane,

' "History and Hope": E.P. Thompson and *The Making of the English Working Class*', 169–212, which has much useful comment on the *Universities and Left Review*, and Soper, 'Socialist Humanism', 217–21. For views somewhat at odds with those of Thompson, see Perry Anderson, 'The Left in the Fifties', *New Left Review*, 29 (January–February 1965), 3–18, which tilts towards the condescending; and Raymond Williams, 'The British Left', *New Left Review*, 30 (March–April 1965), 18–26. For comment on the first Campaign for Nuclear Disarmament, see Richard Taylor and Nigel Young, eds, *Campaigns for Peace: British Peace Movements in the Twentieth Century* (Manchester 1987).

23. On this rupture, see the original combative texts: Perry Anderson, 'Origins of the Present Crisis', *New Left Review*, 23 (January–February 1964), 26–53; Anderson, 'Socialism and Pseudo-Empiricism: The Myths of Edward Thompson', *New Left Review*, 35 (Janury–February 1968), 2–42; Tom Nairn, 'The English Working Class', *New Left Review*, 24 (March–April 1964), 43–57; E.P. Thompson, 'The Peculiarities of the English', *Socialist Register 1965* (London 1965), 311–62. See also Palmer, *Making of E.P. Thompson*, 55–64; Peter Sedgwick, 'The Two New Lefts', in Widgery, ed., *The Left in Britain*, 131–53. The humorous self-characterizations of Thompson and Saville appear in *New Reasoner*, 5 (1958), 152. Note the recent discussion in Lin Chun, *The British New Left* (Edinburgh 1993) and the fictional treatment in Clancy Sigal, *The Secret Defector* (New York 1992).

24. Thompson, 'Remembering C. Wright Mills', *Peace News*, 22, 29 November 1963, quoted in Sedgwick, 'The Two New Lefts', 131; Thompson, 'The Peculiarities of the English', *The Socialist Register 1965* (London 1965), 348; 'E.P. Thompson: Interview', *Visions of History*, 10.

25. Note, in particular, Thompson, 'Through the Smoke of Budapest', *The Reasoner*, 3 (November 1956), reprinted in Widgery, ed., *The Left in Britain*, 66–72, esp. 69; Thompson, 'Socialist Humanism', and 'Agency and Choice'; and the comment on these statements in Palmer, *Making of E.P. Thompson*, 48–51; and Thompson, 'The Peculiarities of the English', in *The Poverty of Theory and Other Essays*, 35–91, esp. 87–8. For statements on revolution, see Thompson, 'Revolution', in Thompson, ed., *Out of Apathy* (London 1960), 287–308; Thompson, 'Revolution Again! Or Shut Your Ears and Run', *New Left Review*, 6 (November–December 1960), esp. 31. On class and base and superstructure, see Ellen Meiksins Wood, 'The Politics of Theory and the Concept of Class: E.P. Thompson and His Critics', *Studies in Political Economy*, 9 (Fall 1982), 45–76; Wood, 'Falling Through the Cracks: E.P. Thompson and the Debate on Base and Superstructure', in Kaye and McClelland, eds, *E.P. Thompson*, 125–52.

26. Thompson, 'A Psessay in Ephology', 3; Thompson, ed., *Out of Apathy*, esp. the essays 'At the Point of Decay' and 'Revolution' by Thompson; and 'The Supply of Demand' (Stuart Hall) and 'Breaking the Chains of Reason' (Alasdair MacIntyre); E.P. Thompson and Raymond Williams, eds, *May Day Manifesto 1968* (Harmondsworth 1968), and the comment on the 1960s in Kate Soper, 'Socialist Humanism', 217–21; Fred Inglis, 'A Difficult Country', *New Universities Quarterly*, 32 (Spring 1978), 224, 226–7; E.P. Thompson to Michael Bess, 2 April 1989, quoted in Bess, 'E.P. Thompson: The Historian as Activist', 25; 'European Nuclear Disarmament: Interview with E.P. Thompson', *Socialist Review*, 58 (July–August 1981), 33; Thompson to Palmer, 1 February 1993. The miners occupied a special, affectionate place in Thompson's understanding of the importance of class struggle in England. See, for instance, Thompson, 'On History, Sociology, and Historical Relevance', *British Journal of Sociology*, 27

(1976), 387–402; and, most importantly, the evocative tribute in Thompson, 'A Special Case', *New Society*, 24 February 1972, reprinted in Thompson, *Writing by Candlelight* (London 1980), 65–76.

27. See Raphael Samuel, 'Born Again Socialism'; and Clancy Sigal, 'A Rootless American', in Oxford University Socialist Discussion Group, ed., *Out of Apathy: Voices of the New Left Thirty Years On* (London 1989), esp. 49, 133. For a fictional portrait of Dorothy and Edward from Sigal, see *Weekend in Dinlock* (London 1960), 82–3.

28. C. Wright Mills, *The Marxists* (New York 1967), 97–9.

## Chapter 3

1. Perry Anderson, 'Diary', *London Review of Books*, 21 October 1993, 24–5.

2. Thompson, *The Making of the English Working Class* (1968), 13 (all references to this text in this section will be to this edition). Hobsbawm points out that according to the Arts and Humanities Citation Index, Thompson was cited more frequently than any other historian in the twentieth-century world, and that he was, indeed, one of the 250 most frequently cited authors of all time. Hobsbawm, 'E.P. Thompson: Obituary', *The Independent*, 30 August 1993.

3. On the descriptive side, see especially Harvey J. Kaye, *The British Marxist Historians* (Oxford 1984), 167–220; Kaye, *The Education of Desire: Marxists and the Writing of History* (New York 1992), 98–115; E.K. Trimberger, 'E.P. Thompson: Understanding the Process of History', in Theda Skocpol, ed., *Vision and Method in Historical Sociology* (Cambridge 1984), 211–43. For the influence on American social history, see Alan Dawley, 'E.P. Thompson and the Peculiarities of the Americans', *Radical History Review*, 19 (1978–9), 33–59. Note also F.K. Donnelly, 'Ideology and Early English Working-Class History: Edward Thompson and His Critics', *Social History*, 3 (1976), 219–38.

4. Anthony Giddens, 'Out of the Orrery: E.P. Thompson on Consciousness and History', in Giddens, *Social Theory and Modern Sociology* (Stanford, CA 1987), 203–24; Renato Rosaldo, 'Celebrating Thompson's Heroes: Social Analysis in History and Anthropology', in Kaye and McClelland, eds, *E.P. Thompson*, 103–24; Suzanne Desan, 'Crowds, Community, and Ritual in the Work of E.P. Thompson and Natalie Davis', in Lynn Hunt, ed., *The New Cultural History* (Berkeley, CA 1989), 47–71.

5. See, for instance, Richard Johnson, 'Edward Thompson, Eugene Genovese, and Socialist-Humanist History', *History Workshop Journal*, 6 (Autumn 1978), 79–100; Johnson, 'Culture and the Historians', and 'Three Problematics: Elements of a Theory of Working-Class Culture', in John Clarke, Chas Critcher and Richard Johnson, eds, *Working-Class Culture: Studies in History and Theory* (London 1979), 41–71, 201–37; Gregor McLennan, 'E.P. Thompson and the Discipline of Historical Context', and 'Philosophy and History: Some Issues in Recent Marxist History'; and Richard Johnson, 'Reading for the Best Marx: History-Writing and Historical Abstraction', in Richard Johnson, Gregor McLennan, Bill Schwarz and David Sutton, eds, *Making Histories: Studies in History-Writing and Politics* (London 1982), 96–204.

6. Anderson, *Arguments within English Marxism*, esp. 16–58; Geoff Eley, 'Edward

Thompson, Social History and Political Culture: The Making of a Working-Class Public, 1780–1850', and William H. Sewell, 'How Classes Are Made: Critical Reflections on E.P. Thompson's Theory of Working-Class Formation', in Kaye and McClelland, eds, *E.P. Thompson*, 12–77; Craig Calhoun, *The Question of Class Struggle: Social Foundations of Popular Radicalism During the Industrial Revolution* (Chicago 1982); E.J. Hobsbawm, 'The Formation of British Working-Class Culture', and 'The Making of the Working Class, 1870–1914', in Hobsbawm, *Workers: Worlds of Labor* (New York 1984), 176–213.

7.  I regard as useful Catherine Hall, 'The Tale of Samuel and Jemima: Gender and Working-class Culture in Nineteenth-century England', in Kaye and McClelland, eds, *E.P. Thompson*, 78–102; James Epstein, 'Understanding the Cap of Liberty: Symbolic Practice and Social Conflict in Early Nineteenth-Century England', *Past & Present*, 122 (1989), 75–118. If there is indeed a point in Joan W. Scott, 'Women in *The Making of the English Working Class*', in Scott, *Gender and the Politics of History* (New York 1988), 68–92, and Scott, 'Experience', in Judith Butler and Joan W. Scott, eds, *Feminists Theorize the Political* (New York 1992), 22–40 – *and there is* – it is nevertheless squandered in obscurantism and a disturbing capacity to misread. My own views are put forward in Palmer, *Descent into Discourse: The Reification of Language and the Writing of Social History* (Philadelphia 1990), 78–86, and I remain unrepentant. Thompson, of course, would have replied to Scott had not ill-health and pressing political and writing commitments in the last years of his life made this impossible. It is perhaps appropriate, therefore, to quote from personal correspondence.

> I've glanced through Joan *very* fast, and it's a quite different piece from her first shot at this at the AHA. Indeed at several places she's arguing opposite points. She's obviously heard on the gossip network that I was cross about her misquotes. So she's taken those out. It's a more intelligent, more interesting piece, and she's determined to get me, one way or the other. She's introduced one or two *new* misquotations & I'm convinced she's a victim of word–blindness, which is to be pitied in her since it makes preoccupation with Language & Discourse difficult. ... Her book hasn't got to this side yet. I *will* someday write a comment. (Thompson to Palmer, 17 March 1989)

> This Scott is better than first version, & she has a point about gendered class. I didn't do it ... it *was* so gendered. As regards Barbara Taylor, her women (of course I didn't know 1/4 as much as she found out) didn't appear in *Making* for the boring academic reason they weren't 'my period' – they mostly got going after 1830 and I could only wave a hand toward them. Scott's version 1 was even sillier on Joanna Southcott. I'm convinced she hasn't even read John Harrison's sane and sympathetic account of her. I liked v. much the way you exposed her mis-use of 'paradox of feeling'. But all you do is expose yourself as an Idiot, brother: there's NO Way you can win against that on-rolling fashion-machine – you simply point yourself out to be rolled over next. I accept Jim Epstein's review of *Making* on women ... in recent *P & P*. (Thompson to Palmer, 26 May 1989)

8.  For exceptions, see Henry Abelove's brief but often suggestive comments in his review of *The Poverty of Theory* in *History and Theory*, 21 (1980), 132–42; and McShane's ' "History and Hope": E.P. Thompson and *The Making of the English Working Class*', which, while overly in the mode of intellectual history, does try to excavate the relationship between Romanticism, Marxism, and Thompson's

writing of working-class history.

9.   E.P. Thompson, 'Homage to Tom Maguire', in Asa Briggs and John Saville, eds, *Essays in Labour History* (London 1960), 276–316; Hogben, 'E.P. Thompson, Historian and Peace Activist', *Whig-Standard Magazine*, 4 June 1988, 9; Scott, 'Voluntary Exile from History's Mainstream', *Times Higher Education Supplement*, 27 June 1980, 7; 'E.P. Thompson: Interview', *Visions of History*, 6–7, 14–15; Sheila Rowbotham, 'In Search of Carpenter', in Rowbotham, *Dreams and Dilemmas: Collected Writings* (London 1983), 242–3, explaining Rowbotham and Jeffrey Weeks, *Socialism and the New Life: The Personal and Sexual Politics of Edward Carpenter and Havelock Ellis* (London 1977). Note also Rowbotham's comment in 'Search and Subject, Threading Circumstance', in *Dreams and Dilemmas*, 171–2; and, on listening, Bess, 'E.P. Thompson: the Historian as Activist', 19–38.

10.   Thompson, *The Making of the English Working Class*, 258, 296, 346, 351, 384, 820. Also Thompson, 'Blake's Tone', *London Review of Books*; Sewell, 'Thompson's Theory of Working-Class Formation', 75. Thompson, 'Powers and Names', *London Review of Books*, 23 January 1986, 10.

11.   Thompson, *The Making of the English Working Class*, 195, 203; Tim Mason, 'The Making of the English Working Class', *History Workshop Journal*, 7 (1979), 224–5; Thompson, 'Responses to Reality', *New Society* (4 October 1973), 33–5; and, for Thompson's understandings of where other work has surpassed his own: Thompson, 'The Very Type of the "Respectable" Artisan', *New Society* (3 May 1979), 275–7 (reviewing Prothero's *Artisans and Politics in Early 19th Century London: John Gast and His Times*) or, in the case of an even more critical review, Thompson, 'Testing Class Struggle', *Times Literary Supplement*, 3 March 1974 (reviewing Foster's *Class Struggle and the Industrial Revolution*).

12.   Thompson, *The Making of the English Working Class*, 915.

13.   Thompson, *Education and Experience*, 13–14 and, for an interesting statement on experiential versus experience, see Sewell, 'Thompson's Theory of Working-Class Formation', 67–8. It is perhaps within an appreciation of this context of ideological pressure that Jacques Rancière's *The Nights of Labor: The Workers' Dream in Nineteenth-Century France* (Philadelphia 1989) can be read against its author's interpretive grain.

14.   Thompson, 'The Peculiarities of the English', *Socialist Register, 1965*, 311–62; and, for an extension of the 'warrening' argument, John Saville, *1848: The British State and the Chartist Movement* (Cambridge 1987), 208–10; Palmer, *Making of E.P. Thompson*, 65–82; and Stuart Macintyre, 'The Making of the Australian Working Class: An Historiographical Survey', *Historical Studies*, 18 (1978), 233–53 (for influence of *The Making* abroad); Thompson, 'Responses to Reality', *New Society* (4 October 1973), 33–5.

15.   For Thompson's teaching at Warwick, I rely on the relevant discussion in Robert W. Malcolmson, John Rule and Peter Searby, 'Edward Thompson as a Teacher: Yorkshire and Warwick', in Malcolmson and Rule, eds, *Protest and Survival*, esp. 17–18; Douglas Hay, 'Edward Thompson as a Teacher', comments at a Memorial for E.P. Thompson, York University, 15 September 1993; Anna Davin, 'Memories of E.P. Thompson', 1, 15. To suggest, as does Anderson's *London Review of Books* 'Diary', that the move from industrial-capitalist Halifax, Yorkshire to the countryside of Wick Episcopi, Worcester-shire implied a shift in political sensitivities that prefigured Thompson's increasing distance from class and a consequent 'modulation in his writing' is

to push a geographical determinism rather far. Anderson's interesting abbreviations concerning Thompson's intellectual and political voice can, of course, be interpreted differently.

16. Consider the case of Thompson's shifting interpretation of the wife sale. In *The Making of the English Working Class* (1963), 410–11 it is acknowledged that the practice was used as a form of divorce when no other possibilities existed for the poor to address marital breakdown. But in the main, Thompson considered the ritual barbaric. Five years later, in the 1968 edition (451), these comments were excised. More considered comment was later offered piecemeal in a series of essays: Thompson, 'Anthropology and the Discipline of Historical Context', 52, 55; Thompson, 'Folklore, Anthropology, and Social History', *Indian Historical Review*, 3 (1978), 247–66, with comment on the wife sale on 252–3, and on Brand, 248–51; Thompson, 'Eighteenth-Century English Society: Class Struggle without Class', *Social History*, 3 (1978), 156. Other work: 'Rough Music: Le charivari anglais', *Annales: E.S.C.*, 27 (1972), 285–312; 'The Grid of Inheritance: A Comment', in Jack Goody, Joan Thirsk and E.P. Thompson, eds, *Family and Inheritance: Rural Society in Western Europe, 1200–1800* (London 1976), 328–60; 'Patrician Society, Plebeian Culture', *Society for the Study of Labour History Bulletin*, 27 (1973), 26–7; 'Patrician Society, Plebeian Culture', *Journal of Social History*, 7 (1974), 381–405; 'Time, Work-Discipline and Industrial Capitalism', *Past & Present*, 38 (December 1967), 56–97; 'The Moral Economy of the English Crowd in the Eighteenth Century', *Past & Present*, 50 (1971), 76–136. The student is quoted in Malcolmson, Rule and Searby, 'Edward Thompson as a Teacher: Yorkshire and Warwick', 18; note also Christopher Hitchens, 'Minority Report', *The Nation* (27 September 1993), 306. For the intellectual impact of this period, see the creative applications of Thompson's insights in two books by James C. Scott: *Weapons of the Weak: Everyday Forms of Peasant Resistance* (New Haven, CT 1985); *Domination and the Arts of Resistance: Hidden Transcripts* (New Haven, CT 1990).

17. See, for instance, E.P. Thompson, 'Mayhew and the *Morning Chronicle*', in Eileen Yeo and E.P. Thompson, eds, *The Unknown Mayhew* (New York 1971), 11–50.

18. See the often anonymous reviews: Thompson, 'Man Bites Yeoman', *Times Literary Supplement* (11 December 1969), 1413–16; Thompson, 'Glandular Aggression', *New Society* (19 January 1967), 100–01; Thompson, 'Land of Our Fathers', *Times Literary Supplement* (16 February 1967), 117–18; Thompson, 'Law as Part of a Culture', *Times Literary Supplement* (24 April 1969), 425–7; Thompson, 'The Book of Numbers', *Times Literary Supplement* (9 December 1965), 1117–18; and note, for a later statement on another Laslett text: 'Under the Same Roof-Tree', *Times Literary Supplement* (4 May 1973), 485–7; Thompson, 'History from Below', *Times Literary Supplement* (7 April 1966), 279–80; and Thompson, 'Preface', in Staughton Lynd, *Class Conflict, Slavery, and the United States Constitution* (New York 1967), ix–xiii. For more on the discipline of historical context, see Thompson, 'Anthropology and the Discipline of Historical Context', *Midland History*, 1 (1972), 41–55. On Thompson's appearance, note Robert Malcolmson, 'E.P. Thompson, 1924–1993: Mentor Extraordinaire', *Queen's Quarterly*, 100 (Fall 1993), pp. 742–8.

19. See Douglas Hay, Peter Linebaugh, John G. Rule, E.P. Thompson and Carl Winslow, *Albion's Fatal Tree: Crime and Society in Eighteenth-Century England* (New York 1975); E.P. Thompson, *Whigs and Hunters: The Origin of the Black Act* (London 1977) – this second edition offering, on 301–11, Thompson's response to hostile critics, especially John Cannon, *History* (October 1976);

J.C.D. Clark, 'The Namierism of the Left', *Cambridge Review*, 22 October 1976. Valued exchanges took place around Alexander Pope and the Windsor Blacks. See Pat Rogers, 'A Pope Family Scandal', *Times Literary Supplement* (31 August 1973), 1005; Thompson, 'Alexander Pope and the Windsor Blacks', ibid. (7 September 1973), 1031–3; Howard Erskine–Hill, 'Alexander Pope and the Windsor Forest Blacks', ibid. (14 September 1973), 1056; Andrew Varney, 'Pope and the Windsor Blacks', ibid. (21 September 1973). Stone, 'Whigs, Marxists, and Poachers', *New York Review of Books*, is, in its American distanced way, more good-humoured than much of the antagonistic conservatism of Clark–Cannon. For more elaboration on the content of this work, see Palmer, *Making of E.P. Thompson*, 83–103.

# Chapter 4

1. 'Herbert G. Gutman: Interview', *Visions of History*, 201. Thompson's view of Gutman appears in 'The Mind of a Historian', a review of a posthumously published collection of Gutman's essays, *Power and Culture* (1987), which appeared in *Dissent* (Fall 1988), 493–6.

2. E.P. Thompson, 'Highly Confidential: A Personal Comment by the Editor', in Thompson, ed., *Warwick University Ltd: Industry, Management and the Universities* (Middlesex 1970), 157; 'E.P. Thompson: Interview', *Visions of History*, 14; Dorothy Thompson, 'Introduction', *Outsiders*.

3. Thompson, 'Mayhew and the *Morning Chronicle*', in Yeo and Thompson, eds, *The Unknown Mayhew*, 16; Thompson, 'Highly Confidential', in *Warwick*, 155. On British universities and the student revolt of 1968, see David Caute, *The Year of the Barricades: A Journey Through 1968* (New York 1988), 345–74. For a personal account of one of Thompson's first North American students, see Peter Linebaugh, 'From the Upper West Side to Wick Episcopi', *New Left Review*, 201 (September/October 1993), 18–25. I have also benefited from hearing Barbara Winslow's remarks at the AHA Thompson Memorial, San Francisco, 8 January 1994; and the comment in Davin, 'Memories of E.P. Thompson', pp. 1, 15–16.

4. The above paragraph draws on Thompson, *Warwick*.

5. Note E.P. Thompson, 'The Business University', and 'A Report on Lord Radcliffe', articles which originally appeared in *New Society* in 1970, reprinted in Thompson, *Writing by Candlelight* (London 1980), 30–38; Melvyn Dubofsky, unpublished recollection of E.P. Thompson, Conversational Monitor System, September 1993; Bess, 'E.P. Thompson: The Historian as Activist', 25–6, where Bess draws obliquely on Thompson's journalistic comment on the 1978 Official Secrets Trial against Crispin Aubrey, John Berry and Duncan Campbell (The ABC Trial). This writing is now conveniently gathered together in 'An Elizabethan Diary', 'The State versus its "Enemies"', and 'A State of Blackmail', in *Writing by Candlelight*, 91–134. See Thompson, *Warwick*, esp. for reply to Bess, 152–8.

6. Thompson, 'My Study' (September 1973) in *The Heavy Dancers*, 339. A first published statement on Blake appeared in Thompson, 'London', in Phillips, ed., *Interpreting Blake*, 5–31.

7. Many earlier citations could be marshalled here. The following should suffice.

On the compressed essay, see in particular: Thompson, 'Eighteenth-Century English Society: Class Struggle without Class', *Social History*, 3 (1978), 133–65; Thompson, 'Folklore, Anthropology, and Social History', *Indian Historical Review*, 3 (1978), 247–66. Among the reviews by Thompson: 'Happy Families', *New Society* (8 September 1977), 499–501; 'Sold Like a Sheep for a Pound', *New Society* (14 December 1978), 645–8; 'The Very Type of the "Respectable Artisan"', *New Society* (3 May 1979), 275–7; 'English Daughter', *New Society* (3 March 1977), 455–8; 'Review of *English Hunger and Industrial Disorders*', *Economic History Review*, 27 (1974), 480–84; 'Testing Class Struggle', *Times Higher Education Supplement* (8 March 1974).

8. Some relevant writings – 'Sir, Writing by Candlelight', 'Yesterday's Manikin', 'A Special Case', and 'A Question of Manners' – appear in Thompson, *Writing by Candlelight*, 39–84.

9. Thompson, 'An Open Letter to Leszek Kolakowski', originally in *The Socialist Register 1973*, reprinted in *The Poverty of Theory*, 93–192, esp. 124, 186–7.

10. Thompson, 'Testing Class Struggle', *Times Higher Education Supplement*, 3 March 1974; Thompson, 'Caudwell', *Socialist Register 1977*, esp. 271; Thompson, *Morris* (1977); Thompson, 'Romanticism, Utopianism and Moralism', 83–112, esp. 'Afternote', 112. For Williams and Marxism, see, among many possible texts: Raymond Williams, 'Base and Superstructure in Marxist Cultural Theory', *New Left Review*, 82 (1973), 3–16; Williams, *Marxism and Literature* (London 1977); Williams, *Politics and Letters: Interviews with New Left Review* (London 1979); Williams, *Problems in Materialism and Culture* (London 1980). For the Thompson–Williams relationship, see Thompson's reviews and obituary: 'The Long Revolution, I', *New Left Review*, 9 (1961), 24–33; 'The Long Revolution, II', *New Left Review*, 10 (1961), 34–9; 'A Nice Place to Visit', *New York Review of Books*, 22 (6 February 1975), 34–7; 'Last Dispatches from the Border Country: Raymond Williams', *The Nation* (5 March 1988), 310–12, where Thompson notes that in his *NYRB* review of Williams's *The Country and The City*, the editors excised all references to capitalism.

11. E.P. Thompson, 'The Poverty of Theory: or an Orrery of Errors', in *The Poverty of Theory and Other Essays*, 193–397, esp. 205, 373.

12. Ibid., 380, 384.

13. See Conor Cruise O'Brien, 'No to a Nauseous Marxist–Methodist Cocktail', *The Observer*, 28 January 1979; Thompson, 'The Acceptable Faces of Marxism', *The Observer*, 4 February 1979, reprinted as 'The Great Fear of Marxism', in *Writing by Candlelight*, 181–6.

14. See the conveniently assembled pieces of journalism in *Writing by Candlelight*, noting also Thompson, *Whigs and Hunters* (1975), 258–69. Earlier interventions include Thompson's effort to stave off the privatization of the public library, saving old books from the clutches of the market, and his materialist commentary on the American Bi-centennial: 'In Citizens' Bad Books', *New Society* (28 March 1974), 778–80; 'C is for Country, A is for Anniversary, S is for Solicitude, H is for History', *New York Times*, 26 April 1976. The jury system would later be the subject of Thompson's Meiklejohn Lecture, Brown University, 1980. See 'Subduing the Jury, I', *London Review of Books* (4 December 1986), 7–9; 'Subduing the Jury, II', *London Review of Books* (18 December 1986), 12–13. Note Bernard Crick, 'Thompson and Liberty!' (a review of *Writing by Candlelight*) *Manchester Guardian Weekly*, 11 May 1980.

15. Perry Anderson, *Arguments within English Marxism*, 201–5; Interview with E.P.

Thompson, 'Recovering the Libertarian Tradition', *The Leveller* (22 January 1979), 20–22. Anderson points out that Thompson's position in the late 1970s differed in emphasis from that of the very early 1970s, where he specifically rejected the limitation of oppositional politics to defensive containment. He quotes Thompson, *Warwick*, 159:

> The logic of the whole conflict leads not just to a defensive position (of establishing traditional safeguards for 'academic freedom'), but must lead on to a positive and far-reaching reconstruction of the University's self-government and of its relations to the community. We have forced matters to a point where we must demand a more democratic constitution than any existing university enjoys, or nothing – and perhaps something very much worse than nothing – will have been won.

16. There is no need to cite every reply to Thompson's *The Poverty of Theory*. Anderson's *Arguments within English Marxism* is still among the most useful. For a sample of this literature, see: Paul Q. Hirst, 'The Necessity of Theory – A Critique of E.P. Thompson's *The Poverty of Theory*', in Hirst, *Marxism and Historical Writing* (London 1985), 57–90, first published in *Economy and Society* (1979); the contributions of Terry Eagleton and others in *Literature and History*, 5 (Autumn 1979), 139–64; a number of articles in *New Statesman*, including Raphael Samuel, 'History Workshop 1: Truth is Partisan' (15 February 1980), 247–9; Gavin Kitching, 'History Workshop 5: A View from the Stalls', (14 March 1980), 398–9. The debate at St Paul's, edited for publication, appears in Raphael Samuel, ed., *People's History and Socialist Theory* (London 1981), 375–401. For an essay that steps back from the immediacy of the debate, considering it in the context of a different – later – time, and alongside other issues of theory, see Robert Gray, 'History, Marxism, and Theory', in Kaye and McClelland, eds, *E.P. Thompson*, 153–82. See also Thompson to Palmer, 15 October 1980. Note also Anderson, 'Diary', *London Review of Books*, 24; Philip Corrigan, 'Bread and Knowledge Politics: E.P. Thompson (1924–1993)', *left history*, 1 (Fall 1993), 103–10.

## Chapter 5

1. Thompson, 'Protest and Revive', *END Journal*, 37 (1989), 38; Hitchens, 'Minority Report', *The Nation* (27 September 1993), 306; Kazin, 'The Last Socialist', *Washington Post*; and, for an account of the huge anti-nuclear peace rallies of 1981, *Morning Star*, 26 October 1981. The quote is not actually from Blake, but is adapted from a seventeenth-century New Model Army marching song, which Thompson locates within a general antinomian impulse. See E.P. Thompson, *Witness Against the Beast: William Blake and the Moral Law* (New York 1993), 23.

2. Thompson, 'Protest and Revive', 37–41 (quote from 36–7), this review essay being one of the best short introductions to Thompson's account of his early peace movement activities. On the history of the peace movement, see, besides this review, Richard Taylor and Nigel Young, eds, *Campaigns for Peace: British Peace Movements in the Twentieth Century* (Manchester 1987). For his father's poem, see E.J. Thompson, 'Commentary', in *The Thracian Stranger*, 104.

3. For brief introductions to Thompson and these years, see Michael D. Bess, 'E.P. Thompson: Historian as Activist', 29–38; Martin Shaw, 'From Total War

to Democratic Peace: Exterminism and Historical Pacifism', in Kaye and McClelland, eds, *E.P. Thompson*, 233–51. There is a rather sterile account of the revived Campaign for Nuclear Disarmament in Great Britain in Paul Byrne, *The Campaign for Nuclear Disarmament* (London 1988).

4. The initial writings 'The Doomsday Consensus' and 'European Nuclear Disarmament' are now reprinted in *Writing by Candlelight*, 259–86.

5. See E.P. Thompson, *Protest and Survive* (London 1980), esp. 28–33. My copy of the pamphlet, a second edition and fourth printing, contains a copy of the END appeal as a centrepiece. This statement and the original pamphlet also appeared in E.P. Thompson and Dan Smith, eds, *Protest and Survive* (Harmondsworth 1980), a Penguin edition with a number of additional essays by END advocates. See also 'European Nuclear Disarmament: An Interview with E.P. Thompson', *Socialist Review*, 58 (1981), 9–34; 'Thompson's Doomsday Warning', *The Sunday Times*, 8 June 1980.

6. The sources that could be cited here are legion. For a general statement and selected citation of evidence, see Bess, 'E.P. Thompson: The Historian as Activist', 33–4. On the Oxford debate with Howard, which drew a crowd of over a thousand, see Paul Flather, 'When the Worst Form of Defence is the Best Form of Attack', *Times Higher Education Supplement*, 20 February 1981. From my own files I can pull the following: 'An Interview with E.P. Thompson', a Communiqué programme broadcast on 28 August 1981 by National Public Radio; E.P. Thompson, 'The END of the Line', *Bulletin of the Atomic Scientists* (January 1981), 6–13; Thompson, 'Double Standards', *Morning Star*, 1 February 1982; Thompson, 'A Letter to America', *The Nation* (24 January 1981), 68–75; Jeffrey Simpson, 'Shelving Anti-Arms Talks Backfires on BBC', *Globe*, 5 September 1981; Beth Richards, 'Canada Can Be Leader: E.P. Thompson Tells Toronto Audience', *The Peace Calendar*, 1 (September 1983), 1, 4; Jane Gadd, 'Peace Activist at Loss on Failure of Protests', *Globe*, 26 August 1983; Olivia Ward, 'Perspective: Peace: A Pessimist Soldiers On', *Toronto Star*, 28 August 1983. Typical correspondence: Thompson to Palmer, 7 June 1980; 20 November 1981; 16 August 1982; Dorothy Thompson to Palmer, 4 June 1983. On the early 1980s disarmament campaign and 1848, see David Held, 'Power and Legitimacy in Contemporary Britain', in Gregor McLennan, David Held and Stuart Hall, eds, *State and Society in Contemporary Britain: A Critical Introduction* (London 1984), 346.

7. Thompson, *Beyond the Cold War: NOT the Dimebleby Lecture* (London 1982), esp. 17, 35–6; Thompson, *Beyond the Cold War: A New Approach to the Arms Race and Nuclear Annihilation* (New York 1982), which also contains 'The War of Thatcher's Face', from *The Times*, 29 April 1982, reprinted on 189–96; Jeffrey Simpson, 'Shelving Anti-Arms Talks Backfires on BBC'; Thompson, *The Defence of Britain* (London 1983), reprinted in Thompson, *The Heavy Dancers*, 69–106.

8. Note in particular the essays in Thompson, *Beyond the Cold War* (1982), published in Great Britain as *Zero Option* (London 1982); Thompson, *The Heavy Dancers*; and, most explicitly, Thompson, *Double Exposure* (London 1985). See also 'Charter 77 Document No. 5/85: The Prague Appeal', 11 March 1985, distributed by Palach Press Ltd, London; Thompson, 'Beyond the Blocs', *END: Journal of European Nuclear Disarmament*, 12 (October–November 1984), 12–15. Background on the question of Eastern European/Soviet dissidents appears in Thompson, 'Detente and Dissent', in Roy Medvedev, *Detente & Socialist Democracy* (New York 1976), 119–38, while a useful discussion appears in Thompson and Racek, 'Freedom and the Bomb', *New Statesman* (24

April 1981), 6–13. For the opposition to Thompson, note the brief discussion and citations in Bess, 'E.P. Thompson: The Historian as Activist', 35–6; Alun Chalfont, 'Arguing About War & Peace: Thompson's "Ban-the-Bomb" Army', *Encounter* (January 1981), 79–87; and, for the Soviet Peace Council attack: Mark Solomon, *Death Waltz to Armageddon: E.P. Thompson and the Peace Movement* (New York 1984).

9. See Ferenc Koszegi and E.P. Thompson, *The New Hungarian Peace Movement* (London 1982), esp. 3, 5, 7, 35–7, 52.

10. E.P. Thompson, 'Notes on Exterminism, the Last Stage of Civilization', *New Left Review*, 121 (1980), 31; and E.P. Thompson *et al.*, *Exterminism and Cold War* (London 1982), esp. 348–9.

11. Among many writings, see E.P. Thompson, 'Agenda: The Ideological Delirium which Strikes Chords in the Worst Traditions of American Populism', *Guardian*, 18 February 1985; Thompson, ed., *Star Wars* (Harmondsworth 1985); Thompson, 'The Pie Isn't in the Sky: Look Who's Really Behind Star Wars', *The Nation* (1 March 1986), 233-8.

12. Mary Kaldor and Paul Anderson, eds, *Mad Dogs: The US Raids on Libya* (London 1986); Thompson to Palmer, 14 March 1985; 19 December 1991; 17 February 1991; 20 September 1986; 17 November 1986; 3 October 1987; Thompson and Racek, 'Freedom and the Bomb', 8–9; Richard Falk and Mary Kaldor, 'An International Citizens' Appeal for Peace and Democracy in the Middle East'/ Emergency Gulf Appeal, END, 10 February 1991.

13. Thompson, *The Defence of Britain*, 2–3, 11–13; Thompson, 'The View from Oxford Street', in *Mad Dogs*, 142–52; Davin, 'Memories of E.P. Thompson', 16. See also Dorothy Thompson, ed., *Over Our Dead Bodies: Women Against the Bomb* (London 1983); and the careful comments in Bess, 'E.P. Thompson: The Historian as Activist', 36–8. Thompson's own assessment of END and the thawing of the second Cold War is in 'Ends and Histories', in Mary Kaldor, ed., *Europe from Below: An East–West Dialogue* (London 1991), 7–25.

# Chapter 6

1. Thompson to Palmer, 22 February 1987; Thompson to Don Akenson, 11 June 1987, copy to Palmer.

2. This draws upon personal correspondence: Thompson to Palmer, 15 September 1987; 3 October 1987; 2 November 1987; 9, 10, 11 November 1987; 4 March 1989; 20 September 1991; 19 December 1991; 1 February 1993; Dorothy Thompson to Palmer, Tuesday (1989?); 1 September (1991?).

3. The above paragraph is perhaps too stark in its assessment of *Customs in Common* (London 1991). What is clear is that Thompson's essays themselves spawned a reinterpretation of eighteenth-century England. Had Thompson had the time and the health to keep abreast of the explosion in eighteenth-century English social history, and to relate his own work to that expansive field, his text would no doubt have evolved differently. As it was, this was impossible, and *Customs in Common* is the achievement of its chapter parts, rather than an achievement taking those parts beyond their own individual – and considerable – significance. So obvious is that significance, however, that

most reviewers acknowledge the status of the text. See, for instance, Linda Colley, 'Perpetual Commotion', *The Independent on Sunday*, 5 January 1992; John Saville, 'Custom Made', *Socialist Review*, January 1992; John Brewer, 'Voice of the Labouring Poor', *Times Literary Supplement* (13 March 1992), 14–15; Peter Linebaugh, 'Commonists of the World Unite!', *Radical History Review*, 56 (1993), 59-67. For Thompson's own assessments, I rely on personal correspondence: Thompson to Palmer, 5 October 1987; 17 March 1989; 26 May 1989; 20 September 1991; 19 December 1991. Perhaps one of the most interesting critical reviews of *Customs in Common*, unique in its careful structuring of the possible relationship between the eighteenth-century essays and the interpretive positions of *The Making of the English Working Class*, is David Levine, 'Proto-nothing', *Social History*, 18 (October 1993), 381–90.

4. E.P. Thompson, *Customs in Common*, esp. 14–15, 179, 184. See also the underappreciated essay E.P. Thompson, 'The Grid of Inheritance: A Comment', in Jack Goody *et al.*, eds, *Family and Inheritance: Rural Society in Western Europe, 1200–1800* (London 1976), 328–60; and for comment on the essays on customary eighteenth-century culture and other Thompson writing, Deborah Valenze and Peter Weiler, 'Edward Palmer Thompson (1924–1993)', 14; or – more idiosyncratic and critical – Levine, 'Proto-nothing'.

5. E.P. Thompson, *'Alien Homage': Edward Thompson and Rabindranath Tagore* (Delhi 1993), quote from vii; E.P. Thompson and E.J. Thompson, 'Memories of Tagore', *London Review of Books*, 22 May 1986, 18–19.

6. Thompson to Palmer, 15 June 1988; 1 February 1993; Dorothy Thompson to Palmer, 1 September 1992.

7. Thompson, 'Powers and Names', *London Review of Books*, 23 January 1986, 9–10; Thompson, 'Ends and Histories', in Kaldor, ed., *Europe from Below*, 23–4.

8. E.P. Thompson, *The Sykaos Papers* (New York 1988), esp. 92–3, 118, 318–19, 359–61, 476–8; Paul Buhle, 'Isn't it Romantic: E.P. Thompson's Global Agenda', *Voice Literary Supplement*, 76 (July 1989), 24–6; Palmer, *Descent into Discourse*, 211–14; Benjamin DeMott, 'The Poet Who Fell to Earth', *New York Times Book Review* (25 September 1988), 12–13. On 15 June 1988 Thompson wrote to me:

> an incredibly mixed reception to *Sykaos*. Clearly I am not to be the flavour-of-the-month of the London trendy left. An assassination in the 'New Statesman' by a reviewer with your own philistine predilections, except that she supposed the book was sci-fi. But very nice reviews in the centrist press, 'Sunday Times' and 'Observer'. I suppose you will mutter that you're not surprised. Advance copies of the US edn shd be going out shortly, I'll ask them to send you one.

See also Perry Anderson, 'Diary', *London Review of Books*, 24. A passage from Edward John Thompson, *Cock Robin's Disease*, 22 seems appropriate: 'Do you mean to say that you have gone on, day after day, writing down words, until you have made a big book – a novel!'

# Chapter 7

1. Thompson, *'Alien Homage'*, 89; Thompson, *The Sykaos Papers*, esp. 460, 467; DeMott, 'The Poet Who Fell to Earth', 12–13.

2. E.P. Thompson, 'Preface', in Lynd, *Class Conflict, Slavery, and the United States Constitution*, ix–xiii; Thompson, 'Theory and Evidence', *History Workshop Journal*, 35 (Spring 1993), 274–5.

3. Thompson, 'An Open Letter to Kolakowski', 109, 183–4; Hill, 'From the Awkward School', *Guardian*, 30 August 1993; Thompson, *Whigs and Hunters* (1975), 260; Thompson to Palmer, 20 September 1991.

4. Suzanne Cassidy, 'A Historian's Alternative Culture', *New York Times Book Review* (25 September 1988), 13; Colley, 'Perpetual Commotion', 26; Thompson, 'Blake's Tone', 12–13; Thompson to Palmer, 20 September 1991; 30 November 1988.

5. Thompson, 'Theory and Evidence', *History Workshop Journal*, 275; Thompson, 'Table Talk about Class', *Listener*, 6 June 1985, 29; Thompson to Palmer, 30 November 1988. As I was writing this essay I was directed by a friend and colleague who is well versed in Thompson's writings to one of his last reviews, a critical engagement with Linda Colley's *Britons: Forging the Nation, 1707–1837* (1992), which, I was told, was his repudiation of class. In fact it was anything but, and Thompson's statement with respect to his *The Making of the English Working Class* that ' "Class" was perhaps overworked in the 1960s and 1970s, and it has become merely boring', is a typical piece of Thompson ironic hyperbole, directed at 'the prevalent view'. On class and its eighteenth- and nineteenth-century origins, Thompson's views in this review are unambiguous: 'I am not ready to capitulate.' See Thompson, 'The Making of A Ruling Class', *Dissent* (Summer 1993), 377–82.

6. Thompson, 'The Long Revolution, I', *New Left Review*, 25. For an account of Williams's hurt response to the Thompson review, see Anderson, 'Diary', *London Review of Books*, 24. Thompson and Williams obviously mended the fences, and Thompson wrote a moving obituary upon Williams's death: Thompson, 'Last Dispatches from the Border Country: Raymond Williams', *The Nation* (5 March 1988), 310–12. Given that Thompson's original polemical brush had tarred Williams with retreating in the face of the genteel politeness of the ruling-class academy, it is noteworthy that his last tribute to Williams stated:

> Those of us who were Raymond's colleagues will miss that strenuous, patient, calming arguing voice very sorely. It is as if a fixed point from which we had been accustomed to take our bearings had suddenly dissolved, a point on the border country between the academy and the activist movement. We must thank him for his years of persistent inquiry.

7. Thompson, *Warwick*, 153–4. I will spare the author of the anti-Thompson letter, dated 26 November 1984, citation.

8. E.P. Thompson, *Witness Against the Beast: William Blake and the Moral Law* (New York 1993); Thompson, 'On the Rant', *London Review of Books*, 9 July 1987, 9–10; also in Geoff Eley and William Hunt, eds, *Reviving the English Revolution: Reflections and Elaborations on the Work of Christopher Hill* (London 1988), 153–61.

9. Thompson, *Witness Against the Beast*, esp. 3–5, 90, 221, 229; Anderson, 'Diary', 24–5; Thompson, 'Ends and Histories', 23–5. The left is liable to miss much of this, as I think is evident in the sympathetic statement in David McNally, 'E.P. Thompson: Class Struggle and Historical Materialism', *International Socialism: A Quarterly Journal of Socialist Theory*, 61 (December 1993), 75–89.

10. Palmer, *The Making of E.P. Thompson*; Gregor McLennan, 'E.P. Thompson and the Discipline of Historical Context', in *Making Histories*, 343 n. 1; Thompson to Palmer, no date (1980); Thompson, *The Making of the English Working Class* (1968), 469–85; Thompson, 'The Secret State', in *Writing by Candlelight*, 171–2; Thompson, 'Benevolent Mr. Goodwin', *London Review of Books* (8 July 1993), 14–15. Sarkar, 'Afterword', *The Other Side of the Medal*, 92, states: 'The tension with inherited Christianity would in some sense persist throughout, and, just possibly, enter into the brilliant and angry chapter Edward Thompson's son would write one day on the "moral machinery" of Methodism . . . .'

11. Thompson, 'Homage to Tom Maguire', in *Essays in Labour History*, 315; Thompson, 'Remembering C. Wright Mills', and 'Homage to Salvadore Allende', in *The Heavy Dancers*, 261, 278; Thompson, 'Homage to Thomas McGrath', *Triquarterly*, 122.

12. Thompson, *The Poverty of Theory*, 234.

# Index